LISREL VI

Analysis of Linear Structural Relationships
by Maximum Likelihood, Instrumental Variables,
and Least Squares Methods

by

Karl G. Jöreskog and Dag Sörbom

University of Uppsala
Department of Statistics
P.O. Box 513
S-751 20 Uppsala
SWEDEN

Fourth Edition
January 1986

LISREL VI

ISBN: 0-89498-024-6

Copyright© 1981, 1984
Scientific Software, Inc.
P.O. Box 536
Mooresville, Indiana 46158 - USA
Phone: 317-831-6296

LISREL® is a registered trademark of
Scientific Software, Inc.

CONTENTS

. . . .

LIST OF COMPUTER EXERCISES

1. Estimating the Disattenuated Correlation
2. The Rod and Frame Test
3. A Circumplex Model
4. Regression of GNP
5. Educational Attainment
6. Intergenerational Social Mobility
7. Role Behavior of Farm Managers
8. Social Status and Social Participation
9. Testing Psychometric Assumptions

PREFACE

LISREL VI is an extension and improvement of LISREL V. Input
for Version VI is downwardly compatible with input for Version V,
with the exception of the OB parameter, which is not supported in
Version VI.

New features of LISREL VI are:

- Procedures for computing automatic starting values have
  been improved and extended to more cases. For many purposes
  these initial values are satisfactory as final estimates; in
  other cases, they provide starting values from which the
  iterative solutions are likely to converge in the smallest
  number of steps.

- The modification index has been improved to correspond more
  closely to the drop in chi-square obtained when a fixed parameter is set free. The index now also shows the extent to
  which parameters subject to an equality constraint depart
  from the assumed equality. The utility of the modification
  index as a guide to improving LISREL models has been greatly
  enhanced.

- The program can now automatically modify a hierarchical
  model by adding the parameter corresponding to the largest
  modification index. Parameters are added sequentially until
  a user-specified significance level is no longer exceeded.

- Parameter estimates for all models may now be obtained by
  any of five statistically well-defined methods: instrumental
  variables, two-stage least squares, ordinary (unweighted)
  least squares, generalized least squares, and maximum likelihood. All methods give consistent estimates for fully
  identified models. The fast, non-iterative instrumental
  variable and two-stage least squares methods are used to
  obtain starting values for the iterative models.

- The user can now plot the fitting criterion for ordinary
  least squares, generalized least squares, and maximum
  likelihood as a function of any parameter, fixed or free,
  over a range of values corresponding to a 95 percent, large-
  sample confidence interval. A quadratic approximation to

i

the function is superimposed to reveal the extent to which, in maximum likelihood estimation, the limiting normal form of the log likelihood function is attained.

- To make the output more readable, the user can now assign names to the latent variables. Other improvements have been made in the readability of the output.

- Free-format input of data has been improved, but all forms of data that run on LISREL V will still run on LISREL VI. Formatted data records may now be as long as 240 characters.

- Technical improvements in the fitting procedures give LISREL VI a better chance of detecting numerically non-identified models. Defaults for the convergence criteria have been set so that only as many iterations are performed as required for three-figure accuracy in all parameters. Users can request more places of precision when greater accuracy is needed.

As in the previous version, the user has the option of estimating parameters by initial non-iterative instrumental variables and two-stage least-squares, by unweighted least-squares (ULS), or by maximum likelihood (ML). The ULS method makes it possible to analyze tetrachoric, biserial and poly-serial correlations computed from dichotomous, ordinal or mixed ordinal and interval data. Multivariate data containing missing values can also be analyzed by this method.

This manual contains fifteen examples covering a wide range of typical LISREL models. The input and output for these models are discussed in detail. A number of computer exercises are also given.

The research on LISREL has been supported by the Bank of
Sweden Tercentenary Foundation first under project *Structural
Equation Models in the Social Sciences* and later under project *Methodology of Evaluation Research*. Our sincere thanks
go to Lotten Gellin and Carin Hyenstrand who typed the manuscript and to our graduate students Barbro Dunér, Gösta Hägglund and Åke Jonsson who helped us check the manuscript.
Our thanks are also due to Lena Lindén for providing the
data for Example 11. We have tried to eliminate all errors
we have found. No doubt, however, some errors may remain
undetected, for which we, ourselves, take full responsibi-
lity.

Uppsala in November 1981

Karl G Jöreskog   Dag Sörbom

PREFACE FOR IBM USERS

The IBM version of LISREL has a system dependent feature
required to implement dynamic core allocation. If the
procedure supplied on the distribution tape is employed,
the feature is controlled by the parameter in the EXEC
procedure statement:

    // EXEC LISREL,SIZE=nnn   where,

        nnn = the number of kilobytes in the run-time computing
              region. This parameter must be large enough to
              accommodate the largest problem in the run.
              Typical sizes may be seen at the end of each
              sample problem printout in the user's guide.
              The last line of each problem printout is "THIS
              PROBLEM COULD HAVE BEEN RUN WITH PARM=nnn."
              This is the minimum value of SIZE for this
              problem. If SIZE is too small, the program will
              print a message indicating the value to which
              SIZE should be set. DEFAULT is 16K if not altered
              in the catalogued procedure.

        The value of SIZE determines the value of REGION on
        the system JOB card. Exact REGION size required may be
        installation dependent, but REGION=(192 + nnn)K (where
        nnn = the SIZE subfield) should be safe.

Unlike previous versions, time allocation for all problems is
not set on the EXEC card of LISREL VI. It is set on the
OUTPUT card separately for each problem.

Explanation of Notational System

Pages, equations, tables and figures are numbered consecutively within chapters. When referring to a page, an equation, a table or a figure in the same chapter, the chapter number is omitted. For example, in Chapter III a reference to (4) is to equation (4) in Chapter III, whereas a reference to (I.4) is to the fourth equation in Chapter I.

Symbols with a $\sim$ under it denote matrices and vectors. These would be boldface in a typeset version. Matrices are denoted by capital letters; vectors are denoted by lower case letters. The transpose of a matrix is denoted by a prime. For example, $\underset{\sim}{\Gamma}'$ is the transpose of $\underset{\sim}{\Gamma}$. All vectors without a prime are column vectors. When a row vector is needed it is denoted as a transpose of a column vector. If $\underset{\sim}{S}$ is a matrix we use s_{ij} to denote a typical element of $\underset{\sim}{S}$. The inverse matrix of $\underset{\sim}{\Sigma}$, say, is written $\underset{\sim}{\Sigma}^{-1}$. The determinant of a square matrix $\underset{\sim}{\Sigma}$, say, is denoted $|\underset{\sim}{\Sigma}|$ and the trace, or sum of diagonal elements, of a square matrix $\underset{\sim}{\Sigma}$, say, is denoted $\text{tr}(\underset{\sim}{\Sigma})$.

Greek letters are used to denote true population parameters and hypothetical latent (unobservable) random variables. For example, in $\underset{\sim}{x} = \underset{\sim}{\Lambda}_x \underset{\sim}{\xi} + \underset{\sim}{\delta}$, $\underset{\sim}{\xi}$ and $\underset{\sim}{\delta}$ are vectors of latent random variables, $\underset{\sim}{x}$ is a vector of observed random variables and $\underset{\sim}{\Lambda}_x$ is a matrix of parameters. Parameter estimates are usually denoted by a hat ($\hat{\ }$) above the corresponding parameter. For example, $\underset{\sim}{\hat{\Lambda}}_x$ denotes the estimate of $\underset{\sim}{\Lambda}_x$, regardless of the method of estimation used.

CHAPTER I

GENERAL DESCRIPTION OF MODELS AND METHODS

I.1 Introduction

Structural equation models have been useful in attacking many substantive problems in the social and behavioral sciences. Such models have been used in the study of macroeconomic policy formation, intergenerational occupational mobility, racial discrimination in employment, housing and earnings, studies of antecedents and consequences of drug use, scholastic achievement and evaluation of social action programs and many other areas. In methodological terms, the models have been referred to as simultaneous equation systems, linear causal analysis, path analysis, structural equation models, dependence analysis, cross-lagged panel correlation technique, etc.

The structural equation model is used to specify the phenomenon under study in terms of putative cause and effect variables and their indicators. Because each equation in the model represents a causal link rather than a mere empirical association, the structural parameters do not, in general, coincide with coefficients of regressions among observed variables. The structural parameters represent relatively unmixed, invariant and autonomous features of the mechanism that generate the observable variables. The use of structural equation models requires statistical tools which are based upon, but which go well beyond, conventional regression analysis and analysis of variance.

Background material on structural equation models may be found
in Heise (1975), Duncan (1975), Goldberger (1972) and Chapter 7
of Goldberger (1964) and in Jöreskog and Sörbom (1979). Two volumes of Blalock (1971, 1974) contain several papers dealing
with basic issues and problems at an elementary level. At a more
advanced level, the two volumes, Goldberger and Duncan (1973)
and Aigner and Goldberger (1977) cover several issues, problems
and applications. Bielby and Hauser (1977) gave an excellent review of the sociological literature on structural equation models.
Bentler (1980) reviewed the psychological and statistical literature on latent variable models.

The LISREL model was introduced by Jöreskog (1973a). More recent
descriptions of it are given by Jöreskog (1977, 1978, 1981a). The
present description of LISREL, however, does not require familia-
rity with these references but is rather self-contained. Numerous
applications of LISREL may be found in journals of psychological,
sociological, econometric and other social sciences.

LISREL is a general computer program for estimating the unknown
coefficients in a set of linear structural equations. The variables in the equation system may be either directly observed variables or unmeasured latent variables (hypothetical construct variables) which are not observed but related to observed variables.
The computer program is based on a general model which is particularly designed to handle models with latent variables, measurement errors and reciprocal causation (simultaneity, interdepen-
dence). In its most general form the model assumes that there is a causal

structure among a set of latent variables. The latent variables appear as underlying causes of the observed variables. Latent variables can also be treated as caused by observed variables or as intervening variables in a causal chain.

The LISREL model consists of two parts: *the measurement model* and *the structural equation model*. The measurement model specifies how the latent variables or hypothetical constructs are measured in terms of the observed variables and is used to describe the measurement properties (validities and reliabilities) of the observed variables. The structural equation model specifies the causal relationships among the latent variables and is used to describe the causal effects and the amount of unexplained variance.

The LISREL model covers a wide range of models useful in the social and behavioral sciences, for example, exploratory and confirmatory factor analysis models, path analysis models, econometric models for time series data, recursive and non-recursive models for cross-sectional and longitudinal data and covariance structure models.

The program can analyze data from a single sample but can also analyze samples from several populations simultaneously. For example, one can test hypotheses of equality of covariance matrices, equality of correlation matrices, equality of regressions, equality of factor patterns, etc. In general, some or all of the parameters can be constrained to be equal in all populations. One

can also estimate mean structures as well as covariance structures. For example, one can estimate constant intercept terms in
the measurement model and in the structural equations and mean values of the latent variables.

This manual proceeds as follows. Chapter I describes the general LISREL model and some of its submodels. It also considers,
in general terms, the methods of identification, estimation and
testing used by the program. Because of the general formulation
in Chapter I the material is rather abstract. Readers who find
Chapter I difficult are recommended to read all the examples in
Chapter III first and then go back to Chapters I and II.

Chapter II gives detailed instructions for the problem run in
general terms and Chapter III gives examples with detailed input and output for several single-sample problems. A separate
chapter (Chapter IV) is devoted to the computation of polychoric
and polyserial correlations, the analysis of such correlations
and the handling of missing observations.

Analysis of data from several samples is considered and illustrated in Chapter V.

I.2 The LISREL Model

In analysis of a single sample there is seldom any interest in
location parameters of the latent variables and in intercept
terms of the equations. Such parameters, however, may be of con-
siderable interest in multi-sample analysis. We shall therefore
postpone the discussion of such problems until Chapter V and
here in Chapter I we shall assume that all variables, observed
as well as latent, are measured in deviations from their means.
The LISREL model can then be defined as follows.

Consider random vectors $\eta' = (\eta_1, \eta_2, \ldots, \eta_m)$ and $\xi' = (\xi_1, \xi_2, \ldots, \xi_n)$ of latent dependent and independent variables, respectively, and the following system of linear structural relations

$$\eta = B\eta + \Gamma\xi + \zeta \tag{I.1}$$

where $B(m \times m)$ and $\Gamma(m \times n)$ are coefficient matrices and
$\zeta' = (\zeta_1, \zeta_2, \ldots, \zeta_m)$ is a random vector of residuals (errors
in equations, random disturbance terms). The elements of B represent direct causal effects of η-variables on other η-va-
riables and the elements of Γ represent direct causal effects
of ξ-variables on η-variables. It is assumed that ζ is uncorrelated with ξ and that $I-B$ is non-singular.

The vectors η and ξ are not observed but instead vectors
$y' = (y_1, y_2, \ldots, y_p)$ and $x' = (x_1, x_2, \ldots, x_q)$ are observed,
such that

$$y = \Lambda_y \eta + \varepsilon \tag{I.2}$$

and

$$x = \Lambda_x \xi + \delta \tag{I.3}$$

where ε and δ are vectors of errors of measurement in y and x, respectively. The matrices Λ_y (p x m) and Λ_x (q x n) are regression matrices of y on η and of x on ξ, respectively. It is convenient to refer to y and x as the observed variables and η and ξ as the latent variables. The errors of measurement are assumed to be uncorrelated with η, ξ and ζ but may be correlated among themselves.

In summary, the general LISREL model is defined by the three equations,

Structural Equation Model: $\eta = B\eta + \Gamma\xi + \zeta$ (I.1)

Measurement Model for y : $y = \Lambda_y \eta + \varepsilon$ (I.2)

Measurement Model for x : $x = \Lambda_x \xi + \delta$ (I.3)

with the assumptions,

   (i) ζ is uncorrelated with ξ

  (ii) ε is uncorrelated with η

 (iii) δ is uncorrelated with ξ

  (iv) ζ, ε and δ are mutually uncorrelated

   (v) B has zeroes in the diagonal and $I - B$ is non-singular.

Note that the structural equation (1) is different from LISREL IV. The matrix B now has zeros in the diagonal and contains the direct effects of each η on other η's. The relationship between the new B, B_V say, and the old B, B_{IV} say, is

$$B_{IV} = I - B_V.$$

The advantage of the new definition of B is illustrated by the model shown in the following path diagram.

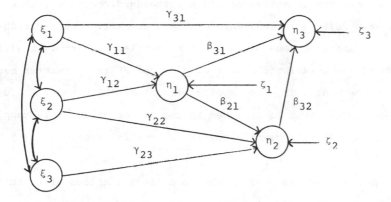

This corresponds to the structural equations

$$
\begin{pmatrix} \eta_1 \\ \eta_2 \\ \eta_3 \end{pmatrix} = \begin{pmatrix} 0 & 0 & 0 \\ \beta_{21} & 0 & 0 \\ \beta_{31} & \beta_{32} & 0 \end{pmatrix} \begin{pmatrix} \eta_1 \\ \eta_2 \\ \eta_3 \end{pmatrix} + \begin{pmatrix} \gamma_{11} & \gamma_{12} & 0 \\ 0 & \gamma_{22} & \gamma_{23} \\ \gamma_{31} & 0 & 0 \end{pmatrix} \begin{pmatrix} \xi_1 \\ \xi_2 \\ \xi_3 \end{pmatrix} + \begin{pmatrix} \zeta_1 \\ \zeta_2 \\ \zeta_3 \end{pmatrix}
$$

Note that the coefficients in B correspond exactly to the direct paths from one η to another η. In LISREL V these path coefficients come out with the correct sign whereas in LISREL IV one had to change their signs.

Since η and ξ are unobserved they do not have a definite scale. Both the origin and the unit of measurement in each latent variable are arbitrary. To define the model properly the origin and the unit of measurement of each latent variable must be assigned. The origin has already been assigned by the assumption that each variable has zero mean. The most convenient way of assigning a unit of measurement is to fix a one in each column of Λ_y and Λ_x. This defines the unit to be the same as in one of the observed variables. Another alternative is to

assume that the latent variables are standardized, i.e., that
they have unit variances. This can be done easily for ξ-variab-
les but cannot be done in LISREL for η-variables since, as will
be seen, the covariance matrix of $\underset{\sim}{\eta}$ is not a free parameter matrix in the model. In every application of a LISREL model the units
of measurement must be assigned in one way or other. The examples
in Chapter III will clarify how it is done in practice.

Let $\underset{\sim}{\Phi}$ (n x n) and $\underset{\sim}{\Psi}$ (m x m) be the covariance matrices of ξ and
$\underset{\sim}{\zeta}$, respectively, and let $\underset{\sim}{\Theta}_\varepsilon$ and $\underset{\sim}{\Theta}_\delta$ be the covariance matrices
of ε and $\underset{\sim}{\delta}$, respectively. Then it follows, from the above assump-
tions, that the covariance matrix $\underset{\sim}{\Sigma}\left[(p + q) \text{ x } (p + q)\right]$ of $\underset{\sim}{z}$ =
= $(\underset{\sim}{y}', \underset{\sim}{x}')'$ is

$$
\underset{\sim}{\Sigma} = \begin{bmatrix}
\underset{\sim}{\Lambda}_y (I - B)^{-1}(\Gamma\Phi\Gamma' + \Psi)(I - B')^{-1}\underset{\sim}{\Lambda}_y' + \underset{\sim}{\Theta}_\varepsilon & \underset{\sim}{\Lambda}_y (I - B)^{-1}\Gamma\Phi\Lambda_x' \\
\underset{\sim}{\Lambda}_x\Phi\Gamma'(I - B')^{-1}\underset{\sim}{\Lambda}_y' & \underset{\sim}{\Lambda}_x\Phi\Lambda_x' + \underset{\sim}{\Theta}_\delta
\end{bmatrix}
\tag{I.4}
$$

The elements of $\underset{\sim}{\Sigma}$ are functions of the elements of $\underset{\sim}{\Lambda}_y$, $\underset{\sim}{\Lambda}_x$, $\underset{\sim}{B}$, $\underset{\sim}{\Gamma}$,
$\underset{\sim}{\Phi}$, $\underset{\sim}{\Psi}$, $\underset{\sim}{\Theta}_\varepsilon$ and $\underset{\sim}{\Theta}_\delta$. In applications some of these elements are fixed
and equal to assigned values. In particular, this is so for ele-
ments of $\underset{\sim}{\Lambda}_y$, $\underset{\sim}{\Lambda}_x$, $\underset{\sim}{B}$ and $\underset{\sim}{\Gamma}$, but it is possible to have fixed values in the other matrices also. For the remaining non-fixed
elements of the eight parameter matrices one or more subsets may
have identical but unknown values. Thus, the elements in $\underset{\sim}{\Lambda}_y$, $\underset{\sim}{\Lambda}_x$,
$\underset{\sim}{B}$, $\underset{\sim}{\Gamma}$, $\underset{\sim}{\Phi}$, $\underset{\sim}{\Psi}$, $\underset{\sim}{\Theta}_\varepsilon$ and $\underset{\sim}{\Theta}_\delta$ are of three kinds:

   (i) <u>fixed parameters</u> that have been assigned given values,

  (ii) <u>constrained parameters</u> that are unknown but equal to
        one or more other parameters and

 (iii) <u>free parameters</u> that are unknown and not constrained
        to be equal to any other parameter.

I.3 Submodels

The general LISREL model involves four kinds of variables in addition to the error variables ζ, ε and δ, namely y-variables, x-variables, η-variables and ξ-variables. The notation for the number of each of these is given in Table 1.

TABLE I.1

Notation for Number of Variables

	Mathematical Notation	LISREL Notation
Number of y-variables	p	NY
Number of x-variables	q	NX
Number of η-variables	m	NE
Number of ξ-variables	n	NK

The general model subsumes many models as special cases. A submodel will be obtained when one or more of NY, NX, NE and NK is not specified, i.e., when one or more of these are default on the MO card (the MO card will be explained in Chapter II). Each submodel involves only some of the eight parameter matrices. The default values for NY, NX, NE and NK has been chosen so as to be able to specify the most common submodels with a minimum of input. A user who is only interested in a particular submodel needs only be concerned with a subset of the eight parameter matrices and does not have to understand the general model.

The common types of submodels are as follows.

1. When only NX and NK are specified the program assumes the model

$$x = \Lambda_x \xi + \delta \tag{I.5}$$

i.e., a measurement model or a factor analysis model. In this case there is no structural equation model of the form (1) and there are no y-variables or η-variables and consequently no measurement model of the form (2). Only one of the three equations (1), (2) and (3) is in operation. The only parameter matrices included in the model are $\underset{\sim}{\Lambda}_x$, $\underset{\sim}{\Phi}$ and $\underset{\sim}{\Theta}_\delta$. An example of this is given in Chapter III.

2. When only NY and NX are specified, the program assumes the model

$$\underset{\sim}{y} = \underset{\sim}{B}\underset{\sim}{y} + \underset{\sim}{\Gamma}\underset{\sim}{x} + \underset{\sim}{\zeta} \qquad (I.6)$$

i.e., a structural equation model for directly observed variables. If, in addition, $\underset{\sim}{B} = \underset{\sim}{0}$, one can have multivariate or univariate regression models and other forms of the general linear model. Technically, when NE and NK are omitted on the MO card the program sets NE = NY, NK = NX, $\underset{\sim}{\Lambda}_y = \underset{\sim}{I}$, $\underset{\sim}{\Theta}_\varepsilon = \underset{\sim}{0}$, $\underset{\sim}{\Lambda}_x = \underset{\sim}{I}$, $\underset{\sim}{\Theta}_\delta = \underset{\sim}{0}$ and $\underset{\sim}{\Phi} = \underset{\sim}{S}_{xx}$. The only parameter matrices involved in the model are $\underset{\sim}{B}$, $\underset{\sim}{\Gamma}$ and $\underset{\sim}{\Psi}$. Examples of this kind of model are given in Chapter III.

3. When only NY, NE and NK are specified the program assumes the model

$$\underset{\sim}{\eta} = \underset{\sim}{B}\underset{\sim}{\eta} + \underset{\sim}{\Gamma}\underset{\sim}{\xi} + \underset{\sim}{\zeta} \qquad (I.7)$$

$$\underset{\sim}{y} = \underset{\sim}{\Lambda}_y\underset{\sim}{\eta} + \underset{\sim}{\varepsilon} \qquad (I.8)$$

or equivalently

$$\underset{\sim}{y} = \underset{\sim}{\Lambda}_y(\underset{\sim}{I} - \underset{\sim}{B})^{-1}(\underset{\sim}{\Gamma}\underset{\sim}{\xi} + \underset{\sim}{\zeta}) + \underset{\sim}{\varepsilon} \qquad (I.9)$$

When $\underset{\sim}{B} = \underset{\sim}{0}$, this becomes

$$\underset{\sim}{y} = \underset{\sim}{\Lambda}_y(\underset{\sim}{\Gamma}\underset{\sim}{\xi} + \underset{\sim}{\zeta}) + \underset{\sim}{\varepsilon} \qquad (I.10)$$

which is a second-order factor analysis model with first-order factor loadings given by $\underset{\sim}{\Lambda}_y$ and second-order factor loadings given by $\underset{\sim}{\Gamma}$. Equation (10) is of the form of Jöreskog's (1969, 1970a, 1973b, 1974) ACOVS-model, so that such models can be handled by LISREL in this way. *Note that the program can handle ξ-variables even though there are no x-variables.* This model involves the following parameter matrices in LISREL $\underset{\sim}{\Lambda}_y$, $\underset{\sim}{\Gamma}$, $\underset{\sim}{\Phi}$, $\underset{\sim}{\Psi}$ and $\underset{\sim}{\Theta}_\varepsilon$.

4. When only NY and NE are given on the MO card the program assumes the model

$$\underset{\sim}{y} = \underset{\sim}{\Lambda}_y \underset{\sim}{\eta} + \underset{\sim}{\varepsilon} \qquad (I.11)$$

$$\underset{\sim}{\eta} = \underset{\sim}{B}\underset{\sim}{\eta} + \underset{\sim}{\zeta} \qquad (I.12)$$

or equivalently

$$\underset{\sim}{y} = \underset{\sim}{\Lambda}_y (\underset{\sim}{I} - \underset{\sim}{B})^{-1} \underset{\sim}{\zeta} + \underset{\sim}{\varepsilon}$$

This is just a special case of case 3 above. In this case the parameter matrices are $\underset{\sim}{\Lambda}_y$, $\underset{\sim}{B}$, $\underset{\sim}{\Psi}$ and $\underset{\sim}{\Theta}_\varepsilon$. When $\underset{\sim}{B} = \underset{\sim}{0}$ this model reduces to

$$\underset{\sim}{y} = \underset{\sim}{\Lambda}_y \underset{\sim}{\zeta} + \underset{\sim}{\varepsilon} \qquad (I.13)$$

with parameter matrices $\underset{\sim}{\Lambda}_y$, $\underset{\sim}{\Psi}$ and $\underset{\sim}{\Theta}_\varepsilon$. This, of course, is a factor analysis model for a set of y-variables, in which the matrix $\underset{\sim}{\Psi}$ plays the role of a factor covariance or correlation matrix. To analyze a factor analysis model one can use either model (5) or model (13) but, as we shall see, because of an option we have added for the matrix $\underset{\sim}{\Phi}$

(see next section), it is slightly more convenient to use model (5).

A summary of the different submodels considered above is given in Table 2.

TABLE I.2

Submodels in LISREL

Type	Specified	Default	Model	Parameters
1	NX,NK	NY,NE	$\underset{\sim}{x}=\underset{\sim}{\Lambda}_x\underset{\sim}{\xi}+\underset{\sim}{\delta}$	$\underset{\sim}{\Lambda}_x,\underset{\sim}{\Phi},\underset{\sim}{\Theta}_\delta$
2A	NY,NX	NE,NK	$\underset{\sim}{y}=\underset{\sim}{B}\underset{\sim}{y}+\underset{\sim}{\Gamma}\underset{\sim}{x}+\underset{\sim}{\zeta}$	$\underset{\sim}{B},\underset{\sim}{\Gamma},\underset{\sim}{\Psi}$
			$\underset{\sim}{y}=\underset{\sim}{\Gamma}\underset{\sim}{x}+\underset{\sim}{\zeta}$	$\underset{\sim}{\Gamma},\underset{\sim}{\Psi}$ (B=0)
2B	NY	NX,NE,NK	$\underset{\sim}{y}=\underset{\sim}{B}\underset{\sim}{y}+\underset{\sim}{\zeta}$	$\underset{\sim}{B},\underset{\sim}{\Psi}$
3A	NY,NE,NK	NX	$\underset{\sim}{y}=\underset{\sim}{\Lambda}_y(\underset{\sim}{I}-\underset{\sim}{B})^{-1}(\underset{\sim}{\Gamma}\underset{\sim}{\xi}+\underset{\sim}{\zeta})+\underset{\sim}{\varepsilon}$	$\underset{\sim}{\Lambda}_y,\underset{\sim}{B},\underset{\sim}{\Gamma},\underset{\sim}{\Phi},\underset{\sim}{\Psi},\underset{\sim}{\Theta}_\varepsilon$
			$\underset{\sim}{y}=\underset{\sim}{\Lambda}_y(\underset{\sim}{\Gamma}\underset{\sim}{\xi}+\underset{\sim}{\zeta})+\underset{\sim}{\varepsilon}$	$\underset{\sim}{\Lambda}_y,\underset{\sim}{\Gamma},\underset{\sim}{\Phi},\underset{\sim}{\Psi},\underset{\sim}{\Theta}_\varepsilon$ (B=0)
3B	NY,NE	NX,NK	$\underset{\sim}{y}=\underset{\sim}{\Lambda}_y(\underset{\sim}{I}-\underset{\sim}{B})^{-1}\underset{\sim}{\zeta}+\underset{\sim}{\varepsilon}$	$\underset{\sim}{\Lambda}_y,\underset{\sim}{B},\underset{\sim}{\Psi},\underset{\sim}{\Theta}_\varepsilon$

I.4 Default Values for Parameter Matrices

There are eight parameter matrices in LISREL: $\underset{\sim}{\Lambda}_y$, $\underset{\sim}{\Lambda}_x$, $\underset{\sim}{B}$, $\underset{\sim}{\Gamma}$, $\underset{\sim}{\Phi}$, $\underset{\sim}{\Psi}$, $\underset{\sim}{\Theta}_\varepsilon$ and $\underset{\sim}{\Theta}_\delta$. The LISREL names for these parameter matrices, their possible forms and default values are given in Table 3.

On the MO card one can make any number of specifications of the form

        MN = AA, BB

where MN is a matrix name (column 3), AA is a matrix form (column 5) and BB is FR (free) or FI (fixed) (column 7). Either AA

TABLE I.3

Parameter Matrices in LISREL

Their Possible Forms and Default Values

Name (1)	LISREL Notation (2)	LISREL Name (3)	Order (4)	Possible Forms (5)	Default Form (6)	Default Mode Fixed-Free (7)
LAMBDA-Y	Λ_y	LY	NYxNE	ID,IZ,ZI,DI,FU	FU	FI
LAMBDA-X	Λ_x	LX	NXxNK	ID,IZ,ZI,DI,FU	FU	FI
BETA	B	BE	NExNE	ZE,SD,FU	ZE	FI
GAMMA	Γ	GA	NExNK	ID,IZ,ZI,DI,FU	FU	FR
PHI	Φ	PH	NKxNK	ID,DI,SY,ST	SY	FR
PSI	Ψ	PS	NExNE	ZE,DI,SY	SY	FR
THETA-EPSILON	Θ_ε	TE	NYxNY	ZE,DI,SY	DI	FR
THETA-DELTA	Θ_δ	TD	NXxNX	ZE,DI,SY	DI	FR

or BB may be omitted in which case the defaults of Table 3 are used. The order of AA and BB is immaterial so that the above specification can also be written MN = BB, AA. The meaning of the possible form values are as follows

ZE = $\underset{\sim}{0}$ (zero matrix)

ID = $\underset{\sim}{I}$ (identity matrix)

IZ = $\begin{bmatrix} \underset{\sim}{I} & \underset{\sim}{0} \end{bmatrix}$ or $\begin{pmatrix} \underset{\sim}{I} \\ \underset{\sim}{0} \end{pmatrix}$ (partitioned identity and zero)

ZI = $\begin{bmatrix} \underset{\sim}{0} & \underset{\sim}{I} \end{bmatrix}$ or $\begin{pmatrix} \underset{\sim}{0} \\ \underset{\sim}{I} \end{pmatrix}$ (partitioned zero and identity)

DI = a diagonal matrix

SD = a subdiagonal matrix, i.e., a lower triangular matrix with diagonal elements equal to zero (refers to B only)

SY = a symmetric matrix which is not diagonal

ST = a symmetric matrix with fixed ones in the diagonal (a correlation matrix)

FU = a rectangular or square non-symmetric matrix.

The program orders the eight parameter matrices in the order $\underset{\sim}{\Lambda}_y$, $\underset{\sim}{\Lambda}_x$, $\underset{\sim}{B}$, $\underset{\sim}{\Gamma}$, $\underset{\sim}{\Phi}$, $\underset{\sim}{\Psi}$, $\underset{\sim}{\Theta}_\epsilon$, $\underset{\sim}{\Theta}_\delta$ and within each matrix, the elements are ordered row-wise. Only the lower triangular parts of the symmetric matrices $\underset{\sim}{\Phi}$, $\underset{\sim}{\Psi}$, $\underset{\sim}{\Theta}_\epsilon$, $\underset{\sim}{\Theta}_\delta$ are counted and if a matrix is specified to be diagonal, only the diagonal elements are counted. Matrices which are specified to be $\underset{\sim}{I}$ (ID) or $\underset{\sim}{0}$ (ZE) are not stored in the computer.

I.5 Specification of Fixed and Free Elements

For each and every element in each of the eight parameter matrices, $\underset{\sim}{\Lambda}_y$, $\underset{\sim}{\Lambda}_x$, $\underset{\sim}{B}$, $\underset{\sim}{\Gamma}$, $\underset{\sim}{\Phi}$, $\underset{\sim}{\Psi}$, $\underset{\sim}{\Theta}_\epsilon$ and $\underset{\sim}{\Theta}_\delta$, the user must specify whether it is a fixed, free or constrained parameter.

Section 1.4 described how one can specify an entire matrix to be fixed or free. Any element which has been fixed (free) in this way can be declared free (fixed) either by giving the coordinates (row and column numbers) of the free elements or by reading in a pattern matrix of zeroes and ones where 0 means a fixed element and 1 a free element. The first method can also be used to specify equality constraints.

For example, if $\Lambda_{\sim y}$ has been specified as fixed (default) and

$$
\Lambda_{\sim y} = \begin{bmatrix} \lambda_1 & 0 & 0 \\ \lambda_2 & 0 & 0 \\ \lambda_2 & \lambda_3 & 0 \\ 0 & \lambda_4 & 0 \\ 0 & \lambda_4 & 0 \\ 0 & 0 & \lambda_5 \\ 0 & 0 & \lambda_5 \\ 0 & 0 & \lambda_6 \end{bmatrix}
$$

one can write

FREE LY(1,1)   LY(2,1)   LY(3,2)   LY(4,2)   LY(6,3)   LY(8,3)

Here we define only one element in each group of constrained
elements as a free parameter. The other constrained elements
are defined in Section I.6. Blanks can be used instead of parenthesis and commas, so that LY(4,2) can also be written LY 4 2.
Instead of using two coordinates, an element can be referred to
by its linear index reading row-wise. Thus LY(4,2) can be written
LY(11) or LY 11 since it is the eleventh element in $\Lambda_{\sim y}$.

In the other alternative, the pattern is specified by reading in
an integer matrix with 1's for free and 0's for fiexed elements
(See Section II.8).

As a second example, consider

$$
B_{\sim} = \begin{bmatrix} 0 & x & x & x & x \\ x & 0 & 0 & 0 & 0 \\ x & 0 & 0 & 0 & 0 \\ 0 & 0 & 0 & 0 & 0 \\ 0 & 0 & 0 & 0 & 0 \end{bmatrix}
$$

where the x's represent free parameters. We show three different ways of specifying the pattern by coordinates

1. Since the first five free elements are in consecutive order
   they can be referred to collectively as BE(1,2)-BE(2,1) (or
   BE(2)-BE(6)). Thus, all free elements can be defined by
   FREE BE(1,2)-BE(2,1) BE(3,1)

2. FREE BE(1,2)-BE(3,1)
   FIX BE(2,2)-BE(2,5)

   The first statement frees β_{12} through β_{31}. The second statement fixes β_{22} through β_{25} thereby overwriting the first.

3. FREE BE(1,2)-BE(5,5)
   FIX BE(2,2)-BE(5,5)
   FREE BE(3,1)

   The first statement frees all elements except β_{11}. The second statement fixes β_{22} through β_{55}. The last statement
   frees β_{31}. Note that every statement overwrites the previous.

If a matrix has been specified as diagonal, only the diagonal
elements are counted. In such a case it is only if the diagonal
elements are of mixed types that the user must specify anything.
For example, if

$$\underset{\sim}{\Psi} = \text{diag} (1, x, x, 0, x, x, x)$$

then one can specify

   FREE PS(2) PS(3) PS(5)-PS(7)
or alternatively

   FREE PS(2)-PS(7)

   FIX PS(4)

Here ψ_{ii} can be referred to as either PS(i,i) or PS(i).

I.6 Specification of Equality Constraints

If there are no equality constraints in the model this step may
be omitted. Otherwise, one specifies a set of equalities, one for
each group of parameters which are constrained to be equal. In
each set of equalities one first defines one element which has
been defined to be a free parameter, then one defines all other
elements in the group.

In the first example in I.5 there are three groups of constrained
elements each containing two parameters. These are specified as

    EQUAL LY(2,1) LY(3,1)

    EQUAL LY(4,2) LY(5,2)

    EQUAL LY(6,3) LY(7,3)

The constrained elements within a group may be elements of any
parameter matrix. For example, $\beta_{35} = \gamma_{41} = \phi_{21}$ is specified as,
assuming γ_{41} has been defined as a free element previously,

    EQUAL GA(4,1) BE(3,5) PH(2,1)

If a matrix is specified to be fully symmetric, only the elements
below and in the diagonal are counted. As far as the program is
concerned, the elements in the upper half of the matrix do not
exist. Thus, there is no need to treat these elements as constrained parameters. However, if the user refers to such an element it is automatically taken to mean the corresponding element
in the lower half. Note also that if the user refers to an element in a symmetric matrix by its linear index, again only the

lower half including the diagonal is counted. For example, if $\underset{\sim}{\Phi}$ is fully symmetric, PH(5) always refers to the element ϕ_{32} in the third row and second column of $\underset{\sim}{\Phi}$.

If a matrix has been specified as $\underset{\sim}{0}$ (ZE) or $\underset{\sim}{I}$ (ID) one cannot refer to any element of this matrix since it is not stored in the computer.

Also, if a matrix has been specified as diagonal (DI) one cannot refer to off-diagonal elements of this matrix since only the diagonal elements are stored in the computer.

Special explanation is needed for the specification of $\underset{\sim}{\Theta}_\varepsilon$ and $\underset{\sim}{\Theta}_\delta$. The default for these is that they are diagonal with free diagonal elements. This is the most common specification. However, if one specifies TE = SY on the MO card this is taken to mean that $\underset{\sim}{\Theta}_\varepsilon$ is symmetric with free diagonal elements and *fixed off-diagonal* elements, and similarly for $\underset{\sim}{\Theta}_\delta$. We have done it in this way, because when $\underset{\sim}{\Theta}_\varepsilon$, say, is not diagonal, usually only a few of the off-diagonal elements are free and these can be declared free by a FR card. Very rarely is one interested in a model where a majority of the elements of $\underset{\sim}{\Theta}_\varepsilon$, say, are to be free. However, if this is the case, one can specify this most easily by writing TE = SY,FR on the MO card and then specify the fixed elements on a FI card.

Summing up the specifications for TE and TD:

1. Default means diagonal and free.

2. TE or TD = SY means symmetric with free diagonal and fixed otherwise.

3. TE or TD = SY,FR means that the whole matrix is free.

I.7 Specification of Non-Zero Fixed Parameters

It should be noted that the specification described in Sections I.5-6 only concerns whether certain parameters are to be fixed or free and do not specify their actual values. The value of each parameter, whether free or fixed, is zero by default. All *non-zero fixed* parameters must be specified by the user. This will be explained in this section.

The value of non-zero fixed parameters are defined either by reading a matrix of real numbers (See Section II.10) or by specifying the fixed value and the matrix (matrices) and coordinates where this value is to be set.

For example, if one wants to specify that $\lambda_{11}^{(y)} = \lambda_{21}^{(y)} = \lambda_{64}^{(y)} = 0.5$, one can write

    VALUE 0.5 LY(1,1) LY(2,1) LY(6,4)

Any real number in any format can be used and this number can be set in any position in any matrix. For example, one can write

    VALUE 1.47E-6 LY(4,2) BE(6,1) PS(5,4) TE(7,3)

Also, as before, every statement of this type overwrites the previous. Thus, one can first set a group of elements equal to 1 and then set some of these equal to 0.5.

I.8 Identification of Models and Parameters

When the model involves latent variables there are usually more unobserved variables than observed variables in the model. For example, the model (5) involves $n+q$ unobserved variables ξ and δ but only q observed variables x. Therefore, the model is not testable or estimable at the level of the variables. However, the model implies that a certain covariance structure, in general given by (4), must hold, and this is usually testable. In this way one can also estimate the parameters of the model. However, before an attempt is made to estimate a model, the identification problem must be examined.

We assume that the distribution of the observed variables is sufficiently well described by the moments of first and second order, so that information contained in moments of higher order may be ignored. In particular, this will hold if the distribution is multivariate normal. Since the mean vector is unconstrained, the distribution of $z = (y', x')'$ is described by the independent parameters in Λ_y, Λ_x, B, Γ, Φ, Ψ, Θ_ε, Θ_δ.

Identifiability depends on the choice of model and on the specification of fixed, constrained and free parameters. Under a given structure, i.e., a given set of values of the parameters in

Λ_y, Λ_x, B, Γ, Φ, Ψ, Θ_ε, Θ_δ generates one and only one Σ, but there may be several structures generating the same Σ. If two or more structures generate the same Σ, the structures are said to be *equivalent*. If a parameter has the same value in all equivalent structures, the parameter is said to be *identified*. If all parameters of the model are identified, the whole model is said to be identified.

Let θ be a vector of all the independent, free and constrained parameters, i.e., counting each distinct constrained parameter once only. The identification problem then is the problem of whether or not θ is determined by Σ.

If a parameter is identified, LISREL can determine several consistent estimators of it (See Section I.10). However, if a parameter is not identified it does not make sense to talk about an estimator of it.

One way to phrase the identification problem is as follows. Suppose the model is correct but we do not know the values of the parameters of the model. Suppose we have all the data we can possibly ask for. The identification problem is concerned with the question: Is there a unique set of parameter values consistent with this data? Some parameters may be *identified*, i.e., uniquely defined in this sense, others may not be so. If all the parameters of the model are identified we say that the whole model is identi-

fied. Otherwise, the model is said to be *non-identified*. If
the model is non-identified it does not mean that everything
is hopeless. Those parameters which are identified will still
be estimated consistently by the program. And for the parameters which are not identified, it may be, for example, that the
sum or the product of two parameters is identified although
each parameter is not separately identified. Although the computer program can estimate models which are non-identified, it
is recommended to deal with such models by adding appropriate
conditions so as to make all the parameters identified. For example, if only the sum of two parameters is identified we may fix one
and estimate the other or we may assume that the two parameters
are equal and estimate the common value. In interpreting the results of an analysis it is necessary to have a complete under-
standing of the identification status of each parameter of the
model.

Since no general and practically useful necessary and sufficient
conditions for identification are available for the general LISREL
model, it is suggested that the identification problem be studied
on a case by case basis by examining the equations

$$\sigma_{ij} = f_{ij}(\underset{\sim}{\theta}) \ , \quad i \leq j \tag{I.14}$$

defining the σ's as functions of $\underset{\sim}{\theta}$.
There are $(p + q)(p + q + 1)/2$ equations in t unknown parameters
θ_1, θ_2,..., θ_t, t being the total number of parameters in the model. Hence, a necessary condition for identification of all para-
meters is that

$$t \leq (p + q)(p + q + 1)/2 \tag{I.15}$$

If a parameter θ can be determined from these equations, this
parameter is identified, otherwise it is not. Often some parameters can be determined in different ways. This gives rise to over-
identifying conditions in $\underset{\sim}{\Sigma}$ which must hold if the model is true.
The equations are usually non-linear, the solution is often com-
plicated and explicit solutions for all θ's seldom exist. However,
it is not necessary to actually solve the equations, but one should
convince oneself about which of the parameters can be solved and
which cannot. Several necessary and sufficient conditions for
identification has been given for some special classes of LISREL
models namely for factor analysis models by Howe (1955), Anderson
and Rubin (1956), Dunn (1973), Jennrich (1978), Algina (1980),
see also Jöreskog and Sörbom (1979) pp 40-43, for simultaneous
structural equation models, see e.g. Goldberger (1964) pp 306-318
and for structural equation models with measurement errors by
Geraci (1976). These conditions may be applied to the measurement
model part and to the structural equation model part separately.
Examples of how the identification problem is solved are given in
Jöreskog (1977, 1981b), Jöreskog and Sörbom (1977) and in Chapter III.

For many users of LISREL, the identification problem may be
too difficult to resolve. There may be a tendency to run the model even though the identification of it is unclear. Therefore it
is a good thing that the computer program checks the positive de-
finiteness of the information matrix. (The information matrix

is the probability limit of the matrix of second order derivatives of the fitting function used to estimate the model, see Section I.10). If the model is identified then the information matrix is almost certainly positive definite. If the information
matrix is singular, the model is not identified and the rank of
the information matrix indicates which parameters are not identified (see Jöreskog, 1981b). One should be aware, however, that
this check is not one hundred percent reliable although experience
indicates that it is nearly so. The check depends on the estimated point in the parameter space at which the information matrix
is evaluated and on the numerical accuracy by which the information matrix is inverted.

Another way to use the program to check the identification status
of the model is the following. Choose a set of reasonable values
for the parameters and compute Σ. (The program can do this for
you.) Then run the program with this Σ as input matrix and estimate θ. If this results in the same estimated values as those used
to generate Σ, then it is most likely that the model is identified.
Otherwise, those parameters which gave a different value are probably not identified.

I.9 Kinds of Input Data and Matrices to Be Analyzed

Equations (1)-(3) represent a model for a population of individuals (observational units). This population is characterized by
the mean vector μ and the parameters θ generating the covariance
matrix Σ in (4). In practice, μ and θ are unknown and must be estimated from data. It is assumed that the data is a random sample
of independent observations from the population.

Any number, k, of input variables may be read by the program. From
these input variables, the p y-variables and q x-variables to be
included in the model are selected in the order the user wants
them.

Let Z be a matrix of raw data of order N x k, with N independent
observations on k input variables. The user may choose to read in

   A. the raw data matrix Z itself
   B. the moment matrix $M = (1/N) Z'Z$, i.e., the matrix of moments
      about zero
   C. the covariance matrix $S = \left[1/(N-1)\right](Z'Z - N\bar{z}\bar{z}')$, where $\bar{z}$
      is the mean vector $(1/N) Z'1$
   D. the correlation matrix $R = D^{-1}SD^{-1}$, where $D = (\text{diag } S)^{\frac{1}{2}}$
      is a diagonal matrix of standard deviations.

The user may also read in a vector of means $\bar{z} = (1/N) Z'1$ and/or
a vector of standard deviations $d = (\sqrt{s_{11}}, \sqrt{s_{22}}, \ldots, \sqrt{s_{kk}})$.

The user may choose to analyze:

    a. the moment matrix $\underset{\sim}{M}$. This should be used whenever there
       are intercept terms in the equations or mean parameters
       of the latent variables, see Chapter V.

    b. the covariance matrix $\underset{\sim}{S}$. This should be used in general.

    c. the correlation matrix $\underset{\sim}{R}$. This could be used if the units
       of measurements in the observed variables are arbitrary
       and irrelevant.

The program can compute $\underset{\sim}{M}$ from $\underset{\sim}{S}$ and $\bar{z}$ and $\underset{\sim}{S}$ from $\underset{\sim}{M}$ and $\bar{z}$. Default values are zero for means and one for standard deviations.
As a consequence, the program can always compute the matrix to be
analyzed ($\underset{\sim}{M}$, $\underset{\sim}{S}$ or $\underset{\sim}{R}$) regardless of what has been read ($\underset{\sim}{Z}$, $\underset{\sim}{M}$, $\underset{\sim}{S}$
or $\underset{\sim}{R}$).

LISREL can handle missing observations and discrete (ordinal)
variables when reading raw data. This will be described in a separate chapter (Chapter IV). This also leads to possibilities for
analyzing matrices of polychoric (including tetrachoric) and polyserial correlations.

Regardless of the kind of input data, the program will compute a
matrix $\underset{\sim}{M}$, $\underset{\sim}{S}$ or $\underset{\sim}{R}$ according to the user's specification. This matrix may be saved on disk to be used again in the next problem.
From this matrix the variables to be included in the analysis
are selected. The p y-variables are selected first and the q

x-variables second. After selection the resulting matrix is partitioned as

$$
\underset{\sim}{S}\left[(p + q) \times (p + q)\right] = \begin{pmatrix} \underset{\sim}{S}_{yy}(p \times p) & \underset{\sim}{S}_{yx}(p \times p) \\ \underset{\sim}{S}_{xy}(q \times p) & \underset{\sim}{S}_{xx}(q \times q) \end{pmatrix}
$$

Here and in the following, the matrix to be analyzed is denoted
$\underset{\sim}{S}$ regardless of whether it is a $\underset{\sim}{M}$, $\underset{\sim}{S}$ or $\underset{\sim}{R}$.

I. 10 Estimation of the Model

It is assumed that the distribution of the observed variables can
be described, at least approximately, by the mean vector and the
covariance matrix, so that information about parameters provided
by moments of higher order may be ignored. (The term covariance
matrix is used here in the general sense of a moment matrix,
which may be a matrix of moments about zero, a matrix of variances and covariances, or a matrix of correlations). The mean
vector is unconstrained, so the estimation is essentially that of
fitting the covariance matrix $\underset{\sim}{\Sigma}$ implied by the model, as given by
(4), to the sample covariance matrix $\underset{\sim}{S}$.

LISREL can obtain five kinds of estimates of parameters:

1.   Instrumental Variables (IV)

2.   Two-Stage Least Squares (TSLS)

3.   Unweighted Least Squares (ULS)

4.   Generalized Least Squares (GLS)

5.   Maximum Likelihood (ML)

All five methods give consistent estimates which means that they
will be close to the true parameter values in large samples
(assuming, of course, that the model is correct). The five types
of estimates differ in several respects. The Two-Stage Least
Squares and the Instrumental Variables methods are ad-hoc procedures which are non-iterative and therefore very fast. They are
described in the next section. The ULS, GLS and ML estimates are
obtained by means of an iterative procedure which minimizes the
particular fitting function by successively improving the parameter estimates. Initial values have to be provided for the iterative procedures as a first approximation of the estimates.

The fitting function for ULS is

$$F = \tfrac{1}{2}\ \text{tr}[(\underset{\sim}{S} - \underset{\sim}{\Sigma})^2] \qquad\qquad (\text{I.16})$$

i.e., half the sum of squares of all the elements of the matrix
$\underset{\sim}{S} - \underset{\sim}{\Sigma}$. The fitting function for GLS,

$$F = \tfrac{1}{2}\ \text{tr}[(\underset{\sim}{I} - \underset{\sim}{S}^{-1}\underset{\sim}{\Sigma})^2]\ , \qquad\qquad (\text{I.17})$$

uses sums of squares weighted by the inverse of the sample
covariance matrix $\underset{\sim}{S}$. Finally, maximum likelihood estimation
minimizes the function

$$F = \log|\underset{\sim}{\Sigma}| + \text{tr}(\underset{\sim}{S}\underset{\sim}{\Sigma}^{-1}) - \log|\underset{\sim}{S}| - (p + q), \qquad (\text{I.18})$$

where, for a square matrix $\underset{\sim}{A}$, $|\underset{\sim}{A}|$ denotes the determinant of $\underset{\sim}{A}$
and $\text{tr}(\underset{\sim}{A})$ denotes the sum of the diagonal elements of $\underset{\sim}{A}$. Each of
the three equations represents a function of the independent
parameters $\underset{\sim}{\theta}$, i.e., the free and constrained elements in $\underset{\sim}{\Lambda}_y$, $\underset{\sim}{\Lambda}_x$,
$\underset{\sim}{B}$, $\underset{\sim}{\Gamma}$, $\underset{\sim}{\Phi}$, $\underset{\sim}{\Psi}$, $\underset{\sim}{\theta}_\epsilon$, and $\underset{\sim}{\theta}_\delta$, and is minimized with respect to these.
The fitting functions are always non-negative. They are equal to
zero only when there is a perfect fit and the fitted $\underset{\sim}{\Sigma}$ equals $\underset{\sim}{S}$.
The fitting function for ULS can be justified without distribu-
tional assumptions. The fitting function for ML is derived from

the maximum likelihood principle based on the assumption that the observed variables have a multinormal distribution (see, e.g., Joreskog, 1967). The GLS estimator is a straightforward application of Aitkin's (1934-35) generalized least squares principle (cf. Joreskog and Goldberger, 1972). GLS and ML estimates have similar asymptotic properties. Under the assumption of multivariate normality both estimators are optimal in the sense of being most precise in large samples. The LISREL program provides large sample standard errors for the GLS and ML parameter estimates. These measure the precision of each parameter estimate. Standard errors are not available for the other three types of estimates (IV, TSLS, and ULS).

The fitting function for ML may also be used to compute parameter estimates even if the distribution of the observed variables deviate moderately from normality, but the standard errors must then be interpreted very cautiously. If the distributions deviate far from normality it is adviseable to "robustify" the elements of S before the analysis, see Gnanadesikan (1977) for methods for assessing multivariate normality and for robust estimates of variances, covariances and correlations.

A requirement for the ML method is that the matrix S is positive definite, and that starting values for the parameter estimates are provided (see next section) such that also the matrix Σ is positive definite. These requirements are not necessary for the ULS method.

A special submodel of the general LISREL model, not mentioned specifically before, is one in which $\xi \equiv x$ so that the x-variab-

les themselves influence the η-variables directly. Example 8 of
Section III.9 is such a model. The x-variables are either random
variables with an unconstrained covariance matrix or a set of
fixed variables.

In this kind of a model we have $\Lambda_x = I$ and $\Theta_\delta = 0$ and Φ is the
covariance matrix of x which is unconstrained. If x is random,
it can be shown that the minimum of the fitting function (ULS or
ML) always occur when $\Phi = S_{xx}$, the sample covariance matrix of x.
When x is fixed, of course, Φ is automatically equal to S_{xx}. Thus,
regardless of whether x is considered fixed or random, we may take $\Phi = S_{xx}$ and hold Φ fixed in the minimization.

This kind of model is so common that it is convenient to introduce a special keyword for it. This keyword   FI, which stands
for FIxed-x, may be given on the MO card, see Section II.6. The
keyword FI automatically implies all of the following

$$NK = NX \qquad \Lambda_x = I, \qquad \Theta_\delta = 0, \qquad \Phi = S_{xx} \text{ (fixed)}$$

In the ML case, the program also adjusts the degrees of freedom
in the model (see next section) so that these will be correct
regardless of whether x is fixed or random.

In the ULS and ML methods, the fitting function $F(\theta)$ is minimized by an iterative procedure, which, starting at the initial
estimates $\theta^{(1)}$ generates successively new points $\theta^{(2)}$, $\theta^{(3)}$ ...

in the parameter space such that $F(\theta^{(s+1)}) < F(\theta^{(s)})$, until convergence is obtained. The minimization method makes use of the
first-order derivatives and approximations (probability limits)
to the second-order derivatives of F. For the ML method, the approximation to the second-order derivatives is the information
matrix which is nearly always positive definite if the model is
identified. For the ML method the information matrix may be computed and used to compute standard errors for all the parameters.
The whole estimated covariance or correlation matrix of all the
estimated parameters may also be obtained.

It may happen that there are several local minima of the fitting
function. The only way to avoid this is to have a model which is
appropriate for the data and a large random sample. Experience
indicates, however, that multiple solutions seldom occur, and
when they do, it is usually with solutions on the boundary of or
outside the admissible parameter space. The computer program does
not constrain variances to be positive, correlations to be less than
one in magnitude, etc. The only constraint imposed by the program
is that the matrix Σ reproduced by the model is positive definite.
Apart from this there is nothing that prevents the program from
going outside the admissible parameter space. Although constrained
estimation would be possible, the minimization algorithm for this
would be much more time-consuming even in the case when the solution is admissible. This would not be worthwhile. If the solution
is in the interior of the admissible parameter space one will just
spend more computer time to find it. If, on the other hand, the so-

lution is inadmissible, the current program will find the solution outside the admissible parameter space whereas a program which uses constrained estimation will find the solution on the boundary of the admissible parameter space. In both cases the conclusions will be that the model is wrong or that the sample size is too small.

It is often possible, though not always, to use various tricks to force the program to stay within the admissible parameter space (for an example, see Jöreskog, 1981b).

I.11 Automatic Starting Values = Initial Estimates

LISREL provides automatic starting values by computing consistent estimates of all the parameters of the model using instrumental variables methods and least squares methods developed by Hägglund (1980, 1981). A technical detailed presentation of these methods as applied to LISREL models will be given elsewhere (Sörbom & Jöreskog, 1982a).Only a brief summary is given here.

When the model fits the data well the starting values produced

by the program are often so close to the ML or ULS solution
that only a few iterations are necessary to compute these solutions. For some models the estimated starting values are identical to the ML estimates. To emphasize the fact that the starting values are estimates in their own right we call them *initial estimates* instead of starting values. The user may choose
to obtain only these initial estimates and not compute the ML
or ULS estimates. In particular, this may be used with large models to save computer time especially when the model is only tentative. In such a situation the initial estimates themselves and/
or other information in the output may suggest how to improve the
model.

In most cases the user would only specify the non-zero value in
each column of Λ_y and Λ_x, necessary to fix the scales for η and
ξ, and leave it to the program to compute starting values for all
the free parameters. However, if the user wishes, he/she may specify starting values for any number of free parameters.

The initial estimates are computed in four steps as follows:

Step 1: Reference variables are determined as follows.

　　　　If the scales for η and ξ have been fixed by assigning

　　　　a non-zero fixed value in each column of Λ_y and Λ_x, the

first reference variable corresponds to the first row
of $\underset{\sim}{\Lambda}$ having at least one non-zero value, where $\underset{\sim}{\Lambda}$ is either
$\underset{\sim}{\Lambda}_y$ or $\underset{\sim}{\Lambda}_x$. The second reference variable corresponds to
the first row of $\underset{\sim}{\Lambda}$ which is linearly independent of the
row corresponding to the first reference variable. The
third reference variable corresponds to the first row of
$\underset{\sim}{\Lambda}$ which is linearly independent of the rows corresponding
to the first and the second reference variables, etc. In
this way m+n reference variables can be determined pro-
vided $\underset{\sim}{\Lambda}_y$ and $\underset{\sim}{\Lambda}_x$ contain m and n linearly independent
rows, respectively. Note that this requires that m $\leq$ p
and n $\leq$ q.

If the scales of $\underset{\sim}{\xi}$ have been fixed by standardizing $\underset{\sim}{\Phi}$,
the program will automatically assign fixed values in the
columns of $\underset{\sim}{\Lambda}_x$, relax the fixed diagonal elements of $\underset{\sim}{\Phi}$ and
use the same procedure as above to determine the reference
variables. When the initial estimates for $\underset{\sim}{\Lambda}_x$ have been determined in Step 2 the program will rescale the ξ-variab-
les so that diag$(\underset{\sim}{\Phi}) = \underset{\sim}{I}$.

Step 2: For each row of $\underset{\sim}{\Lambda}$ ($\underset{\sim}{\Lambda}_y$ or $\underset{\sim}{\Lambda}_x$) the program estimates the
free parameters, if any, which are left zero by the user,
by estimating the linear relation between each observed
variable and the reference variables using all other observed variables as instrumental variables. In this step we
use Hägglund's (1981) FABIN 3 estimators.

Step 3: For given Λ_y and Λ_x we estimate the joint covariance matrix of η and ξ and Θ_ε and Θ_δ by unweighted least squares (ULS) applied to $S - \Sigma$. For given Λ_y and Λ_x this leads to a quadratic function which can be minimized easily. Parameters in Φ, Θ_ε and Θ_δ for which the user has provided a non-zero value are held fixed during this minimization.

Step 4: When the joint covariance matrix of η and ξ has been estimated as in Step 3, the structural equation system can be estimated by instrumental variables methods. We estimate each equation separately using all the ξ-variables as instrumental variables. Again, parameters in B and Γ for which the user has provided a non-zero value are held fixed. The estimates computed in this step are identical to the well-known two-stage least-squares estimators.

The instrumental variables method used in Steps 2 and 4 require that the number of instrumental variables be at least as many as the number of right-hand variables whose parameters are to be estimated. In general, there is no such guarantee (for example, the model may have no ξ-variables). Whenever this condition fails, or if the instrumental variables procedure fails for any other reason, the linear relation is estimated by ordinary least squares (OLS) instead. This may result in estimates which in some cases may be slightly biased (or inconsistent).

I.12 Assessment of Fit

One important part in the application of LISREL is the assessment
of the fit and the detection of lack of fit of the model. LISREL
provides several powerful tools for this purpose.

The first and most obvious way of assessing the goodness of the
model is to examine the results of an analysis. It is recommended
that the user pays careful attention to the following quantities

1. Parameter estimates

2. Standard errors (for ML only)

3. Squared multiple correlations

4. Coefficients of determination

5. Correlations of parameter estimates (for ML only)

If any of the above quantities has an unreasonable value this is
an indication that the model is fundamentally wrong and that it
is not suitable for the data. Examples of such unreasonable values
in the parameter estimates are negative variances, correlations
which are larger than one in magnitude, covariance or correlation
matrices which are not positive definite. Whenever such things
occur the program prints a warning message. Other indications of
a bad model are squared multiple correlations or coefficients of
determination which are negative. Further indications of bad models are standard errors which are extremely large or parameter
estimates which are correlated very highly. This means that the
model is nearly non-identified and that some parameters cannot be
determined from the data.

The program gives squared multiple correlations for each observed variable separately and coefficients of determination for all the observed variables jointly. It also gives squared multiple correlations for each structural equation and coefficients of determination for all structured equations jointly. The squared multiple correlation is a measure of the strength of relationship, and the coefficients of determination is a measure of the strength of several relationships jointly.

These coefficients are defined as follows. The squared multiple correlation for the i:th observed variable is $1 - \hat{\theta}_{ii}/s_{ii}$, where $\hat{\theta}_{ii}$ is the error variance and s_{ii} is the observed variance of the i:th variable. The coefficient of determination is $1 - |\underset{\sim}{\theta}|/|\underset{\sim}{S}|$, where $|\underset{\sim}{\theta}|$ is the determinant of $\underset{\sim}{\theta}$ and $|\underset{\sim}{S}|$ is the determinant of the covariance matrix $\underset{\sim}{S}$ of the observed variables. The measures show how well the observed variables serve, separately or jointly, as measurement instruments for the latent variables. These coefficients are between zero and one, large values being associated with good models.

The squared multiple correlations for the structural equations are defined as

$$1 - Var(\zeta_i)/Var(\eta_i)$$

for the i:th equation and the total coefficient of determination is defined as

$$1 - |\underset{\sim}{\Psi}| / |\text{Cov}(\underset{\sim}{\eta})|$$

for all the structural equations jointly.

The second part of the model evaluation concerns the assessment of the overall fit of the model to the data. The goodness of fit of the whole model may be judged by means of three measures of overall fit. One is the overall χ^2-measure and its associated degrees of freedom and probability level (for ML only). The χ^2-measure is N - 1 times the minimum value of the fitting function for the specified model. If the model is correct and the sample size sufficiently large, the χ^2-measure is the likelihood ratio test statistic for testing the model against the alternative that $\underset{\sim}{\Sigma}$ is unconstrained. The degrees of freedom for χ^2 is

$$df = \tfrac{1}{2}k(k + 1) - t,$$

where k is the number of observed variables analyzed and t is the total number of independent parameters estimated. The probability level of χ^2 is the probability of obtaining a χ^2-value larger than the value actually obtained given that the model is correct.

Although the χ^2-measure may be derived theoretically as a like-lihood ratio test statistic for testing the hypothesis that $\underset{\sim}{\Sigma}$ is of the form implied by the model against the alternative that $\underset{\sim}{\Sigma}$ is unconstrained (see Jöreskog, 1977), it should be emphasized that such a use of χ^2 is not valid in most cases for several rea-sons. Firstly, in most empirical work the model is only tentative and is only regarded as an approximation to reality. From this point of view the statistical problem is not one of testing a given hypothesis (which a priori may be considered false) but rather one of fitting the model to the data and to decide whether the fit is adequate or not. Even if it would be reasonable to take the view that one wants to test the composite hypothesis that the model is true in the total population one must remember that the χ^2 is a valid test statistic only if

1. all the observed variables have a multivariate normal distribution,
2. the analysis is based on the sample covariance matrix $\underset{\sim}{S}$ (standardization is not permitted),
3. the sample size is fairly large.

All these three assumptions are seldom fulfilled in practice.

Instead of regarding χ^2 as a test statistic one should regard it as a goodness (or badness) of fit measure in the sense that large χ^2-values correspond to bad fit and small χ^2-values to good fit. The degrees of freedom serves as a standard by which to judge whether χ^2 is large or small. The χ^2-measure is sensitive to sample size and very sensitive to departures from multivariate normality of the observed variables. Large sample sizes and departures from normality tend to increase χ^2 over and above what can be expected due to specification error in the model. One reasonable way to use χ^2-measures in comparative model fitting is to use χ^2-differences in the following way. If a value of χ^2 is obtained, which is large compared to the number of degrees of freedom, the fit may be examined and assessed by an inspection of the covariance residuals, the normalized residuals and the modifica-

cation indices (see below). Often these quantities will suggest
ways to relax the model somewhat by introducing more parameters.
The new model usually yields a smaller χ^2. A large drop in χ^2,
compared to the difference in degrees of freedom, indicates that
the changes made in the model represent a real improvement. On
the other hand, a drop in χ^2 close to the difference in number of
degrees of freedom indicates that the improvement in fit is obtained by "capitalizing on chance", and the added parameters may
not have real significance and meaning.

The other two measures of overall fit are the goodness-of-fit
index GFI and the root mean square residual RMR. The goodness-
of-fit index is defined as

$$GFI = 1 - \frac{tr(\hat{\underset{\sim}{\Sigma}}^{-1}\underset{\sim}{S} - \underset{\sim}{I})^2}{tr(\hat{\underset{\sim}{\Sigma}}^{-1}\underset{\sim}{S})^2} \qquad \text{for ML}$$

and

$$GFI = 1 - \frac{tr(\underset{\sim}{S} - \hat{\underset{\sim}{\Sigma}})^2}{tr(\underset{\sim}{S}^2)} \qquad \text{for ULS}$$

where $\hat{\underset{\sim}{\Sigma}}$ is the fitted matrix. The goodness-of-fit index adjusted
for degrees of freedom, or the adjusted GFI, AGFI, is defined as

$$AGFI = 1 - [k(k+1)/2d](1 - GFI),$$

where k is as before and d is the degrees of freedom for the model.
This corresponds to using mean squares instead of total sums of
squares in the numerator and denominator of 1 - GFI. Both of these
measures should be between zero and one, although it is theoretically
possible for them to become negative. They are defined differently in the

two cases to correspond most closely to the function being minimized in each case. GFI is a measure of the relative amount of
variances and covariances jointly accounted for by the model.
Unlike χ^2, GFI is independent of the sample size and relatively
robust against departures from normality. Unfortunately, however,
its statistical distribution is unknown, even under idealized
assumptions, so there is no standard to compare it with.

The root mean square residual is defined as

$$RMR = \left[2 \sum_{i=1}^{k} \sum_{j=1}^{i} (s_{ij} - \hat{\sigma}_{ij})^2 / k(k+1) \right]^{\frac{1}{2}}$$

where k is the total number of y- and x-variables in the model.
This is a measure of the average of the residual variances and
covariances. This can only be interpreted in relation to the
sizes of the observed variances and covariances in $\underset{\sim}{S}$.

The root mean square residual can be used to compare the fit of
two different models for the same data. The goodness of fit index can be used for this purpose too but can also be used to compare the fit of models for different data.

It should be emphasized that the measures χ^2, GFI and RMR are
measures of the overall fit of the model to the data and do not
express the quality of the model judged by any other internal or
external criteria. For example, it can happen that the overall
fit of the model is very good but with one or more relationships
in the model very poorly determined, as judged by the squared multiple correlations, or vice versa. Furthermore, if any of the overall measures indicate that the model does not fit the data well,
it does not tell what is wrong with the model or which part of the

model is wrong. A more detailed assessment of fit can be obtained by an inspection of the normalized residuals and/or the modification indices. A normalized residual is $s_{ij} - \hat{\sigma}_{ij}$ divided by the square root of its asymptotic variance which is estimated as $(s_{ii}s_{jj} + s_{ij}^2)/N$. A Q-plot of these residuals gives a very effective summary. Residuals which are larger than two in magnitude are indicative of a specification error in the model and the corresponding indices i and j usually give a hint as to where this error is.

The modification indices are measures associated with the derivatives of the fitting function with respect to the fixed and constrained parameters. For each fixed and constrained parameter the modification index is defined as (N/2) times the ratio between the squared first-order derivative and the second-order derivative. It can be shown that this index equals the expected decrease in χ^2 if a single constraint is relaxed and all estimated parameters are held fixed at their estimated value. These indices therefore, may be judged by means of a χ^2-distribution with 1 degree of freedom. The fixed parameter corresponding to the largest such index is the one which, when relaxed, will improve fit maximally. The improvement in fit is measured by a reduction in χ^2 which is *guaranteed* to be at least as large as the modification index. This procedure seems to work well in practice, as the examples in Chapter III will illustrate, but it is recommended to use it only when relaxing a parameter makes sense from a substantive point of view and when the values of this parameter can be clearly interpreted.

CHAPTER II

DETAILED INSTRUCTIONS FOR THE PROBLEM RUN

II.1 Keywords

The LISREL control cards and data are explained in detail
in this chapter. The input for LISREL is controlled by
certain two-letter keyword card names and keyword parameter
names. The input is actually very easy to set up once
certain basic keywords have been learned. The general
rules for the keywords are given in this chapter. The
examples in the next chapter will clarify how the rules are
applied in practice.

The input for LISREL falls naturally into three groups:
1. Specification of the data
2. Specification of the model
3. Specification of the output
The data is specified by a DA card, the model is defined
by a MO card and the output is specified by a OU card.
These cards are required for every problem. In addition
there must be a title card for each problem. Other cards
may be required to define the data and the model completely.

The term card is used here in the sense of an input record
from a terminal or a punched card. On a terminal the end
of a record is specified by a RETURN character. The first

non-blank character on a LISREL control card must be a
LISREL card name such as DA, MO or OU. A card name may
contain any number of characters but only the first two
are significant. Thus

    DATA

    DATAPARAMETERS

    DATA-PARAMETERS

    DA

are all equivalent as long as they do not contain a blank.

Each LISREL card with a card name may contain parameters
with certain keywords. Parameter names may also contain
any number of characters but only the first two are significant. Blanks are used to separate different keywords
and thus cannot be used within keywords. All LISREL parameters have default values which have been defined so that
one can specify the common types of problems with a minimum
of input. Only parameters which do not have the default
value must be given. Parameters which have a numerical
value is specified by an equal sign and a number. For
example, the parameter NI on the DA card which specifies
the number of input variables (see Section II.2) can be
given as

    DA NI=5

or as

    DATA NINPUTVAR:S=5

There must not be a blank character before the
equal sign. Logical parameters, i.e., parameters which
can take only two "values", are given without the equal
sign. The absence of such a parameter implies the default
value and the presence implies the other value. For example,
the presence of the parameter SE (standard errors) on the
OU card signifies that the user wants the standard errors
to be given in the output. The default is that standard
errors will not be given. Some parameters have values which
are non-numeric. Such values must be given exactly as
defined. For example, one of the three alternative values
of the parameter MA on the DA card is MM (moment matrix)
and this must be given as

    MA=MM

or

    MATRIX=MM

but not as

    MA=MOMMATRIX

If one card is not sufficient for all the parameters, write
a C for CONTINUE or COMMENT and continue on the next card.
Every character appearing after the C on that card will be
ignored by the program. The C must appear in place of a
parameter name, not in place of an equal sign or a parameter
value.

A description of all LISREL control cards follows. The
order among the cards is arbitrary to a certain extent
but they will be presented in the order which seems most
natural.

II.2 Title

The first card for each problem must be a title card containing any information which the user wants to use as a
heading for this problem. Most users will only use a single
title card. However, the program can read any number ($\geq$ 1)
of title cards which may be used to describe the model and
the data. The program will read the title until it finds
a blank in column 80. Therefore column 80 must not be blank
on any title card except the last one. The complete title
will be printed on the first page of the printed output.
The first 79 characters of the title will be printed on
every page of the printed output.

II.3 The DA card

The DATAPARAMETERS card contains the following parameters
which determine the data to be used. In the following,
the underlined characters are the required characters for
each keyword.

NGroups = Number of groups (see V.2)

> Default value = 1

NInpvar = Number of input variables

> Default value = 0

NObs   = Sample size N , i.e., the number of statistical
> units (e.g. persons) on which the NI variables
> have been measured or observed.
>
> Default value = 100
>
> If N is unknown and raw data is to be read,
> set NObs = 0 and the program will compute N
> (see II.4)

MAtrix   Type of matrix to be analyzed

> = MM for a matrix of moments about zero
>
> = CM for a covariance matrix
>
> = KM for a correlation matrix
>
> = AM for an augmented moment matrix (See II.4.4)
>
> Default = CM

It should be noted that the matrix to be analyzed is not
necessarily the same as the matrix that will be read. As
explained in Section I.9, the program can always compute the
matrix to be analyzed regardless of the kind of data that
will be read in.

II.4 Input Data

After the DA card, one will usually read in various kinds of
input data. This is done in the following way: (1) read a card
with a card name which specifies the kind of data that will be
read; (2) read an optional card specifying a format; (3) read a
number of cards containing data given in this format.

The different card names for reading data are

LA for labels

RA for raw data

MM for a moment matrix

CM for a covariance matrix

KM for a correlation matrix

ME for means

SD for standard deviations

Each of these cards may contain three parameters UN, FO
and RE:

UNit = n FOrmat-on-unit-5 REwind

where n is the logical unit number of the disk or tape
where the data are stored, default value = 5, i.e., the
unit where the LISREL control cards are read. If $n \neq 5$,
the format and the data will be read from unit n , i.e.,
another unit than the unit from which the control cards
are read. However, if FO appears, the format is given in
the immediately following record on unit 5. If FO does
not appear, the optional format statement preceeds the data on

unit n. If the format and the data are stored on the ordinary
input unit (unit 5) along with the other control cards, the card
need only contain the keyword card name. If RE appears,
unit n ≠ 5 will be rewound after the data have been
read.

The cards MM, CM and KM may contain one additional parameter explained in II.4.3 and the card RA may contain four
additional parameters explained in Chapter IV.

For fixed-format input, the second card should contain a user-
specified FORTRAN format of at most 80 columns beginning with a
left parenthesis and ending with a right parenthesis. If no
format statement is supplied, the data entries are assumed to be
in free form and have to be separated by blanks or commas (list-
directed input).

II.4.1 Labels (LA)

The user may assign a label for each input variable. The
number of labels to be read is equal to value of NI given on the DA card.
Each label may consist of any number of alphanumeric characters but only the first eight characters will be retained
by the program. If the format is an * in column 1, the
labels are read in free format with blanks as separators
and each label between apostrophes. Otherwise, the labels
must be read by an A-format.

If no labels are read the variables will simply be labeled
1, 2, ..., NI .

II.4.2 Labels for Latent Variables (LK, LE)

The user can now read in labels for the latent variables.
These will be used in the printout, which, as a consequence,
will be much more readable. Several other changes have been
made in the printout to make this more readable.

To read labels for ξ-variables one uses a LK card and to read
labels for η-variables one uses a LE card. The syntax for both
is the same as for the LA card (p. II.7). The example *Nine
Psychological Variables - Confirmatory Factor Analysis* given
at the end of this document illustrates the use of labels for
ξ-variables.

II.4.3 Raw Data (RA)

Raw data are read with one observational unit (person) per
record, i.e., each unit begins on a new line (card). There
must be NI data values on each record. Data records are
read until NObs records have been read or a full record of
only zeroes is encountered or an end-of-file is encountered.
If NObs is unknown, specify NObs=0 on the DA card, and, if
the data matrix is read from unit 5, add a full record
with all zeroes at the end. The number of data records
read will be given in the output and used as NObs in subsequent computations.

If the number of observations NObs is erroneously set too
large, the program will terminate input when a complete
blank or zero observation or an end-of-file card is encountered and will use the correct observation count in the computations.

II.4.4 Moment, Covariance and Correlation Matrices (MM, CM, KM)

All matrices are read row-wise. When reading a symmetric
matrix, the user may choose to read it in three alternative
ways. To read the full matrix, i.e., the elements of the
matrix above as well as below the diagonal, one writes the
parameter keyword FUll on the first card and reads one
record for each row of the matrix, i.e., each row begins
on a new record (card). To read only the lower half of
the matrix, one writes the parameter keyword SYmmetric and
reads each row up to and including the diagonal element and
begins each row on a new record (card). In the default option,
i.e., when neither FU or SY is given, one reads the lower
half of the matrix row-wise as one long record.

The following example illustrates the three alternatives.
Suppose one wants to read the covariance matrix

$$
\underset{\sim}{S} = \begin{bmatrix} 1.13 & -0.87 & 1.08 \\ -0.87 & 2.17 & 1.83 \\ 1.08 & 1.83 & 3.25 \end{bmatrix}
$$

using the format F5.2 . Then the input in the three
alternatives will be (note the blanks)

```
CM FU
(16F5.2)
   113  -87  108
   -87  217  183
   108  183  325
```

```
CM SY
(16F5.2)
   113
  -87   217
  108   183   325
```

```
CM
(16F5.2)
   113  -87   217   108   183   325
```

Another possibility is to read the matrix with a free
format. If blanks are used as delimiters, there is no
distinction between starting a new record for each row and
reading all elements as one long record. When reading
only the lower half of the matrix the parameter SY is redundant. For example, one can read the full matrix by
giving

```
CM FU
*
1.13 -.87 1.08
-.87 2.17 1.83
1.08 1.83 3.25
```

and one can read the lower half as

```
CM
*
1.13 -.87 2.17 1.08 1.83 3.25
```

or equivalently as

```
CM
*
1.13
-.87 2.17
1.08 1.83 3.25
```

II.4.5 Augmented Moment Matrix

Suppose one reads NI = k and MA = AM (Augmented Moment
Matrix) on the DA card (see p. II.5). Let z_{i1}, z_{i2}, ..., x_{ik}
denote the input variables for the i:th unit in the sample,
i = 1, 2, ..., N. Then the program will compute the augmented
moment matrix $\underset{\sim}{M}$ of order (k + 1) x (k + 1) , defined as

$$
\underset{\sim}{M} =
\begin{bmatrix}
m_{11} & & & & \\
m_{21} & m_{22} & & & \\
\cdot & \cdot & & & \\
\cdot & \cdot & & & \\
\cdot & \cdot & & & \\
m_{k1} & m_{k2} & \cdots & m_{kk} & \\
\bar{z}_1 & \bar{z}_2 & \cdots & \bar{z}_k & 1
\end{bmatrix}
$$

where $\quad m_{jk} = (1/N) \sum_{i=1}^{N} z_{ij} z_{ik}$ and $\quad \bar{z}_j = (1/N) \sum_{i=1}^{N} z_{ij}$.

This is the sample moment matrix when the variable "const",
which is equal to one for every sample unit, has been added
as the last variable. This variable will be given the default
label 'CONST'. The program also automatically updates NI
from NI = k to NI = k + 1 .

The augmented moment matrix is needed whenever the model involves constant intercept terms and/or mean values of latent
variables (see pp. V.15-30). Note that the program can compute
the augmented moment matrix regardless of what kind of input
data is actually read in (raw data, covariance matrix, correlation matrix, means and standard deviations) provided, of
course, that information about both means and standard deviations are obtainable from the input.

II.4.6 Means and Standard Deviations (ME, SD)

The means or the standard deviations of the input variables
may be given by first writing an ME or SD card, then a
format card and the means or standard deviations written
as one long record. The record must contain NI data values.

Some of the control cards considered so far will now be
illustrated by means of a small but fairly typical example.
Suppose the three variables are denoted Y, X1 and X2 and
their covariance matrix is given by $\underset{\sim}{S}$ in the previous
subsection. The means are 1.051, 2.185 and 3.753. The
covariance matrix $\underset{\sim}{S}$ and the means are stored in a file
on unit 8. The format for the covariance matrix is also
on unit 8 but not the format for the means. Unit 8 contains
the following

```
(16F5.2)                    Format for covariance matrix
   113           ⎤
  -87   217      ⎥        Covariance matrix
  108   183  325 ⎦
 1051 2185 3753          Means
```

The input on unit 5 may then be

```
LISREL Model for Y, X1 and X2        Title
DA NI=3                              DA card
LA                                   LA card
*                                    Format for labels
'Y'  'X1'  'X2'                      Labels
CM UN=8                              CM card
ME UN=8 FO RE                        ME card
(16F5.3)                             Format for means
```

Unit 8 will be rewound after the means have been read so
that this data may be used immediately in another problem.

II.5 Selection of Variables

The user may select any number out of the NI input variables to be included in the model and choose the order in
which these variables should appear.

To select variables one writes the card SELECT UNIT=n .
A list of selected variables is then read from unit n
(default n = 5). The selected variables should be listed
either by numbers or by labels in the order the user wants
them and the y-variables should be listed first. The list of
selected variables are read in free format and the entries are
separated by blanks or commas. No format card is required.
A / (slash) signals the end of the list of selected variables and must be included regardless of whether the selected variables are listed by numbers or by labels. If all
variables are selected the / (slash) is not required.

If no selection card is read it means that all the input
variables should be included in the analysis and that they are
already in the correct order.

II.6   The MO Card

The MOdelparameters card is used to specify the model to
be estimated. The following parameters may be given on
the MO card

NYvar   = number of y-variables in the model (p)

NXvar   = number of x-variables in the model (q)

NEta   = number of η-variables in the model (m)

NKsi   = number of ξ-variables in the model (n)

When one or more of these are default on the MO card, a
submodel of the general model is obtained, see Section I.3
and Table I.2. For example, if NY and NE are default, one
obtains the submodel

$$\underset{\sim}{x} = \underset{\sim}{\Lambda}_x \underset{\sim}{\xi} + \underset{\sim}{\delta}$$

involving only the three parameter matrices $\underset{\sim}{\Lambda}_x$, $\underset{\sim}{\Phi}$ and
$\underset{\sim}{\Theta}_\delta$. If NE and NK are default, one obtains the submodel

$$\underset{\sim}{y} = B\underset{\sim}{y} + \Gamma\underset{\sim}{x} + \underset{\sim}{\zeta}$$

which involves the parameter matrices B, Γ and Ψ .

For each parameter matrix involved in the model (submodel)
one can write a specification of the form

     MN = AA, BB ,

where MN is a name of a parameter matrix, i.e., one of LY, LX, BE

GA, PH, PS, TE and TD, AA is a matrix form and BB is a

either FI (fixed) or FR (free), see Section I.4 and Table I.3.

For example,

LX = DI, FR

which implies that Λ_x is diagonal with free diagonal elements.

The order of AA and BB may be interchanged so that this

specification can also be written

LX = FR, DI .

Either AA or BB may be omitted in which case the default

values given in Table I.3 will be used. For example

LX = DI

means that Λ_x is a fixed diagonal matrix, and

LX = FR

means that Λ_x is a full matrix with all elements free. Also,

LX may be default entirely on the MO card which implies

that Λ_x is a full fixed matrix.

The user should make a specification of the form

MN = AA, BB

for each matrix in the model (submodel) whose form and/or

fixed-free status differs from the default. Study the

default values in Table I.3 carefully. The defaults have

been chosen so that the most of the commonly used models require a minimum of specifications on the MO card.

One additional parameter may be given on the MO card,
namely the logical parameter $\underline{\text{FI}}$xed x. This signifies that
the x-variables are fixed (non-random) as opposed to random
variables. If FI is given on the MO card, the program
automatically sets NK = NX, $\underset{\sim}{\Lambda}_x = \underset{\sim}{I}$, $\underset{\sim}{\Theta}_\delta = \underset{\sim}{0}$, $\underset{\sim}{\Phi} = \underset{\sim}{S}_{xx}$ (fixed),
i.e., $\underset{\sim}{\xi} \equiv \underset{\sim}{x}$. This specification may also be used even
if the x-variables are random if $\underset{\sim}{\xi} = \underset{\sim}{x}$ and the covariance
matrix of x is unconstrained, i.e., if all the elements
of $\underset{\sim}{\Phi} = \text{Cov}(\underset{\sim}{x})$ are free. The FI specification is automatically included if both NE and NK are default on the MO
card, i.e., for the model

$$\underset{\sim}{y} = \underset{\sim\sim}{By} + \underset{\sim\sim}{\Gamma x} + \underset{\sim}{\zeta}$$

the program automatically takes x to be a set of fixed
variables (predetermined or exogenous).

II.7   The FR and FI Cards

On the MO card one can specify that an entire parameter
matrix is to be fixed or free, i.e., that $\underline{\text{all}}$ the elements
of the matrix are fixed or free. The $\underline{\text{FR}}$ee and $\underline{\text{FI}}$x cards can
be used to define the fixed-free status of single matrix
elements. For example, if $\underset{\sim}{\Lambda}_x$ has been declared free on
the MO card by the specification LX = FR , the elements
$\lambda_{12}^{(x)}$, $\lambda_{22}^{(x)}$, $\lambda_{31}^{(x)}$ and $\lambda_{41}^{(x)}$ can be declared fixed by the
card

FIx LX(1,2) LX(2,2) LX(3,1) LX(4,1) .

Here blanks are used as delimiters between the matrix elements. Blanks may also be used instead of the parantheses and the comma. Thus the above card can also be written

FI LX 1 2   LX 2 2   LX 3 1   LX 4 1

Any specification on a FR or FI card overwrites any previous specification made for the elements listed on that card. Thus, for example,

FR BE(2,1) LY(5,2) LY(4,1) PS(1,1)

declares the elements β_{21}, $\lambda_{52}^{(y)}$, $\lambda_{41}^{(y)}$ and ψ_{11} to be free regardless of their previous fixed-free status. Similarly,

FI LX(2,1) LX(3,1) GA(1,1) PS(2,1)

declares the elements $\lambda_{21}^{(x)}$, $\lambda_{31}^{(x)}$, γ_{11} and ψ_{21} to be fixed regardless of their previous fixed-free status.

If one wants to declare a range of parameters which are in consecutive order (see I.4)   to be free or fixed, one can use a hyphen (-). For example,

FRee BE(1,2) GA(1,1) GA(2,2)-GA(2,5)

defines β_{12}, γ_{11}, γ_{22}, γ_{23}, γ_{24} and γ_{25} to be free.

There are two important rules which one must remember in
FR and FI cards:

1) If a matrix has been specified as ZE or ID on the MO
    card, one cannot refer to any element of this matrix
    since this is not stored in the computer.

2) If a matrix has been specified as DI on the MO card,
    one cannot refer to any off-diagonal element of this
    matrix since only the diagonal elements are stored.

II.8   The PA Card

When a matrix contains many fixed and free elements, the
method of specifying their fixed-free status by means of
a FR or a FI card is inconvenient. In this case one can
use a PAttern card instead. A PA card is a signal to the
program to read a pattern matrix of zeroes and ones, where
a zero means a fixed element and a one means a free element.

To read a pattern matrix, one should first read a card:

    PA MN

where MN is the name of the matrix, LY, BE, PS etc. This
is followed by a format card specifying an integer format
or an * and a pattern matrix of zeroes and ones. The

pattern matrix is read as one long vector reading row-wise,
but, by specifying the format properly, one can arrange to
read the pattern as a matrix. The following are four
alternative ways of reading the pattern matrix for

$$\Gamma = \begin{bmatrix} \text{free} & \text{fixed} & \text{fixed} \\ \text{fixed} & \text{free} & \text{free} \end{bmatrix}$$

1. PA GA
    (6I1)
    100011

2. PA GA
    (3I1)
    100
    011

3. PA GA
    *
    1 0 0 0 1 1

4. PA GA
    *
    1 0 0
    0 1 1

If a matrix is symmetric, only the elements in the lower
half, including the diagonal should be read. If a matrix
is specified to be diagonal, only the diagonal elements
should be read. For example, if $\Phi(4 \times 4)$ is symmetric
with fixed diagonal elements and free off-diagonal elements,
and if $\Psi(4 \times 4)$ is diagonal, with elements ψ_{11} and ψ_{33}
fixed and ψ_{22} and ψ_{44} free, the pattern matrices are
read as

for Φ :

    PA PH
    *
    0 1 0 1 1 0 1 1 1 0

and for $\underset{\sim}{\Psi}$:

```
PA PS
*
0 1 0 1
```

The pattern matrices can also be read from unit   n   by
specifying UNit = n   on the PA card.

II.9   The EQ Card

The EQual card is used to specify equality constraints,
see Section I.6 .   One simply lists those elements which
are supposed to be equal.   Each group of parameters constrained to be equal must be defined on a new EQual card.
The first parameter listed in each group is usually defined as a free parameter separately.   If one card is not
sufficient to list all the constrained parameters in a
group put a   C   in place of a matrix name and continue on
the next card.   For example,

    EQUAL LY(3,4) LY(4,4) BE(2,1)-BE(2,4) C
    GA(4,6) TE(5,2)

defines $\lambda_{34}^{(y)} = \lambda_{44}^{(y)} = \beta_{21} = \beta_{22} = \beta_{23} = \beta_{24} = \gamma_{46} = \theta_{52}^{(\varepsilon)}$

One can also use an EQ card to fix parameters.   If $\lambda_{34}^{(y)}$ is
a fixed parameter in the example above, then all the other
parameters will be fixed and equal to the value of $\lambda_{34}^{(y)}$.

II.10   The PL Card

For any given solution, the user may choose to plot the fitting
function (ULS, GLS or ML) against any parameter, whether fixed
or free. Any number of such plots may be requested in each run.
For free parameters the range of the abscissa in the plot is
chosen to correspond to an approximate 95 % confidence interval.
For fixed parameters the range of the ordinate correspond approximately to the modification index. The plot contains two
curves, one being the exact fitting function, the other being
a quadratic approximation to it. The extent to which these
curves coincide give an indication of how good the normality
approximation is.

For example, to plot the parameters $\lambda_{21}^{(x)}$, ϕ_{32} and γ_{53}
one uses

        PL   LX(2,1)   PH(3,2)   GA(5.3)

The syntax of the PL card is the same as that of the FR and
FI cards (p. II.15).

II.11   The NF Card

A most remarkable feature in LISREL VI is the automatic model modification.

An option is available to let the program automatically modify the model sequentially, by freeing in each step, that fixed parameter or that equality constraint, which corresponds to the largest modification index and continue to do so for as long as this index is statistically significant. The user can specify the significance level and any parameters which must not be set free during this process.

The user should use this option with careful judgement. Only such parameters and constraints should be relaxed that make sense from a substantive point of view.

To use the automatic model modification one writes the logical parameter AM on the OU card. The significance level for the modification index may also be specified on the OU card as SL = 5, i.e. 5 %. The default value is SL = 1. Parameters which must not be set free are specified on a NF (Never Free) card. For example, if it is not meaningful to relax $\lambda_{31}^{(x)}$, $\lambda_{41}^{(x)}$, $\lambda_{52}^{(x)}$, $\lambda_{62}^{(x)}$, say, one writes

     NF   LX(3,1)   LX(4,1)   LX(5,2)   LX(6,2) .

The syntax for the NF card is the same as that of the FR and FI cards (p. II.15).

It should be noted that only fixed and constrained parameters included in the original model will be relaxed during the automatic model modification. For example, if Θ_δ is diagonal no off-diagonal elements of Θ_δ will be relaxed. If one wants to have the possibility of relaxing off-diagonal elements of Θ_δ one must specify TD = SY on the MO card even if Θ_δ is diagonal in the original model.

II.12 The VA and ST Cards

The VAlue and the STarting-value cards are used to define
non-zero values for fixed parameters and can also be used
to specify starting values for free parameters, see Sections
I.7 and I.11. The VA and ST cards are equivalent and can be
used synonymously. Both cards reads a number and inserts
it in the locations given by a list of matrix elements.
For example,

    VA 1.5 LX(2,1) LY(6,2) GA(1,2)

assigns the value 1.5 to $\lambda_{21}^{(x)}$, $\lambda_{62}^{(y)}$ and γ_{12}. As a
second example, suppose that B is subdiagonal, Ψ is
symmetric and Θ_ε is diagonal with the following starting
values for the free parameters

$$
B = \begin{bmatrix} 0 & 0 & 0 \\ 0.5 & 0 & 0 \\ 0.5 & 0.5 & 0 \end{bmatrix}
\qquad
\Psi = \begin{bmatrix} 1.5 & & \\ 0.5 & 1.9 & \\ 0.7 & 0.5 & 1.5 \end{bmatrix}
$$

$$\Theta_\varepsilon = \text{diag } (1.5, 1.5, 1.5)$$

The starting values for the free parameters can then be
set by the following ST cards.

START   0.5 BE(2,1) BE(3,1)-BE(3,2) PS(2,1) PS(3,2)

START   1.5 PS(1,1) PS(3,3) TE(1)-TE(3)

START   1.9 PS(2,2)

START   0.7 PS(3,1)

Whenever a range of elements is specified, only those elements in this range which' have been specified as non-fixed
(free or constrained) elements will be set. Thus, the first of
the ST cards above can also be written

START 0.5 BE(1,1)-B(3,3) PS(2,1) PS(3,2)

with the same effect.

All non-fixed elements in all parameter matrices can be
set at the same starting value by

START 0.5 ALL

II.13 The MA Card

If there are many different non-zero fixed values in a
matrix the above method of specifying them will be inconvenient. In this case one may use a MAtrix card instead.
The MA card signals that one wants to read a matrix of
real numbers.

To read a matrix of values, read first a card

   MATRIX MN

where MN is the name of the matrix and then a format card
or a card with an * in column 1. The matrix is then read
row-wise as one long vector. For the matrices Λ_y, Λ_x, B
and Γ one can, by specifying the format properly, arrange

to read so that each row begins on a new card and this can also be done with an * card. If the matrix is symmetric, the lower half, including the diagonal, should be read as one long vector reading row-wise. If the matrix has been specified as diagonal, only the diagonal elements should be read.

Using the example of the previous section the matrices B, Ψ and Θ_ε could be read as

```
MA BE
(3F1.1)
000
500
550
MA PS
*
1.5 0.5 1.9 0.7 0.5 1.5
MA TE
*
1.5 1.5 1.5
```

These matrices can also be read from unit n by adding UNIT=n and possibly FO and RE on the MA card.

When using a free format (*) it is possible to read only a leading subset of elements in a matrix by terminating the list with a / (slash).

II.14   The OU Card

Parameter estimates may now be obtained by anyone of five different methods: IV (instrumental variables), TSLS (two-stage least squares), ULS (unweighted least squares), GLS (generalized least squares) and ML (maximum likelihood). All methods give consistent estimates for fully identified models. IV and TSLS are fast non-iterative methods which may be used conveniently with large models. ULS-, GLS- and ML-estimates are computed iteratively using starting values which are automatically produced by IV or TSLS.

Anyone of the following five logical parameters may be given on the OU-card: IV, TS, UL, GL and ML. The result is as follows

    IV: Only the IV-estimates are computed
    TS: Only the TSLS-estimates are computed
    UL: Both IV- and ULS-estimates are computed
    GL: Both TSLS- and GLS-estimates are computed
    ML: Both TSLS- and ML-estimates are computed

If none of these are given, ML is assumed. The IO (Initial estimates Only) parameter is equivalent to TS. If two or more of these parameters are given on the OU card, it is the last one that counts.

A related parameter is
    NS: Do not compute initial estimates; start iteration
        by steepest descent from the given starting point.

The other parameters determine which output the user wants to print. The standard output is always obtained. This consists of the log of read control cards, the title with parameter listing, the parameter specifications, the matrix to be analyzed, the initial estimates, the LISREL estimates (ML or ULS) and the overall goodness-of-fit measures. All other output is controlled by the following parameters.

PT	Print technical output
SE	Print standard errors
TV	Print t-values
PC	Print correlations of estimates
RS	Print $\hat{\Sigma}$, residuals $S-\hat{\Sigma}$, normalized residuals and Q-plot
EF	Print total effects
VA	Print variances and covariances
MR	Equivalent to RS and EF and VA
MI	Print modification indices
FS	Print factor scores regression
FD	Print first derivatives
SS	Print standardized solution
AL	Print all output
TO	Print with 80 characters/record. Default 132 characters

NDEC = number of decimals (0-8) on the printed output.
 If ND=9 the output will be printed with the format
 D 11.4. Default is ND=3.

The meaning and interpretation of all standard and optional output is discussed in the next chapter in connection with the examples.

One additional parameter is the following

 TM = maximum number of CPU-seconds allowed for this problem (default = 60)

If TM seconds are exceeded, the iterations are stopped and the current "solution" is written on unit 7 unless another unit is specified on the OU card, see below. The "solution" LY, LX, BE, GA, PH, PS, TE and TD is written in format (5D14.7, A2, I2, I6) where the last 10 columns of each record contains the name of the matrix, the group number and the record number within the matrix.

This termination of the program will also occur if the program iterates for more than 250 iterations or if numerical instabilities are encountered.

In addition to the above parameters one can specify on the OU card that certain parts of the results should be saved on a tape or disk. To do this, set

MN = n

where MN is the matrix to be saved and n the logical unit where it is to be saved. MN may be LY, LX, BE, GA, PH, PS, TE, TD, MA, EC. The first eight matrices refer to the LISREL solution. MA is the matrix analyzed ($\underset{\sim}{M}$, $\underset{\sim}{S}$ or $\underset{\sim}{R}$) <u>before</u> selection and EC is the covariance matrix of the ML estimators. For example, to save $\hat{\Lambda}_{\underset{\sim}{y}}$ and $\hat{B}$ on unit 8, $\underset{\sim}{S}$ on unit 21 and the covariance matrix of the estimators on unit 22, put LY=8 BE=8 MA=21 EC=22. These matrices are then written in format (5D14.7, A2, I2, I6) with the last 10 columns of each record containing the name of the matrix, the group number and the record number within the matrix.

All parameters on the OU card may be default but a card
with the two letters OU must be included. This is always
the last card for each problem.

II.15 Order of LISREL Control Cards

The order of the LISREL control cards is arbitrary except
for the following conditions

1) A title card must always come first, immediately
    followed by a DA card.

2) The OU card must always be last.

3) FR, FI, EQ, PA, VA, ST and MA cards must always come
    after the MO card.

4) The MO card is optional only if no LISREL model is
    analyzed. If the MO card is missing only the matrix
    to be analyzed will be given. Otherwise, the MO card
    must be given.

II.16 Stacked Data

After all the data for one problem or one group have
been read, the program will automatically read the data
for the next problem (if NGroup=1) or the next group
(if NGroup>1) unless an end-of-file is encountered. Any
number of problems and groups of data may be stacked
together and analyzed in one run.

II.17 Free-Format Reading

Unlike LISREL V, free format reading is now handled by our own
general subroutines. Both labels and numeric data may be read
in free format. The format card containing an * in column 1 is
no longer necessary but is still optional. Blanks and commas
are used as delimiters. The return character is ignored until
all items have been read or a slash / is encountered. If a /
is found, the remaining items are set equal to the default
value, which is zero for numeric data and equal to the default
label for labels. The default labels for input variables are
VAR 1, VAR 2, ... The default labels for ξ-variables are
KSI 1, KSI 2, ... The default labels for η-variables are
ETA 1, ETA 2, ... See also section "Labels for Latent Variables" below.

Example 1a: *Suppose that NI = 4 and one reads*

    LA
    'FAEDUC'   'MOEDUC'/

Variables 3 and 4 will then be labelled VAR 3 and VAR 4.

Example 1b: *Suppose instead that we want to assign the labels*
'FAEDUC' and 'MOEDUC' to input variables 1 and 3 and that we
do not care about labels for variables 2 and 4. This can be
done as follows

    LA
    'FAEDUC',,'MOEDUC'/

Note the two commas in the middle.

In general, the effect of two consecutive commas is that one
default value (in this case, one default label) will be inserted.
Three consecutive commas implies that two default values will be
inserted, etc.

Example 2: *Suppose the symmetric matrix* $\underset{\sim}{\Phi}$ *is of order*
10 x 10 and partitioned as

$$\underset{\sim}{\Phi} = \begin{bmatrix} \underset{\sim}{I} & \\ \underset{\sim}{0} & \underset{\sim}{0} \end{bmatrix}$$

where $\underset{\sim}{I}$ *is an identity matrix of order 5 x 5 , say. One*
can read this matrix as

```
    MA   PH
    1
    0 1
    0 0 1
    0 0 0 1
    0 0 0 0 1/
```

Data containing repetitions of the same number or group of
numbers can be read very conveniently. For example, the matrix
$\underset{\sim}{\Phi}$ in Example 2 can also be read as

```
    MA   PH
    1 0 1 2*0 1 3*0 1 4*0 1/
```

Here 3*0 is equivalent to 0 0 0 . Alternatively, 3*0 can
also be written as ,,,, .

Example 3: *Suppose one wants to read the following pattern*
matrix for $\underset{\sim x}{\Lambda}$.

$$\begin{bmatrix} 1 & 0 & 0 \\ 1 & 0 & 0 \\ 1 & 0 & 0 \\ 0 & 1 & 0 \\ 0 & 1 & 0 \\ 0 & 1 & 0 \\ 0 & 0 & 1 \\ 0 & 0 & 1 \\ 0 & 0 & 1 \end{bmatrix}$$

1 = *a free parameter*
0 = *a fixed parameter*

This can be read as

```
PA  LX
3*(1 0 0)  3*(0 1 0)  3*(0 0 1)
```

or even more simply (by omitting the asterisks) as

```
PA  LX
3(1 0 0)  3(0 1 0)  3(0 0 1)
```

II.18 Formats

When reading formatted data, all formats in LISREL V must be
at most 80 characters. This is sometimes too restrictive. It
has therefore been changed in LISREL VI so that three lines of
80 characters may be used. This can be changed, if necessary,
by the new parameter MF which specifies the maximum number of
format lines (each having 80 characters) to be used in formats.
The default value for MF is 3. MF should be given on the OU card.

CHAPTER III

EXAMPLES AND EXERCISES

III.1   Path Diagrams

A number of examples have been chosen to cover a majority
of the most common LISREL applications. For each example
the LISREL input and most of the LISREL printout is presented and explained. In particular, it is emphasized
how easy it is in each case to set up the model specification. A number of computer exercises are also given.
It is instructive to try to do these exercises.

In presenting and discussing a LISREL model it is often
useful to draw a path diagram. If certain rules are
followed in the path diagram it is possible to derive the
model equations from the path diagram and to derive the
LISREL parameter matrices. The following conventions
for path diagrams are made. These are illustrated here
by the path diagram for Example 1 given in Figure 1.

1. Observed variables such as x- and y-variables are en-
    closed in squares or rectangles. Latent variables
    such as ξ- and η-variables are enclosed in circles
    or ellipses. Measurement errors such as δ- and ε-
    variables and random disturbances such as ζ-variables
    are included in the path diagram but are not enclosed.

FIGURE III.1

Path Diagram for Ability and Aspiration

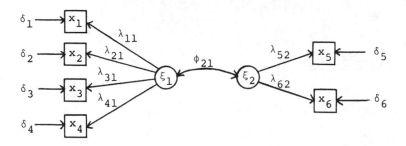

2.   A one-way arrow between two variables indicate a
     postulated direct influence of one variable on another.
     A two-way arrow between two variables indicates that
     these variables may be correlated without any causal
     interpretation.

3.   Coefficients are associated to each arrow as follows.
     Arrows from ξ-variables to x-variables are denoted $\lambda^{(x)}$
     Arrows from η-variables to y-variables are denoted $\lambda^{(y)}$
     Arrows from η-variables to η-variables are denoted β
     Arrows from ξ-variables to η-variables are denoted γ
     Arrows from ξ-variables to ξ-variables are denoted ϕ
     Arrows from ζ-variables to ζ-variables are denoted ψ
     (The path diagram in Figure 1 has no η- and ζ-variables
     so there are no $\lambda^{(y)}, \beta$, γ and ψ coefficients.   For
     this reason the superscript x on λ has been omitted.)
     Each coefficient has two subscripts, the first being the
     subscript of the variable where the arrow is pointing to

and the second being the subscript of the variable where
the arrow is coming from. For two-way arrows the two
subscripts may be interchanged so that $\phi_{21} = \phi_{12}$ in
Figure 1. Arrows which have no coefficient in the
path diagram are assumed to have a coefficient of one.

4. All direct influences of one variable on another must
    be included in the path diagram. Hence the non-
    existence of an arrow between two variables means that
    it is assumed that these two variables are not directly
    related.

If the above conventions for path diagrams are followed
it is always possible to write the corresponding equations
by means of the following general rules:

A. For each variable which has a one-way arrow pointing
    to it there will be one equation in which this variable
    is a left-hand variable.

B. The right-hand side of each equation is the sum of a
    number of terms equal to the number of one-way arrows
    pointing to that variable and each term is the product
    of the coefficient associated with the arrow and the
    variable from which the arrow is coming.

Following these rules we can now write the equations for the
path diagram in Figure 1:

$$x_1 = \lambda_{11}\xi_1 + \delta_1$$

$$x_2 = \lambda_{21}\xi_1 + \delta_2$$

$$x_3 = \lambda_{31}\xi_1 + \delta_3$$

$$x_4 = \lambda_{41}\xi_1 + \delta_4$$

$$x_5 = \lambda_{52}\xi_2 + \delta_5$$

$$x_6 = \lambda_{62}\xi_2 + \delta_6$$

Note that the second subscript of λ is equal to the subscript of the variable following λ and the first subscript is equal to the subscript of the left-hand variable.

These equations can be written in matrix form as

$$
\begin{pmatrix} x_1 \\ x_2 \\ x_3 \\ x_4 \\ x_5 \\ x_6 \end{pmatrix}
=
\begin{pmatrix} \lambda_{11} & 0 \\ \lambda_{21} & 0 \\ \lambda_{31} & 0 \\ \lambda_{41} & 0 \\ 0 & \lambda_{52} \\ 0 & \lambda_{62} \end{pmatrix}
\begin{pmatrix} \xi_1 \\ \xi_2 \end{pmatrix}
+
\begin{pmatrix} \delta_1 \\ \delta_2 \\ \delta_3 \\ \delta_4 \\ \delta_5 \\ \delta_6 \end{pmatrix}
$$

or

$$\underset{\sim}{x} = \underset{\sim}{\Lambda}_x \underset{\sim}{\xi} + \underset{\sim}{\delta} \; .$$

Note that the subscripts on λ correspond to the row and column of $\underset{\sim}{\Lambda}_x$ where the coefficient appears.

III.2 Example 1: Ability and Aspiration

*Calsyn & Kenny (1977) presented the correlation matrix in
Table 1 based on 556 white eighth-grade students. The
measures are*

x_1 = *self-concept of ability*

x_2 = *perceived parental evaluation*

x_3 = *perceived teacher evaluation*

x_4 = *perceived friend's evaluation*

x_5 = *educational aspiration*

x_6 = *college plans*

We analyze a model in which x_1, x_2, x_3 *and* x_4 *are
assumed to be indicators of "ability" and* x_5 *and* x_6
*are assumed to be indicators of "aspiration". We are
primarily interested in estimating the correlation between
true ability and true aspiration.*

TABLE III.1

Correlations Among Ability and Aspiration Measures

x_1	1.00					
x_2	0.73	1.00				
x_3	0.70	0.68	1.00			
x_4	0.58	0.61	0.57	1.00		
x_5	0.46	0.43	0.40	0.37	1.00	
x_6	0.56	0.52	0.48	0.41	0.72	1.00

The path diagram for this model is given in Figure 1 and was discussed previously.

The model, which is of the form of the first submodel in Table I.2 , includes only three parameter matrices namely Λ_x, Φ and Θ_δ , where Λ_x is a 6 x 2 matrix of factor loadings, Φ is a 2 x 2 correlation matrix and Θ_δ is a diagonal matrix with error variances in the diagonal. The LISREL input is as follows.

```
ABILITY AND ASPIRATION
DA NI=6 NO=556 MA=KM
LA
*
'S-C ABIL' 'P P EVAL' 'P T EVAL' 'P F EVAL'
'EDUC ASP' 'COL PLAN'
KM SY
(20F4.2)
 100
  73 100
  70  68 100
  58  61  57 100
  46  43  40  37 100
  56  52  48  41  72 100
MO NX=6 NK=2 PH=ST
FR LX(1,1) LX(2,1) LX(3,1) LX(4,1) LX(5,2) LX(6,2)
OU SE TV RS VA MI FS
```

The specification MA=KM on the DA card is not necessary. Since no standard deviations are read, the program takes them to be ones. Therefore, if MA=KM is omitted, the program computes the covariance matrix from the input corre-lation matrix and the unit standard deviations and the re-sult is identical to the input matrix.

Λ_x and Θ_δ are default on the MO card which means that Λ_x is a full matrix of fixed zeroes and Θ_δ is a diagonal

matrix with free diagonal elements. The declaration PH=ST
means that the two factors are standardized and that their
correlation is a free parameter to be estimated. After
the MO card the only thing that one needs to do is to specify
which factor loadings are to be estimated. These free
elements of Λ_x are given by the FR card. This means that
variables 1 and 5 will be chosen as reference variables in
Step 1 of the starting values procedure, see I.11.

We shall now describe the most important parts of the
printed output. The program lists all the LISREL control cards
that have been read by the program. This list looks as shown
below.

ABILITY AND ASPIRATION

THE FOLLOWING LISREL CONTROL LINES HAVE BEEN READ

```
DA NI=6 NO=556 MA=KM
LA
KM SY
MO NX=6 NK=2 PH=ST
FR LX(1,1) LX(2,1) LX(3,1) LX(4,1) LX(5,2) LX(6,2)
OU SE TV RS VA MI FS
```


The advantage of giving this information in the printout
is that it is always documented which input was used to
produce the output. If something is wrong, the user can
see in the output what was wrong in the input. Syntax

errors in the LISREL control cards will result in error
messages being printed within the above list.

The standard output always include the matrix to be analyzed
and the parameter specifications. The matrix to be analyzed
in this example comes out as

ABILITY AND ASPIRATION

CORRELATION MATRIX TO BE ANALYZED

	S-C ABIL	P P EVAL	P T EVAL	P F EVAL	EDUC ASP	COL PLA
S-C ABIL	1.000					
P P EVAL	0.730	1.000				
P T EVAL	0.700	0.680	1.000			
P F EVAL	0.580	0.610	0.570	1.000		
EDUC ASP	0.460	0.430	0.400	0.370	1.000	
COL PLAN	0.560	0.520	0.480	0.410	0.720	1.00

DETERMINANT = 0.368514D-01

The determinant given below the matrix is a measure of the
"ill-conditioning" of the matrix. If the determinant is
very small relative to the magnitude of the diagonal elements, this is an indication that there are one or more
nearly perfect linear relationships among the observed
variables. In such a case it is best to delete one or
more variables or to use the ULS method instead of the ML
method.

The tables of parameter specifications consist of integer
matrices corresponding to the parameter matrices. In each
matrix an element is an integer equal to the index of the
corresponding parameter in the sequence of independent
parameters. Elements corresponding to fixed parameters
are zero and elements constrained to be equal have the
same index value. Recall that LISREL orders the parameter

matrices $\Lambda_{\sim y}$, $\Lambda_{\sim x}$, B, Γ , Φ , Ψ , $\Theta_{\sim\varepsilon}$, $\Theta_{\sim\delta}$ and the elements row-wise within matrices. The parameter specifications for the example looks as follows.

ABILITY AND ASPIRATION

PARAMETER SPECIFICATIONS

LAMBDA X

	KSI 1	KSI 2
S-C ABIL	1	0
P P EVAL	2	0
P T EVAL	3	0
P F EVAL	4	0
EDUC ASP	0	5
COL PLAN	0	6

PHI

	KSI 1	KSI 2
KSI 1	0	
KSI 2	7	0

THETA DELTA

	S-C ABIL	P P EVAL	P T EVAL	P F EVAL	EDUC ASP	COL PLAN
1	8	9	10	11	12	13

The initial estimates computed by LISREL, using the procedure described in Section I.11 are as follows.

ABILITY AND ASPIRATION

INITIAL ESTIMATES (TSLS)

LAMBDA X

	KSI 1	KSI 2
S-C ABIL	0.866	0.0
P P EVAL	0.847	0.0
P T EVAL	0.801	0.0
P F EVAL	0.702	0.0
EDUC ASP	0.0	0.780
COL PLAN	0.0	0.923

PHI

	KSI 1	KSI 2
KSI 1	1.000	
KSI 2	0.664	1.000

THETA DELTA

S-C ABIL	P P EVAL	P T EVAL	P F EVAL	EDUC ASP	COL PLAN
0.250	0.282	0.359	0.508	0.392	0.148

SQUARED MULTIPLE CORRELATIONS FOR X - VARIABLES

S-C ABIL	P P EVAL	P T EVAL	P F EVAL	EDUC ASP	COL PLAN
0.750	0.718	0.641	0.492	0.608	0.852

TOTAL COEFFICIENT OF DETERMINATION FOR X - VARIABLES IS 0.980

A comparison of these estimates with those of the final ML solution ·given on the next page reveals that they are very accurate. No difference is larger than 0.02.

The table of LISREL estimates obtained by the maximum likelihood method and given on the next page.

In addition to the usual parameter estimates of $\underset{\sim}{\Lambda}_x$, $\underset{\sim}{\Phi}$ and $\underset{\sim}{\Theta}_\delta$, the program gives squared multiple correlations for each observed variable separately and coefficients of determination for all the observed variables jointly.

ABILITY AND ASPIRATION

LISREL ESTIMATES (MAXIMUM LIKELIHOOD)

LAMBDA X

	KSI 1	KSI 2
S-C ABIL	0.863	0.0
P P EVAL	0.849	0.0
P T EVAL	0.805	0.0
P F EVAL	0.695	0.0
EDUC ASP	0.0	0.775
COL PLAN	0.0	0.929

PHI

	KSI 1	KSI 2
KSI 1	1.000	
KSI 2	0.666	1.000

THETA DELTA

S-C ABIL	P P EVAL	P T EVAL	P F EVAL	EDUC ASP	COL PLAN
0.255	0.279	0.352	0.517	0.399	0.137

SQUARED MULTIPLE CORRELATIONS FOR X - VARIABLES

S-C ABIL	P P EVAL	P T EVAL	P F EVAL	EDUC ASP	COL PLAN
0.745	0.721	0.648	0.483	0.601	0.863

TOTAL COEFFICIENT OF DETERMINATION FOR X - VARIABLES IS 0.981

MEASURES OF GOODNESS OF FIT FOR THE WHOLE MODEL :

CHI-SQUARE WITH 8 DEGREES OF FREEDOM IS   9.26 (PROB. LEVEL = 0.321)

GOODNESS OF FIT INDEX IS 0.994

ADJUSTED GOODNESS OF FIT INDEX IS 0.985

ROOT MEAN SQUARE RESIDUAL IS   0.012

These coefficients were defined in Section I.12.

In this example, the squared multiple correlation for x_i
is the reliability of x_i and the coefficient of determination of $\underset{\sim}{x}$ is a generalized measure of reliability for
the whole measurement model. The latter measure shows how

well all the x-variables jointly serve as measurement in-
struments for all the ξ-variables jointly. In this case
the total coefficient of determination is remarkably high,
0.98, indicating that the measurement model is very good.
Of the measures of ξ_1 (ability), x_1 (self-concept of
ability) is the most reliable and of the two indicators
of ξ_2 (aspiration), x_6 (college plans) is the most reliable.

The last four lines of the above table give the four
measures of the overall fit of the whole model.

For the example of ability and aspiration, all four measures of fit indicate that the model fits the data very
well. The two tables on the next page give the standard
errors and the t-values for all the estimated parameters
of the model. The t-value for a parameter is defined as
the parameter estimate divided by its standard error.
This can be used to test whether the true parameter is
zero. Parameters whose t-values are larger than two in
magnitude are normally judged to be different from zero.
Here it is seen that all parameters are highly significant.
The correlation between true ability and true aspiration
is estimated as 0.67 with a standard error of 0.03. It
should be emphasized that this is not a correlation between
any linear combinations of observed variables. It is the
estimated correlation between two latent unobservable variables. A comparison with the observed correlations shows

ABILITY AND ASPIRATION

STANDARD ERRORS

LAMBDA X

	KSI 1	KSI 2
S-C ABIL	0.035	0.0
P P EVAL	0.035	0.0
P T EVAL	0.036	0.0
P F EVAL	0.039	0.0
EDUC ASP	0.0	0.040
COL PLAN	0.0	0.039

PHI

	KSI 1	KSI 2
KSI 1	0.0	
KSI 2	0.031	0.0

THETA DELTA

S-C ABIL	P P EVAL	P T EVAL	P F EVAL	EDUC ASP	COL PLAN
0.023	0.024	0.027	0.035	0.038	0.044

ABILITY AND ASPIRATION

T-VALUES

LAMBDA X

	KSI 1	KSI 2
S-C ABIL	24.561	0.0
P P EVAL	23.958	0.0
P T EVAL	22.115	0.0
P F EVAL	17.996	0.0
EDUC ASP	0.0	19.206
COL PLAN	0.0	23.571

PHI

	KSI 1	KSI 2
KSI 1	0.0	
KSI 2	21.528	0.0

THETA DELTA

S-C ABIL	P P EVAL	P T EVAL	P F EVAL	EDUC ASP	COL PLAN
10.908	11.549	13.070	14.877	10.453	3.151

that the estimated correlation between ability and aspiration is higher than the correlations between anyone of
the observed ability measures and anyone of the observed
aspiration measures, so that these correlations underesti-
mates the true correlation.

We now return to the detailed examination of the fit of
the model. For this purpose, LISREL provides a printed
section labeled RESIDUALS. This is shown below.

ABILITY AND ASPIRATION

FITTED MOMENTS AND RESIDUALS

FITTED MOMENTS

	S-C ABIL	P P EVAL	P T EVAL	P F EVAL	EDUC ASP	COL PLAN
S-C ABIL	1.000					
P P EVAL	0.733	1.000				
P T EVAL	0.695	0.684	1.000			
P F EVAL	0.600	0.591	0.560	1.000		
EDUC ASP	0.446	0.439	0.416	0.359	1.000	
COL PLAN	0.534	0.526	0.498	0.430	0.720	1.000

FITTED RESIDUALS

	S-C ABIL	P P EVAL	P T EVAL	P F EVAL	EDUC ASP	COL PLAN
S-C ABIL	-0.000					
P P EVAL	-0.003	0.000				
P T EVAL	0.005	-0.004	0.000			
P F EVAL	-0.020	0.019	0.010	-0.000		
EDUC ASP	0.014	-0.009	-0.016	0.011	-0.000	
COL PLAN	0.026	-0.006	-0.018	-0.020	-0.000	0.000

NORMALIZED RESIDUALS

	S-C ABIL	P P EVAL	P T EVAL	P F EVAL	EDUC ASP	COL PLAN
S-C ABIL	-0.000					
P P EVAL	-0.060	0.000				
P T EVAL	0.098	-0.073	0.000			
P F EVAL	-0.407	0.395	0.211	-0.000		
EDUC ASP	0.305	-0.187	-0.344	0.242	-0.000	
COL PLAN	0.533	-0.120	-0.387	-0.441	-0.000	0.000

This section of the printed output contains three symmetric matrices. The first is the fitted $\hat{\Sigma}$ and the second is the matrix of residual variances and covariances $S - \hat{\Sigma}$. As already mentioned the size of these residuals must always be judged relative to the size of the elements of S. This may be easy when S is a correlation matrix but is more difficult when S is a covariance matrix or a moment matrix, especially if the size of the covariances or moments vary considerably within the matrix. For this reason we have provided in LISREL what we call NORMALIZED RESIDUALS, see Section I.12. Each normalized residual is approximately a standard normal variable. These normalized residuals are correlated from cell to cell but are nevertheless useful in judging the fit of the model and in detecting lack of fit. If the normalized residual in cell (i,j) is larger than two in magnitude this is an indication that the model does not account for s_{ij} sufficiently well.

An effective summary of the fit, as judged by all the normalized residuals jointly, is given by the Q-plot of the normalized residuals. For our example this is given on the next page. The Q-plot is a plot of the normalized residuals against normal quantiles but for computational convenience we have chosen the normalized residuals as the abscissa. Each single point is represented by an x and multiple points by an * . The 45-degree line is given by small dots.

ABILITY AND ASPIRATION

QPLOT OF NORMALIZED RESIDUALS

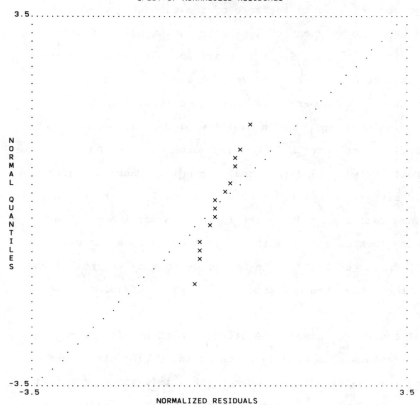

In most LISREL models there are a few elements of Σ
which fit the data trivially in the sense that there is
one free parameter per such element. For example, for
every free parameter in Θ_δ and Θ_ϵ, the corresponding
element of Σ will fit trivially. Elements of Σ which
fit the data trivially correspond to residuals and normalized residuals which are zero. Such zero normalized
residuals are omitted in the Q-plot.

The Q-plot may be examined as follows. By visual inspection, fit a straight line to the plotted points. If the
slope of this line is larger than one, as compared with
the 45-degree line, this is indicative of a good fit.
Slopes which are close to one correspond to moderate fits
and slopes which are smaller than one to poor fits. Non-
linearities in the plotted points are indicative of specification errors in the model or of departures from normality.

The user may request various variances and covariances to
be printed by specifying VA on the OU card. The variances
and covariances are given by covariance matrices between
(y,η), (y,ξ), (x,η), (x,ξ), (η,ξ) and (η,η). In our
example, only the covariance matrix (x,ξ) is relevant.
This is given on the next page.

ABILITY AND ASPIRATION

VARIANCES AND COVARIANCES

X - KSI

	KSI 1	KSI 2
S-C ABIL	0.863	0.575
P P EVAL	0.849	0.566
P T EVAL	0.805	0.536
P F EVAL	0.695	0.463
EDUC ASP	0.516	0.775
COL PLAN	0.619	0.929

In this case, since both x and ξ are standardized, these are correlations. It should be pointed out, however, that the elements of $\hat{\Lambda}_x$ are not in general correlations even if both x and ξ are standardized. The elements of $\hat{\Lambda}_x$ are regression coefficients and, as such, they can exceed the value one even though both x and ξ are standardized. The covariance matrix between x and ξ, on the other hand, is given by the matrix $\hat{\Lambda}_x \hat{\Phi}$ where $\hat{\Phi}$ is the covariance matrix of ξ. When both x and ξ are standardized $\hat{\Lambda}_x \hat{\Phi}$ is a part of a correlation matrix so that its elements are correlations. This is the matrix given above.

The next section of the printed output is the table of modification indices. When a model has been judged not to fit the data adequately by any grounds previously considered, the question arises how the model should be modified to fit the data better. What the model should be cannot be decided on a purely statistical basis, however. The best situation

is if there is a substantive theory that can be used to
decide how the model should be changed. However, in many cases
the theory does not provide such information. In such cases
it is useful to have some information from the data analysis
that would lead to a decision on how to modify the model.
This is provided by the modification indices. For each
parameter which is fixed in the model there is a modification index equal to the expected decrease in χ^2 if this
single parameter *alone* would be free. These modification
indices can therefore be examined in relation to a χ^2 distribution with one degree of freedom. (If a modification
index for a fixed parameter is zero it means that this parameter will not be identified if it is set free; modification indices for parameters which have been estimated as free parameters are automatically zero.)

A practical procedure is the following. Find the largest
modification index for all fixed parameters. If this is
larger than five, set this parameter free and reestimate
the model. The decrease in χ^2 for the new model as compared with the old should be <u>at least</u> equal to the modification index. Often the decrease in χ^2 will be much larger
than the modification index. If the fit of the model is
still bad this procedure can be repeated. Do not relax
more than one parameter each time since the modification
indices can change drastically from one solution to the
next. Technical information about the modification indices
will be given in Sörbom & Jöreskog (1982b).

ABILITY AND ASPIRATION

MODIFICATION INDICES

LAMBDA X

	KSI 1	KSI 2
S-C ABIL	0.0	4.006
P P EVAL	0.0	0.260
P T EVAL	0.0	1.353
P F EVAL	0.0	0.441
EDUC ASP	0.0	0.0
COL PLAN	0.0	0.0

PHI

	KSI 1	KSI 2
KSI 1	0.0	
KSI 2	0.0	0.0

THETA DELTA

S-C ABIL	P P EVAL	P T EVAL	P F EVAL	EDUC ASP	COL PLAN
0.0	0.0	0.0	0.0	0.0	0.0

MAXIMUM MODIFICATION INDEX IS   4.01 FOR ELEMENT (1, 2) OF LAMBDA X

The last part of the printed output for this example that
will be given here is the factor scores regressions given
by the program as

ABILITY AND ASPIRATION

FACTOR SCORES REGRESSIONS

KSI

	S-C ABIL	P P EVAL	P T EVAL	P F EVAL	EDUC ASP	COL PLAN
KSI 1	0.341	0.307	0.230	0.135	0.024	0.085
KSI 2	0.043	0.038	0.029	0.017	0.205	0.717

THE PROBLEM REQUIRED   449 DOUBLE PRECISION WORDS, THE CPU-TIME WAS   0.24 SECONDS

These coefficients represent the estimated bivariate regression of ξ_1 and ξ_2 on all the observed variables
and have been computed by the formula $\underset{\sim}{A} = \hat{\underset{\sim}{\Phi}}\hat{\underset{\sim}{\Lambda}}'\hat{\underset{\sim x}{\Sigma}}^{-1}$ (see
Lawley & Maxwell, 1971, p. 109). The matrix $\underset{\sim}{A}$ may be
saved on a file and used to compute estimated factor scores
$\hat{\underset{\sim}{\xi}}_\alpha$ for any person with observed scores $\underset{\sim}{x}_\alpha$, say, by the
formula

$$\hat{\underset{\sim}{\xi}}_\alpha = \underset{\sim}{A}\underset{\sim}{x}_\alpha \ .$$

When the LISREL model involves both ξ- and η-variables
the factor scores regression will be computed by regressing
all the ξ- and η-variables on all the observed variables.

Computer Exercise 1: Estimating the Disattenuated Correlation

Two tests x_1 and x_2 are 15-item vocabulary tests administered under liberal time limits. Two other tests y_1 and
y_2 are highly speeded 75-item vocabulary tests. The covariance matrix from Lord (1957) is (N = 649)

	x_1	x_2	y_1	y_2
x_1	86.3979			
x_2	57.7751	86.2632		
y_1	56.8651	59.3177	97.2850	
y_2	58.8986	59.6683	73.8201	97.8192

Estimate the disattenuated correlation between x and y
and test whether this is one. Also, test whether the two
pairs of tests are parallel.

Computer Exercise 2: The Rod and Frame Test

The Rod and Frame (RF) test is used as a measure of field
dependence. A subject is seated in a darkened room on a chair
which may be tilted to the left or to the right. In front of
him is a luminous rod located in a luminous square frame.
The chair, frame and rod are tilted to pre-specified positions.
By operating push buttons connected to an electric motor the
subject is to move the rod to the vertical position. The score
on the trial is the angle of the rod from the vertical. This
can assume positive and negative values. Each subject under-
goes 12 trials. The last two columns of the design matrix $\underset{\sim}{A}$
below give initial positions of the frame and chair for each
trial.

$$
\underset{\sim}{A} =
\begin{bmatrix}
1 & 1 & 1 \\
1 & -1 & -1 \\
1 & 1 & 1 \\
1 & -1 & -1 \\
1 & -1 & 1 \\
1 & 1 & -1 \\
1 & -1 & 1 \\
1 & 1 & -1 \\
1 & 1 & 0 \\
1 & -1 & 0 \\
1 & 1 & 0 \\
1 & -1 & 0
\end{bmatrix}
$$

Inter Trial Covariance Matrix for the Rod and Frame Test

	1	2	3	4	5	6	7	8	9	10	11	12
1	51.6											
2	-27.7	72.1										
3	38.9	-41.1	69.9									
4	-36.4	40.7	-39.1	75.8								
5	13.8	-5.2	17.9	1.9	84.8							
6	-13.6	10.9	9.5	17.8	-37.4	91.1						
7	21.5	-9.4	8.5	-13.1	59.7	-54.4	79.9					
8	-12.8	17.2	-3.1	22.0	-43.3	52.7	-49.9	87.2				
9	11.0	-8.9	19.2	-11.2	-12.6	21.9	-10.6	17.5	27.6			
10	-4.5	10.2	-7.6	12.7	20.4	-11.5	16.5	-14.8	-8.8	19.9		
11	9.2	-.3	18.9	-13.6	-3.9	19.0	-8.3	13.1	17.7	-2.8	27.3	
12	-3.7	7.5	-4.5	12.8	19.9	-8.8	15.5	-8.6	-5.4	13.3	-1.0	16.0

A value of +1 denotes that the position of the frame or chair was at +28° from the vertical, a value of -1 denotes that the angle was -28° and a value of 0 denotes that the initial position was vertical (Browne, 1970).

The covariance matrix between trials of the RF-test obtained from a sample of 107 eighteen year old males are given on the previous page.

Estimate the variance components associated with the general bias, frame effect, chair effect and error.

Computer Exercise 3: A Circumplex Model

A circumplex is an ordering of variables along a circle such that points which are closer together on the circle have higher correlations than those which are further apart on the circle.

The variables whose correlations are given on p. 25 are assumed to form a perfect circumplex. Test the hypothesis that the data is consistent with the circular correlation pattern.

$$P = \begin{bmatrix} 1 & & & & & \\ \rho_1 & 1 & & & & \\ \rho_2 & \rho_1 & 1 & & & \\ \rho_3 & \rho_2 & \rho_1 & 1 & & \\ \rho_2 & \rho_3 & \rho_2 & \rho_1 & 1 & \\ \rho_1 & \rho_2 & \rho_3 & \rho_2 & \rho_1 & 1 \end{bmatrix}$$

Intercorrelations among tests of six different kinds of abilities for 710 Chicago school children (Guttman, 1954).

Test	1	2	3	4	5	6
1. Association	1.000					
2. Incomplete Words	0.446	1.000				
3. Multiplication	0.321	0.388	1.000			
4. Dot Patterns	0.213	0.313	0.396	1.000		
5. ABC	0.234	0.208	0.325	0.352	1.000	
6. Directions	0.442	0.330	0.328	0.247	0.347	1.000

TABLE III.2

Scores for Fifteen College Freshmen on Five Educational Measures

Observation	y_1	y_2	x_1	x_2	x_3
1	.8	2.0	72	114	17.3
2	2.2	2.2	78	117	17.6
3	1.6	2.0	84	117	15.0
4	2.6	3.7	95	120	18.0
5	2.7	3.2	88	117	18.7
6	2.1	3.2	83	123	17.9
7	3.1	3.7	92	118	17.3
8	3.0	3.1	86	114	18.1
9	3.2	2.6	88	114	16.0
10	2.6	3.2	80	115	16.4
11	2.7	2.8	87	114	17.6
12	3.0	2.4	94	112	19.5
13	1.6	1.4	73	115	12.7
14	.9	1.0	80	111	17.0
15	1.9	1.2	83	112	16.1

III.3 Example 2: Prediction of grade averages

Finn (1974) presents the data given in Table 2 (p. 25). These data represent the scores of fifteen freshmen at a large midwestern university on five educational measures. The five measures are

y_1 = *grade average for required courses taken*

y_2 = *grade average for elective courses taken*

x_1 = *high-school general knowledge test, taken previous year*

x_2 = *IQ score from previous year*

x_3 = *educational motivation score from previous year*

We examine the predictive value of x_1, x_2 *and* x_3 *in predicting the grade averages* y_1 *and* y_2 .

Consider the bivariate regression of y_1 and y_2 on x_1, x_2 and x_3, i.e.,

$$y_1 = \gamma_{11}x_1 + \gamma_{12}x_2 + \gamma_{13}x_3 + \zeta_1 \qquad (III.1)$$

$$y_2 = \gamma_{21}x_1 + \gamma_{22}x_2 + \gamma_{23}x_3 + \zeta_2 \qquad (III.2)$$

or in matrix form

$$\underset{\sim}{y} = \underset{\sim\sim}{\Gamma x} + \underset{\sim}{\zeta},$$

where $\underset{\sim}{\Gamma}$ is the regression matrix of order 2 x 3. This is a LISREL model of the form (I.6) with $\underset{\sim}{B} = \underset{\sim}{0}$, the default value for $\underset{\sim}{B}$, $\underset{\sim}{\Gamma}$ a full free matrix, $\underset{\sim}{\Phi}$ unconstrained and $\underset{\sim}{\Psi}$ a symmetric and free matrix. A path diagram of this model is shown in Figure 2.

FIGURE III.2

Path Diagram for Prediction of Grade Averages

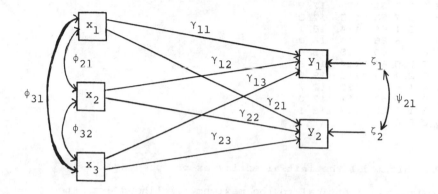

Since both NE and NK are default, the matrix Φ is handled automatically. The other three matrices have their default values. Therefore, the LISREL input for such a model is extremely simple, as shown below.

```
PREDICTION OF GRADE AVERAGES
DA NI=5
RA UN=8
MO NY=2 NX=3
OU TV SE
```

The raw data is read from a file on unit 8 and is pre-ceded by a format which in this case is an asterisk in-dicating free-format reading with blanks as separators. The data on unit 8 is shown on the next page.

```
*              DATA FOR PREDICTION OF GRADE AVERAGES
0.8  2.0  72.   114.   17.3
2.2  2.2  78.   117.   17.6
1.6  2.0  84.   117.   15.
2.6  3.7  95.   120.   18.
2.7  3.2  88.   117.   18.7
2.1  3.2  83.   123.   17.9
3.1  3.7  92.   118.   17.3
3.0  3.1  86.   114.   18.1
3.2  2.6  88.   114.   16.0
2.6  3.2  80.   115.   16.4
2.7  2.8  87.   114.   17.6
3.0  2.4  94.   112.   19.5
1.6  1.4  73.   115.   12.7
0.9  1.0  80.   111.   17.0
1.9  1.2  83.   112.   16.1
0    0    0     0      0
```

For this model the initial estimates produced by the program are identical to the maximum likelihood estimates as is seen on pp. 29-30. This is a consequence of the fact that, as a covariance structure, this model is just identified with zero degrees of freedom and fits the data perfectly, see the three measures of overall fit. The model is only useful to the extent it gives information about the relative importance of the x-variables as predictors of the two grade averages.

In this case when $\underset{\sim}{\eta} = \underset{\sim}{y}$ and $\underset{\sim}{\zeta}$ is the vector of regression residuals, the squared multiple correlations for each equation can be interpreted as the proportion of variance in each y-variable explained by the three x-variables. Here this is somewhat higher for y_2 than for y_1.

PREDICTION OF GRADE AVERAGES

INITIAL ESTIMATES (TSLS)

GAMMA

	VAR 3	VAR 4	VAR 5
VAR 1	0.085	0.008	-0.015
VAR 2	0.047	0.145	0.126

PHI

	VAR 3	VAR 4	VAR 5
VAR 3	47.457		
VAR 4	4.100	10.267	
VAR 5	6.261	0.557	2.694

PSI

	VAR 1	VAR 2
VAR 1	0.257	
VAR 2	0.169	0.237

SQUARED MULTIPLE CORRELATIONS FOR STRUCTURAL EQUATIONS

VAR 1	VAR 2
0.568	0.685

TOTAL COEFFICIENT OF DETERMINATION FOR STRUCTURAL EQUATIONS IS 0.850

PREDICTION OF GRADE AVERAGES

LISREL ESTIMATES (MAXIMUM LIKELIHOOD)

GAMMA

	VAR 3	VAR 4	VAR 5
VAR 1	0.085	0.008	-0.015
VAR 2	0.047	0.145	0.126

PHI

	VAR 3	VAR 4	VAR 5
VAR 3	47.457		
VAR 4	4.100	10.267	
VAR 5	6.261	0.557	2.694

PSI

	VAR 1	VAR 2
VAR 1	0.257	
VAR 2	0.169	0.237

SQUARED MULTIPLE CORRELATIONS FOR STRUCTURAL EQUATIONS

VAR 1	VAR 2
0.568	0.685

TOTAL COEFFICIENT OF DETERMINATION FOR STRUCTURAL EQUATIONS IS 0.850

MEASURES OF GOODNESS OF FIT FOR THE WHOLE MODEL :

CHI-SQUARE WITH   0 DEGREES OF FREEDOM IS   -0.00 (PROB. LEVEL = 1.000)

GOODNESS OF FIT INDEX IS 1.000

ROOT MEAN SQUARE RESIDUAL IS   0.000

The standard errors and the t-values are given below.

PREDICTION OF GRADE AVERAGES

STANDARD ERRORS

GAMMA

	VAR 3	VAR 4	VAR 5
VAR 1	0.027	0.049	0.112
VAR 2	0.026	0.047	0.107

PHI

	VAR 3	VAR 4	VAR 5
VAR 3	0.0		
VAR 4	0.0	0.0	
VAR 5	0.0	0.0	0.0

PSI

	VAR 1	VAR 2
VAR 1	0.109	
VAR 2	0.090	0.101

PREDICTION OF GRADE AVERAGES

T-VALUES

GAMMA

	VAR 3	VAR 4	VAR 5
VAR 1	3.168	0.169	-0.134
VAR 2	1.823	3.117	1.170

PHI

	VAR 3	VAR 4	VAR 5
VAR 3	0.0		
VAR 4	0.0	0.0	
VAR 5	0.0	0.0	0.0

PSI

	VAR 1	VAR 2
VAR 1	2.345	
VAR 2	1.875	2.345

The t-values reveal immediately that only x_1 is a significant predictor of y_1 and only x_2 is a significant predictor of y_2. The variable x_3 is not significant for either purpose. It should be noted, however, that the sample size is too small to draw any safe conclusions.

The final line of the printed output is the following self-explanatory message from the program.

THE PROBLEM REQUIRED   402 DOUBLE PRECISION WORDS, THE CPU-TIME WAS   0.08 SECONDS

The problem was run on a PRIME 750 computer.

A final comment on this example concerns the possibility of including constant intercept terms in the equations (1) and (2). It is quite possible to estimate such constant terms in the model. The only changes necessary to do this is to specify MA = MM on the DA card, indicating that the moment matrix (MM) should be analyzed rather than the co-variance matrix, and to include in the raw data one additional x-variable equal to one for all observations. The constant intercept terms will appear in the column of Γ corresponding to this variable. Further information about the analysis of moment matrices will be given in Chapter V.

Computer Exercise 4:   Regression of GNP

Goldberger (1964, p 187) presented the following data on y = gross national product in billions of dollars, x_1 = labor inputs in millions on man-years, x_2 = real capital in billions of dollars and x_3 is the time in years measured from 1928.

The data consists of 23 annual observations for the United States 1929-1941 and 1946-1955.

	x_1	x_2	x_3	y
1929	47	54	1	142
1930	43	59	2	127
1931	39	57	3	118
1932	34	48	4	98
1933	34	36	5	94
1934	36	24	6	102
1935	38	19	7	116
1936	41	18	8	128
1937	42	22	9	140
1938	37	24	10	131
1939	40	23	11	143
1940	42	27	12	157
1941	47	36	13	182
1946	51	9	18	209
1947	53	25	19	214
1948	53	39	20	225
1949	50	51	21	221
1950	52	62	22	243
1951	54	75	23	257
1952	54	94	24	265
1953	55	108	25	276
1954	52	118	26	271
1955	54	124	27	291

Estimate the regression of y on x_1, x_2 and x_3 and the standard errors of the regression coefficients.

III.4 Example 3: Ambition and Attainment

Kerchoff (1974, p. 46) reports the correlations between a number of variables for 767 twelfth-grade males. Some of these correlations are given in Table 3. The variables, in the order they appear in the table, are

x_1 = *intelligence*

x_2 = *number of siblings*

x_3 = *father's education*

x_4 = *father's occupation*

y_1 = *grades*

y_2 = *educational expectation*

y_3 = *occupational aspiration*

Kenny (1979, pp 47-73) reanalyzed these data according to the recursive system shown in Figure 3. This is a rather typical model for sociological attainment studies. We shall use these data and this model to illustrate the simplicity of the LISREL input and also to explain some new sections of the printout.

TABLE III.3

Correlations for Background, Ambition and Attainment Variables

x_1	1.000						
x_2	-.100	1.000					
x_3	.277	-.152	1.000				
x_4	.250	-.108	.611	1.000			
y_1	.572	-.105	.294	.248	1.000		
y_2	.489	-.213	.446	.410	.597	1.000	
y_3	.335	-.153	.303	.331	.478	.651	1.000

FIGURE III.3

Path Diagram for Recursive Model of Ambition and Attainment

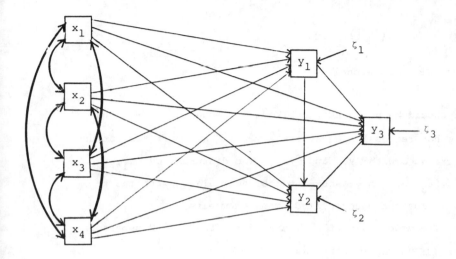

The model is a completely recursive system with exogenous variables x_1, x_2, x_3 and x_4 and jointly dependent variables y_1, y_2 and y_3. To avoid cluttering the figure we have omitted all the coefficients in Figure 3. The structural equations are

$$y_1 = \gamma_{11}x_1 + \gamma_{12}x_2 + \gamma_{13}x_3 + \gamma_{14}x_4 + \zeta_1 \qquad \text{(III.3)}$$

$$y_2 = \beta_{21}y_1 + \gamma_{21}x_1 + \gamma_{22}x_2 + \gamma_{23}x_3 + \gamma_{24}x_4 + \zeta_2 \qquad \text{(III.4)}$$

$$y_3 = \beta_{31}y_1 + \beta_{32}y_2 + \gamma_{31}x_1 + \gamma_{32}x_2 + \gamma_{33}x_3 + \gamma_{34}x_4 + \zeta_3 \quad \text{(III.5)}$$

or in matrix form

$$\begin{pmatrix} y_1 \\ y_2 \\ y_3 \end{pmatrix} = \begin{pmatrix} 0 & 0 & 0 \\ \beta_{21} & 0 & 0 \\ \beta_{31} & \beta_{32} & 0 \end{pmatrix} \begin{pmatrix} y_1 \\ y_2 \\ y_3 \end{pmatrix} + \begin{pmatrix} \gamma_{11} & \gamma_{12} & \gamma_{13} & \gamma_{14} \\ \gamma_{21} & \gamma_{22} & \gamma_{23} & \gamma_{24} \\ \gamma_{31} & \gamma_{32} & \gamma_{33} & \gamma_{34} \end{pmatrix} \begin{pmatrix} x_1 \\ x_2 \\ x_3 \\ x_4 \end{pmatrix} + \begin{pmatrix} \zeta_1 \\ \zeta_2 \\ \zeta_3 \end{pmatrix}$$

i.e., $\quad \underset{\sim}{y} = B\underset{\sim}{y} + \Gamma\underset{\sim}{x} + \underset{\sim}{\zeta}$

with $\underset{\sim}{B}$ subdiagonal.

It should be noted that unlike (3), equations (4) and (5) are not regression equations since ζ_2 and ζ_3 are not un-correlated with y_1 and y_2. The disturbances ζ_1, ζ_2 and ζ_3 are only assumed to be uncorrelated with the x-variables and uncorrelated among themselves.

The model is of the general form (I.6) with $\underset{\sim}{B}$ subdiagonal. The LISREL input for this model is

```
AMBITION AND ATTAINMENT
DA NI=7 NO=767
KM SY
(16F5 3)
 1000
 -100 1000
  277 -152 1000
  250 -108  611 1000
  572 -105  294  248 1000
  489 -213  446  410  597 1000
  335 -153  303  331  478  651 1000
LA
*
'INTEL' 'SIBL' 'FA-ED' 'FA-OCC' 'GRADES' 'EDASP' 'OCCASP'
SE
5 6 7 1 2 3 4
MO NY=3 NX=4 BE=SD PS=DI
OU SE TV EF VA
```

The SE card is necessary to reorder the variables so that the three y-variables come first.

The model involves four parameter matrices $\underset{\sim}{B}$, $\underset{\sim}{\Gamma}$, $\underset{\sim}{\Phi}$, and $\underset{\sim}{\Psi}$: $\underset{\sim}{B}$ is declared subdiagonal on the MO card, $\underset{\sim}{\Gamma}$ is

full and free by default and $\underset{\sim}{\Psi}$ is declared diagonal on
the MO card. The matrix $\underset{\sim}{\Phi}$ is automatically handled
because both NE and NK are default on the MO card, see I.3
point 2. No other model specification is necessary.

When there are no apriori fixed elements among the β's
or γ's, the model is just identified and fits the data
perfectly. The initial estimates are identical to the
maximum likelihood estimates. The ML estimates are given
on the next page.

It is obvious from the model in Figure 3 that there are
both direct and indirect effects of the x-variables on
y_2 and y_3 . For example, the direct effect of x_1 on
y_2 is $\gamma_{21} = 0.160$ and the indirect effect of x_1 on
y_2 via y_1 is $\gamma_{11}\beta_{21} = 0.526 \cdot 0.405 = 0.213$. The sum
of the direct effect and all indirect effects are called
total effects (see e.g. Duncan, 1975, Kenny, 1979, pp 70-73,
Alwin & Hauser, 1975, and Graff & Schmidt, 1981). These
total effects are given by LISREL if the user writes EF
on the OU card. In general, LISREL gives four matrices
representing the total effects of $\underset{\sim}{\xi}$ on $\underset{\sim}{\eta}$, of $\underset{\sim}{\xi}$ on
$\underset{\sim}{y}$, of $\underset{\sim}{\eta}$ on $\underset{\sim}{\eta}$ and of $\underset{\sim}{\eta}$ on $\underset{\sim}{y}$, respectively. In
this case when $\underset{\sim}{\eta} \equiv \underset{\sim}{y}$ and $\underset{\sim}{\xi} \equiv \underset{\sim}{x}$ only two of these
matrices are relevant. The total effects are given on the
page following the next. It is seen that the total effect
of x_1 on y_2 is 0.373. This is the sum of the direct
effect of 0.160 and the indirect effect 0.213 computed above.

AMBITION AND ATTAINMENT

LISREL ESTIMATES (MAXIMUM LIKELIHOOD)

BETA

	GRADES	EDUC ASP	OCC ASP
GRADES	0.0	0.0	0.0
EDUC ASP	0.405	0.0	0.0
OCC ASP	0.158	0.550	0.0

GAMMA

	INTELL	SIBLINGS	FA-ED	FA-OCC
GRADES	0.526	-0.030	0.119	0.041
EDUC ASP	0.160	-0.112	0.173	0.152
OCC ASP	-0.039	-0.019	-0.041	0.100

PHI

	INTELL	SIBLINGS	FA-ED	FA-OCC
INTELL	1.000			
SIBLINGS	-0.100	1.000		
FA-ED	0.277	-0.152	1.000	
FA-OCC	0.250	-0.108	0.611	1.000

PSI

GRADES	EDUC ASP	OCC ASP
0.651	0.517	0.557

SQUARED MULTIPLE CORRELATIONS FOR STRUCTURAL EQUATIONS

GRADES	EDUC ASP	OCC ASP
0.349	0.483	0.443

TOTAL COEFFICIENT OF DETERMINATION FOR STRUCTURAL EQUATIONS IS 0.484

MEASURES OF GOODNESS OF FIT FOR THE WHOLE MODEL :

CHI-SQUARE WITH 0 DEGREES OF FREEDOM IS -0.00 (PROB. LEVEL = 1.000)

GOODNESS OF FIT INDEX IS 1.000

ROOT MEAN SQUARE RESIDUAL IS 0.000

AMBITION AND ATTAINMENT
TOTAL EFFECTS

TOTAL EFFECTS OF X ON Y

	INTELL	SIBLINGS	FA-ED	FA-OCC
GRADES	.526	-.030	.119	.041
EDUC ASP	.373	-.124	.221	.168
OCC ASP	.249	-.092	.099	.198

TOTAL EFFECTS OF Y ON Y

	GRADES	EDUC ASP	OCC ASP
GRADES	.000	.000	.000
EDUC ASP	.405	.000	.000
OCC ASP	.381	.550	.000

LARGEST EIGENVALUE OF (I-B)*(I-B)-TRANSPOSED (STABILITY INDEX) IS   .349

The general formulas for direct, indirect and total
effects are given in Table 4.

TABLE III.4

Decomposition of Effects

Effects on $\underset{\sim}{\eta}$

	by $\underset{\sim}{\xi}$	by $\underset{\sim}{\eta}$
Direct Effect	$\underset{\sim}{\Gamma}$	$\underset{\sim}{B}$
Indirect Effect	$(\underset{\sim}{I} - \underset{\sim}{B})^{-1}\underset{\sim}{\Gamma} - \underset{\sim}{\Gamma}$	$(\underset{\sim}{I} - \underset{\sim}{B})^{-1} - \underset{\sim}{I} - \underset{\sim}{B}$
Total Effect	$(\underset{\sim}{I} - \underset{\sim}{B})^{-1}\underset{\sim}{\Gamma}$	$(\underset{\sim}{I} - \underset{\sim}{B})^{-1} - \underset{\sim}{I}$

Effects on $\underset{\sim}{y}$

	by $\underset{\sim}{\xi}$	by $\underset{\sim}{\eta}$
Direct Effect	$\underset{\sim}{\Lambda}_y\underset{\sim}{\Gamma}$	$\underset{\sim}{\Lambda}_y$
Indirect Effect	$\underset{\sim}{\Lambda}_y(\underset{\sim}{I} - \underset{\sim}{B})^{-1}\underset{\sim}{\Gamma} - \underset{\sim}{\Lambda}_y\underset{\sim}{\Gamma}$	$\underset{\sim}{\Lambda}_y(\underset{\sim}{I} - \underset{\sim}{B})^{-1} - \underset{\sim}{\Lambda}_y$
Total Effect	$\underset{\sim}{\Lambda}_y(\underset{\sim}{I} - \underset{\sim}{B})^{-1}\underset{\sim}{\Gamma}$	$\underset{\sim}{\Lambda}_y(\underset{\sim}{I} - \underset{\sim}{B})^{-1}$

The t-values for the solution of example 3 reveals that the effects γ_{12}, γ_{14}, γ_{31}, γ_{32} and γ_{33} may not be significant. A test of the hypothesis that these five γ's are zero can be obtained by running the model again, inserting a card

        FIX GA(1,2) GA(1,4) GA(3,1)-GA(3,3)

after the MO card. This "new" model does not fit the data perfectly and the χ^2 with five degrees of freedom for this model is a valid test statistic for testing the hypothesis. The value of χ^2 is 5.42 indicating that the hypothesis cannot be rejected.

Computer Exercise 5:   Educational Attainment

Wiley (1973) used a subset of variables from Sewell, Haller & Ohlendorf (1970) to estimate the following structural equation model

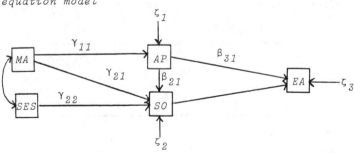

The variables and their intercorrelations ($N \approx 3500$) are

	MA	SES	AP	SO	EA
Mental ability	1.000				
Socioeconomic status	.288	1.000			
Academic performance	.589	.194	1.000		
Significant others' influence	.438	.359	.473	1.000	
Educational aspiration	.418	.380	.459	.611	1.000

A. *Estimate this model. Does the model fit the data? If not, how should it be modified to fit the data better?*

B. *Assuming that there is measurement error in the SO-variable, can the model still be estimated? If so, what is the reliability of SO?*

Computer Exercise 6: Intergenerational Social Mobility

The observed correlations among father and son status variables were as follows in one study (Blau & Duncan, 1967, p. 169). (Sample size unknown.)

FaEd	FaOcc	SoEd	SoOcc
1.000	.516	.453	.322
	1.000	.438	.405
		1.000	.596
			1.000

A. *Suppose a complete recursive model applies in the popu-*
    lation being studied. Estimate all the path coefficients
    and other parameters of the model.

B. *Using Ed and Occ as indicators of social status (SES),*
    estimate the correlation between father's and son's SES.

III.5 Example 4: Klein's Model I of US Economy

Klein's (1950) Model I is a classical econometric model
which has been used extensively as a benchmark problem
for studying econometric methods. It is an eight-equation
system based on annual data for the United States in the
period between the two World Wars. It is dynamic in the
sense that elements of time play important roles in the
model.

Following Goldberger's (1964, pp 303-325) formulation of
the model it will be illustrated how LISREL VI can be used
to estimate econometric models of this kind. In particular,
the example illustrates how one can handle identities,
i.e., exact equations, in the model. The three behavioral
equations of Klein's Model I are

$$C_t = a_1 P_t + a_2 P_{t-1} + a_3 W_t + \zeta_1 \tag{III.6}$$

$$I_t = b_1 P_t + b_2 P_{t-1} + b_3 K_{t-1} + \zeta_2 \tag{III.7}$$

$$W_t^* = c_1 E_t + c_2 E_{t-1} + c_3 A + \zeta_3 \qquad \text{(III.8)}$$

In addition to these stochastic equations the model includes five identities:

$$P_t = Y_t - W_t \qquad \text{(III.9)}$$

$$Y_t = C_t + I_t + G_t - T_t \qquad \text{(III.10)}$$

$$K_t = K_{t-1} + I_t \qquad \text{(III.11)}$$

$$W_t = W_t^* + W_t^{**} \qquad \text{(III.12)}$$

$$E_t = Y_t + T_t - W_t^{**} \qquad \text{(III.13)}$$

The endogenous variables are

C_t = *Aggregate Consumption* (y_1)
I_t = *Net Investment* (y_2)
W_t^* = *Private Wage Bill* (y_3)
P_t = *Total Profits* (y_4)
Y_t = *Total Income* (y_5)
K_t = *End-of-year Capital Stock* (y_6)
W_t = *Total Wage Bill* (y_7)
E_t = *Total Production of Private Industry* (y_8)

The predetermined variables are the exogenous variables

W_t^{**} = *Government Wage Bill* (x_1)
T_t = *Taxes* (x_2)

G_t = *Government Non-Wage Expenditures* (x_3)

A_t = *Time in years from 1931* (x_4)

and the lagged endogenous variables $P_{t-1}(x_5)$, $K_{t-1}(x_6)$ *and* $E_{t-1}(x_7)$. *All variables except* A_t *are in billions of 1934 dollars.*

Rules for identification of a model of this type have been given by econometricians, see e.g. Goldberger (1964, pp 313-318). A necessary condition for identification of each equation is that the number of x-variables excluded from the equation must be at least as great as one less the number of y-variables included in the equation. For example, in the consumption function (6), there are 3 y-variables included (C_t, P_t and W_t) and 6 x-variables excluded (W_t^{**}, T_t, G_t, A_t, K_{t-1} and E_{t-1}) so that the condition is fulfilled. Similarly, it can be verified that the condition is met also for equations (7) and (8).

There is also a sufficient condition for identification, the so called rank condition, but this is often difficult to verify in practice.

The model can be formulated as a LISREL submodel of the form (I.6) with NY = 8 and NX = 7 and with $\underset{\sim}{B}$ and $\underset{\sim}{\Gamma}$ as

$$
\underset{\sim}{B} =
\begin{bmatrix}
0 & 0 & 0 & a_1 & 0 & 0 & a_3 & 0 \\
0 & 0 & 0 & b_1 & 0 & 0 & 0 & 0 \\
0 & 0 & 0 & 0 & 0 & 0 & 0 & c_1 \\
0 & 0 & 0 & 0 & 1 & 0 & -1 & 0 \\
1 & 1 & 0 & 0 & 0 & 0 & 0 & 0 \\
0 & 1 & 0 & 0 & 0 & 0 & 0 & 0 \\
0 & 0 & 1 & 0 & 0 & 0 & 0 & 0 \\
0 & 0 & 0 & 0 & 1 & 0 & 0 & 0
\end{bmatrix}
\begin{matrix}
C_t \\ I_t \\ W_t^* \\ P_t \\ Y_t \\ K_t \\ W_t \\ E_t
\end{matrix}
$$

$$
 \quad C_t \quad I_t \quad W_t^* \quad P_t \quad Y_t \quad K_t \quad W_t \quad E_t
$$

$$
\underset{\sim}{\Gamma} =
\begin{bmatrix}
0 & 0 & 0 & 0 & a_2 & 0 & 0 \\
0 & 0 & 0 & 0 & b_2 & b_3 & 0 \\
0 & 0 & 0 & c_3 & 0 & 0 & c_2 \\
0 & 0 & 0 & 0 & 0 & 0 & 0 \\
0 & -1 & 1 & 0 & 0 & 0 & 0 \\
0 & 0 & 0 & 0 & 0 & 1 & 0 \\
1 & 0 & 0 & 0 & 0 & 0 & 0 \\
-1 & 1 & 0 & 0 & 0 & 0 & 0
\end{bmatrix}
\begin{matrix}
C_t \\ I_t \\ W_t^* \\ P_t \\ Y_t \\ K_t \\ W_t \\ E_t
\end{matrix}
$$

$$
 \quad W_t^{**} \quad T_t \quad G_t \quad A_t \quad P_{t-1} \quad K_{t-1} \quad E_{t-1}
$$

and with

$$
\underset{\sim}{\Psi} = \begin{bmatrix}
\psi_{11} & & & & & & & \\
\psi_{21} & \psi_{22} & & & & & & \\
\psi_{31} & \psi_{32} & \psi_{33} & & & & & \\
0 & 0 & 0 & 0 & & & & \\
0 & 0 & 0 & 0 & 0 & & & \\
0 & 0 & 0 & 0 & 0 & 0 & & \\
0 & 0 & 0 & 0 & 0 & 0 & 0 & \\
0 & 0 & 0 & 0 & 0 & 0 & 0 & 0
\end{bmatrix}
$$

Note that, as a consequence of the identities in the model, the last five rows of B, Γ and $\underset{\sim}{\Psi}$ do not contain any parameters to be estimated. Another consequence of the identities is that both $\underset{\sim}{\Sigma}$ and $\underset{\sim}{S}$ will be singular matrices if one uses all the 15 variables in the model. This makes it impossible to use the ML-method since this requires both $\underset{\sim}{\Sigma}$ and $\underset{\sim}{S}$ to be positive definite. However, five of the y-variables are of course redundant. By eliminating them, ML estimation is in fact possible as will be demonstrated. First, however, consider the initial estimates and the ULS-estimates.

Annual time series data for 1921-1941 are given in Table 5, which has been computed from Theil's (1975) Table 9.1. The labels and the raw data with their formats are stored on logical unit 8. The input for a ULS run is shown on page 48.

TABLE III.5

Time Series Data for Klein's Model I

t	C_t	P_{t-1}	W^*_t	I_t	K_{t-1}	E_{t-1}	W^{**}_t	T_t	A_t	P_t	K_t	E_t	W_t	Y_t	G_t
1921	41.9	12.7	25.5	-0.2	182.8	44.9	2.7	7.7	-10.0	12.4	182.6	45.6	28.2	40.6	6.6
1922	45.0	12.4	29.3	1.9	182.6	45.6	2.9	3.9	-9.0	16.9	184.5	50.1	32.2	49.1	6.1
1923	49.2	16.9	34.1	5.2	184.5	50.1	2.9	4.7	-8.0	18.4	189.7	57.2	37.0	55.4	5.7
1924	50.6	18.4	33.9	3.0	189.7	57.2	3.1	3.8	-7.0	19.4	192.7	57.1	37.0	56.4	6.6
1925	52.6	19.4	35.4	5.1	192.7	57.1	3.2	5.5	-6.0	20.1	197.8	61.0	38.6	58.7	6.5
1926	55.1	20.1	37.4	5.6	197.8	61.0	3.3	7.0	-5.0	19.6	203.4	64.0	40.7	60.3	6.6
1927	56.2	19.6	37.9	4.2	203.4	64.0	3.6	6.7	-4.0	19.8	207.6	64.4	41.5	61.3	7.6
1928	57.3	19.8	39.2	3.0	207.6	64.4	3.7	4.2	-3.0	21.1	210.6	64.5	42.9	64.0	7.9
1929	57.8	21.1	41.3	5.1	210.6	64.5	4.0	4.0	-2.0	21.7	215.7	67.0	45.3	67.0	8.1
1930	55.0	21.7	37.9	1.0	215.7	67.0	4.2	7.7	-1.0	15.6	216.7	61.2	42.1	57.7	9.4
1931	50.9	15.6	34.5	-3.4	216.7	61.2	4.8	7.5	0.0	11.4	213.3	53.4	39.3	50.7	10.7
1932	45.6	11.4	29.0	-6.2	213.3	53.4	5.3	8.3	1.0	7.0	207.1	44.3	34.3	41.3	10.2
1933	46.5	7.0	28.5	-5.1	207.1	44.3	5.6	5.4	2.0	11.2	202.0	45.1	34.1	45.3	9.3
1934	48.7	11.2	30.6	-3.0	202.0	45.1	6.0	6.8	3.0	12.3	199.0	49.7	36.6	48.9	10.0
1935	51.3	12.3	33.2	-1.3	199.0	49.7	6.1	7.2	4.0	14.0	197.7	54.4	39.3	53.3	10.5
1936	57.7	14.0	36.8	2.1	197.7	54.4	7.4	8.3	5.0	17.6	199.8	62.7	44.2	61.8	10.3
1937	58.7	17.6	41.0	2.0	199.8	62.7	6.7	7.7	6.0	17.3	201.8	65.0	47.7	65.0	11.0
1938	57.5	17.3	38.2	-1.9	201.8	65.0	7.7	7.4	7.0	15.3	199.9	60.9	45.9	61.2	13.0
1939	61.6	15.3	41.6	1.3	199.9	60.9	7.8	8.9	8.0	19.0	201.2	69.5	49.4	68.4	14.4
1940	65.0	19.0	45.0	3.3	201.2	69.5	8.0	9.6	9.0	21.1	204.5	75.7	53.0	74.1	15.4
1941	69.7	21.1	53.3	4.9	204.5	75.7	8.5	11.6	10.0	23.5	209.4	88.4	61.8	85.3	22.3

```
KLEIN'S MODEL I ESTIMATED BY ULS
DA NI=15 NO=21
LA UN=8
RA UN=8
SE
1 4 3 10 14 11 13 12 7 8 15 9 2 5 6
MO NY=8 NX=7 BE=FU GA=FI PS=FI
FR BE(1,4) BE(1,7) BE(2,4) BE(3,8)
FR GA(1,5) GA(2,6) GA(3,4) GA(3,7)
FR PS(1,1)-PS(3,3)
VA 1 BE(4,5) BE(5,1) BE(5,2) BE(6,2) BE(7,3) BE(8,5) C
GA(5,3) GA(6,6) GA(7,1) GA(8,2)
VA -1 BE(4,7) GA(5,2) GA(8,1)
OU UL
```

The variables in Table 5 are not in the same order as in the model. The selection card puts them in the order y_1, y_2, ..., y_8, x_1, x_2, ..., x_7 . Since both NE and NK are default on the MO card, FIxed x is already implied, so the only parameter matrices needed are B, Γ and Ψ . B is declared FUll on the MO card and is fixed by default. Γ is declared FIxed on the MO card and is full by default. Ψ is declared FIxed on the MO card and is symmetric by default. After the MO card the only thing that needs to be done is to define the free elements and the values of the non-zero fixed elements. This is done by the FR and VA cards.

The results of the ULS run give two different sets of estimates for the structural parameters. The estimates are given in Table 6. The initial estimates in this case are the wellknown two-stage least-squares estimates.

TABLE III.6

Parameter Estimates for Klein's Model I

Parameter	IV Estimates	ULS estimates	ML estimates
a_1	0.02	0.04	-0.23
a_2	0.22	0.21	0.38
a_3	0.81	0.81	0.80
b_1	0.15	0.05	-0.80
b_2	0.62	0.68	1.05
b_3	-0.16	-0.17	-0.15
c_1	0.44	0.39	0.24
c_2	0.15	0.20	0.28
c_3	0.13	0.15	0.23

The ULS estimates are not identical to any known estimates.
Consider what ULS is doing. ULS minimizes the sum of
squares of all the elements of the matrix

$$\underset{\sim}{S} - \underset{\sim}{\Sigma} = \begin{pmatrix} \underset{\sim}{S}_{yy} & \underset{\sim}{S}_{yx} \\ \underset{\sim}{S}_{xy} & \underset{\sim}{S}_{xx} \end{pmatrix} - \begin{pmatrix} \underset{\sim}{\Sigma}_{yy} & \underset{\sim}{\Sigma}_{yx} \\ \underset{\sim}{\Sigma}_{xy} & \underset{\sim}{\Sigma}_{xx} \end{pmatrix}$$

For simplicity, assume that there are no identities in
the model. Then

$$\underset{\sim}{\Sigma}_{yy} = \underset{\sim}{\Pi}\underset{\sim}{\Phi}\underset{\sim}{\Pi}' + \underset{\sim}{\Psi}*$$

$$\Sigma_{yx} = \Pi\Phi$$

$$\Sigma_{xx} = \Phi$$

where

$$\Pi = (I - B)^{-1}\Gamma$$

$$\Psi^* = (I - B)^{-1}\Psi(I - B')^{-1}$$

are the reduced form regression matrix and the reduced form residual covariance matrix implied by the model. Since both Φ and Ψ are unconstrained, the sums of squares of $S_{yy} - \Sigma_{yy}$ and $S_{xx} - \Sigma_{xx}$ can be made zero regardless of the values of the parameters in B and Γ by choosing $\Phi = S_{xx}$ and $\Psi = (I - B)S_{yy}(I - B') - \Gamma S_{xx}\Gamma'$. It follows that the ULS estimates of B and Γ are those which minimize the sum of squares of

$$S_{yx} - (I - B)^{-1}\Gamma S_{xx} .$$

Other alternative estimates could be obtained by minimizing the sum of squares of

$$S_{yx}S_{xx}^{-1} - (I - B)^{-1}\Gamma$$

or the sum of squares of

$$(\underset{\sim}{I} - \underset{\sim}{B})\underset{\sim\sim}{S}_{yx} - \underset{\sim\sim}{\Gamma S}_{xx} .$$

The latter has a simple closed form solution.

The estimation of Klein's Model I by the ML method will be considered next. As already noted, the covariance matrices $\underset{\sim}{\Sigma}$ and $\underset{\sim}{S}$ as well as the data matrix in Table 5 are singular because of the five identities in the model. The rank of these matrices is not 15 but 10. It is poss- ible to solve the identities (9) - (13) for the redundant variables P_t, Y_t, K_t, W_t and E_t in terms of the other 10 variables and substitute these solutions into the be- havioral equations (6) - (8). This results in a system with 3 y-variables and 7 x-variables and with coefficients which are linear combinations of the structural parameters in (6) - (8). While it is possible to estimate such a system also (see e.g. Jöreskog, 1973a), this approach, which is rather complicated, is unnecessary since LISREL will estimate the model (6) - (13) directly if one treats all the y-variables as η-variables of which only the first 3 are observed. Thus the LISREL specification

$$\underset{\sim}{y}' = (C_t, I_t, W_t^*)$$

$$\underset{\sim}{\eta}' = (C_t, I_t, W_t^*, P_t, Y_t, K_t, W_t, E_t)$$

$$\underset{\sim}{x}' \equiv \underset{\sim}{\xi}' = (W_t^{**}, T_t, G_t, A_t, P_{t-1}, K_{t-1}, E_{t-1}) .$$

The $\Lambda_{\sim y}$-matrix is

$$\Lambda_{\sim y} = \begin{bmatrix} 1 & 0 & 0 & 0 & 0 & 0 & 0 & 0 \\ 0 & 1 & 0 & 0 & 0 & 0 & 0 & 0 \\ 0 & 0 & 1 & 0 & 0 & 0 & 0 & 0 \end{bmatrix}$$

This is the matrix form called IZ in Table I.3. The matrices $\underset{\sim}{B}$, $\underset{\sim}{\Gamma}$ and $\underset{\sim}{\Psi}$ are the same as before. The input for the ML solution is as follows

```
KLEIN'S MODEL I ESTIMATED BY ML
DA NI=15 NO=21
LA UN=8
RA UN=8
SE
1 4 3 7 8 15 9 2 5 6/
MO NY=3 NE=8 NX=7 FI LY=IZ BE=FU GA=FI PS=FI TE=ZE
FR BE(1,4) BE(1,7) BE(2,4) BE(3,8)
FR GA(1,5) GA(2,5) GA(2,6) GA(3,4) GA(3,7)
FR PS(1,1)-PS(3,3)
VA 1 BE(4,5) BE(5,1) BE(5,2) BE(6,2) BE(7,3) BE(8,5) C
GA(5,3) GA(6,6) GA(7,1) GA(8,2)
VA -1 BE(4,7) GA(5,2) GA(8,1)
ST 5 PS(1,1) PS(2,2) PS(3,3)
OU NS
```

The input data is the same as before. However, in this case $NY = 3$ and $NX = 7$ so only 10 variables are selected (note that the data on P_t, Y_t, K_t, W_t and E_t is not used). The MO card specifies $NE = 8$. Since only NK is default on the MO card one must use FI to specify FIxed x and $LY = IZ$ and $TE = ZE$ to specify that $y' = (\eta_1, \eta_2, \eta_3)$. Otherwise, the MO, FR and VA cards are the same as in the previous run. One further complication arises. Since

there are more η-variables than y-variables the assumption
for the starting value algorithm is not fulfilled (see
Section I.11). One must provide such starting values
that Σ becomes positive definite at the starting point.
This is simply done by putting something positive in the
first three diagonal elements of $\underset{\sim}{\Psi}$, as shown by the ST
card in the above input. It is also recommended to write
the parameter NS on the OU card to tell the program to use
the steepest descent method to improve the starting point
before the real minimization of the fitting function begins.

The ML estimates of the structural parameters are given
in the right-most column of Table 6. It is seen that the
ML estimates are considerably different from the initial
estimates and the ULS estimates which are more close to
each other.

The ML estimates for econometric models of the form considered in this section are sometimes called FIML (Full
Information Maximum Likelihood) estimates or FILGRV (Full
Information Least Generalized Residual Variance) estimates.
It has been shown that these estimates minimize the generalized variance of the reduced form residuals, i.e., the
determinant of the reduced form residual covariance matrix
(see e.g. Jöreskog, 1973a). Hence the ML estimates can be
justified without the assumption of normality. The user
should be warned not to rely heavily on the standard errors
and/or the χ^2- measure of fit, since they depend on both

the assumption of normality and a large sample. Also, because autocorrelation is often present in time series data, the assumption of independent observations is questionable.

III.6   Example 5: Stability of Alienation

LISREL may be useful in analyzing data from longitudinal studies in psychology, education and sociology. In the sociological literature there has been a number of articles concerned with the specification of models incorporating causation and measurement errors, and analysis of data from panel studies, see e.g. Bohrnstedt (1969), Heise (1969, 1970), Duncan (1969, 1972). Jöreskog & Sörbom (1976, 1977) and Jöreskog (1979b) discuss statistical models and methods for analysis of longitudinal data.

Wheaton et al (1977) reports on a study concerned with the stability over time of attitudes such as alienation and the relation to background variables such as education and occupation. Data on attitude scales were collected from 932 persons in two rural regions in Illinois at three points in time: 1966, 1967 and 1971. The variables used for the present example are the Anomia subscale and the Powerlessness subscale, taken to be indicators of Alienation. This example uses data from 1967 and 1971 only. The background variables are the respondent's education (years of schooling completed) and

Duncan's Socioeconomic Index (SEI). These are taken to be indicators of the respondent's socioeconomic status (SES). The sample covariance matrix of the six observed variables is given in Table 7.

Two models will be considered as given in Figure 4 A-B. In this path diagram we have abandoned our tradition to label the coefficients with two indices according to the model and the rules given in III.1. In Figures 4 A-B we have simply labeled the coefficients with one index instead. The variables in the model are

y_1 = Anomia 67 $\qquad$ y_3 = Anomia 71

y_2 = Powerlessness 67 $\qquad$ y_4 = Powerlessness 71

x_1 = Education $\qquad$ x_2 = SEI

ξ = SES $\qquad$ η_1 = Alienation 67

$\qquad\qquad\qquad\qquad$ η_2 = Alienation 71

The covariance matrix of the observed variables is given in Table 7.

The model is specified as

$$\begin{pmatrix} y_1 \\ y_2 \\ y_3 \\ y_4 \end{pmatrix} = \begin{pmatrix} 1 & 0 \\ \lambda_1 & 0 \\ 0 & 1 \\ 0 & \lambda_2 \end{pmatrix} \begin{pmatrix} \eta_1 \\ \eta_2 \end{pmatrix} + \begin{pmatrix} \varepsilon_1 \\ \varepsilon_2 \\ \varepsilon_3 \\ \varepsilon_4 \end{pmatrix} \qquad \text{(III.14)}$$

FIGURE III.4

Models for the Study of Stability of Alienation

Fig. 4 A

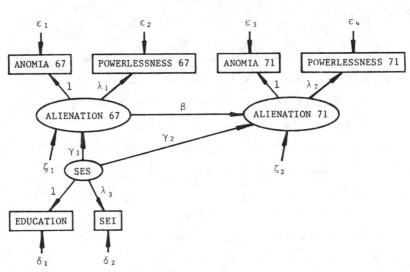

Fig. 4 B

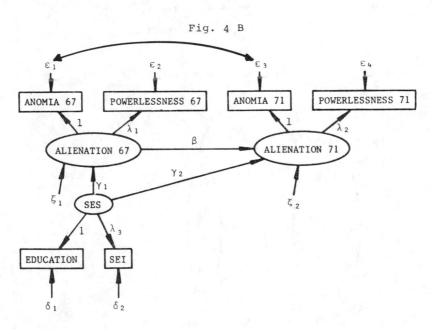

TABLE III.7

Covariance Matrix for Variables in the

Stability of Alienation Example

	y_1	y_2	y_3	y_4	x_1	x_2
y_1	11.834					
y_2	6.947	9.364				
y_3	6.819	5.091	12.532			
y_4	4.783	5.028	7.495	9.986		
x_1	-3.839	-3.889	-3.841	-3.625	9.610	
x_2	-21.899	-18.831	-21.748	-18.775	35.522	450.288

$$\begin{pmatrix} x_1 \\ x_2 \end{pmatrix} = \begin{pmatrix} 1 \\ \lambda_3 \end{pmatrix} \xi + \begin{pmatrix} \delta_1 \\ \delta_2 \end{pmatrix} \qquad \text{(III.15)}$$

$$\begin{pmatrix} \eta_1 \\ \eta_2 \end{pmatrix} = \begin{pmatrix} 0 & 0 \\ \beta & 0 \end{pmatrix} \begin{pmatrix} \eta_1 \\ \eta_2 \end{pmatrix} + \begin{pmatrix} \gamma_1 \\ \gamma_2 \end{pmatrix} \xi + \begin{pmatrix} \zeta_1 \\ \zeta_2 \end{pmatrix} . \qquad \text{(III.16)}$$

It is assumed that ζ_1 and ζ_2 are uncorrelated. The scales for η_1, η_2 and ξ have been chosen to be the same as for y_1, y_3 and x_1, respectively. In Model A all four ε-terms are uncorrelated whereas in Model B, ε_1 and ε_3 are correlated.

Consider first the identification of the model. Let $\phi = \text{Var}(\xi)$. We have six observed variables with 21 variances and covariances. Model 4A has 15 parameters (3 λ's, 1 β, 2 γ's, 1 ϕ, 2 ψ's and 6 θ's) so that if all these are identified the model will have 6 degrees of freedom.

The reduced form of (16) is

$$\eta_1 = \gamma_1 \xi + \zeta_1$$

$$\begin{aligned} \eta_2 &= (\gamma_2 + \beta \gamma_1)\xi + (\zeta_2 + \beta \zeta_1) \\ &= \pi \xi + \nu , \text{ say.} \end{aligned}$$

We have

$$\text{Cov}(y_1, x_1) = \text{Cov}(\eta_1, x_1) = \gamma_1\phi \qquad\qquad \text{(III.17)}$$

$$\text{Cov}(y_2, x_1) = \lambda_1\text{Cov}(\eta_1, x_1) = \lambda_1\gamma_1\phi \qquad\qquad \text{(III.18)}$$

$$\text{Cov}(y_3, x_1) = \text{Cov}(\eta_2, x_1) = \pi\,\phi \qquad\qquad \text{(III.19)}$$

$$\text{Cov}(y_4, x_1) = \lambda_2\text{Cov}(\eta_2, x_1) = \lambda_2\pi\,\phi \qquad\qquad \text{(III.20)}$$

If we use x_2 instead of x_1 in these equations, all four right sides will be multiplied by λ_3 . Hence, λ_3 is overdetermined since

$$\lambda_3 = \text{Cov}(y_i, x_2)/\text{Cov}(y_i, x_1) \qquad i = 1,\ 2,\ 3,\ 4.$$

With λ_3 determined, ϕ is determined by

$$\text{Cov}(x_1, x_2) = \lambda_3\phi\ .$$

With ϕ determined, equations (17) - (20) determine γ_1, λ_1, π and λ_2 , respectively. Furthermore,

$$\text{Cov}(y_1, y_2) = \lambda_1\ \text{Var}(\eta_1) = \lambda_1(\gamma_1^{\,2}\phi + \psi_{11})\ ,$$

which determines ψ_{11}, and

$$\text{Cov}(y_3, y_4) = \lambda_2\ \text{Var}(\eta_2) = \lambda_2[\pi^2\phi + \text{Var}(\nu)]$$

which determines

$$\text{Var}(\nu) = \psi_{22} + \beta^2 \psi_{11} \, .$$

For given λ_1, λ_2, γ_1, π, ϕ and ψ_{11} the four equations

$$\text{Cov}(y_1, y_3) = \gamma_1 \pi \phi + \beta \psi_{11} \, , \qquad\qquad\qquad \text{(III.21)}$$

$$\text{Cov}(y_1, y_4) = \lambda_2 (\gamma_1 \pi \phi + \beta \psi_{11}) \, , \qquad\qquad \text{(III.22)}$$

$$\text{Cov}(y_2, \dot{y}_3) = \lambda_1 (\gamma_1 \pi \phi + \beta \psi_{11}) \, , \qquad\qquad \text{(III.23)}$$

$$\text{Cov}(y_2, y_4) = \lambda_1 \lambda_2 (\gamma_1 \pi \phi + \beta \psi_{11}) \, , \qquad\quad \text{(III.24)}$$

show that β is overdetermined. Then, with β determined, $\gamma_2 = \pi - \beta \gamma_1$ and ψ_{22} are obtained. The error variances $\theta_{ii}^{(\varepsilon)}$ are determined from $\text{Var}(y_i)$, $i = 1, 2, 3, 4$ and $\theta_{ii}^{(\delta)}$ from $\text{Var}(x_i)$, $i = 1, 2$. Hence it is clear that model 4A is identified and has six independent restrictions on $\underset{\sim}{\Sigma}$.

In model 4B there is one more parameter namely $\theta_{31}^{(\varepsilon)}$. This is added to the right side of (21). However, since anyone of (22), (23) or (24) can be used to determine β it is clear that $\theta_{31}^{(\varepsilon)}$ is determined by (21). Hence model 4B is also identified and has five degrees of freedom.

The input for Model A is shown on the next page.

STABILITY OF ALIENATION   MODEL A

THE FOLLOWING LISREL CONTROL LINES HAVE BEEN READ :

```
DA NI=6 NO=932
CM
*
11.834 6.947 9.364 6.819 5.091 12.532
4.783 5.028 7.495 9.986 -3.839 -3.889
-3.841 -3.625 9.61 -21.899 -18.831
-21.748 -18.775 35.522 450.288
LA
(6A8)
MO NY=4 NX=2 NE=2 NK=1 BE=SD PS=DI TD=SY TE=SY
FR LY 2 1 LY 4 2 IX 2 1
ST 1 LY 1 1 LY 3 2 LX 1 1
OU SE TV RS EF VA MI AM PT
```

The model includes all eight parameter matrices but only
two need to be declared on the MO card: $\underset{\sim}{B}$ is subdiagonal
and $\underset{\sim}{\Psi}$ is diagonal. The free parameters λ_1, λ_2 and λ_3
in $\underset{\sim}{\Lambda}_y$ and $\underset{\sim}{\Lambda}_x$ must be declared free by a FR card. One
element in each column of $\underset{\sim}{\Lambda}_y$ and $\underset{\sim}{\Lambda}_x$ are assigned the
value one to fix the scales for η_1, η_2 and ξ . Note
that neither ξ nor η_1 or η_2 are standardized in this
example.

The value of χ^2 for this model is 71.47 with six degrees of
freedom. This is not considered an acceptable fit. We
must therefore look for some way of modifying the model.
As in many other longitudinal studies, where the same
measures are repeated over time, there is a tendency for
the measurement errors in these measures to correlate over
time due to retest effects. This suggests that the most
likely improvement of the model is obtained by freeing
the elements θ_{31} and θ_{42} of $\underset{\sim}{\Theta}_\epsilon$. But let us not take
this for granted. Instead let us see what the modification

indices tell us. The modification indices for model A are given below.

STABILITY OF ALIENATION   MODEL A

MODIFICATION INDICES

LAMBDA Y

	ETA 1	ETA 2
ANOM 67	0.0	3.480
POWL 67	0.0	3.479
ANOM 71	2.490	0.0
POWL 71	2.489	0.0

LAMBDA X

	KSI 1
EDUC	0.0
SEI	0.0

BETA

	ETA 1	ETA 2
ETA 1	0.0	0.0
ETA 2	0.0	0.0

GAMMA

	KSI 1
ETA 1	0.0
ETA 2	0.0

PHI

	KSI 1
KSI 1	0.0

PSI

ETA 1	ETA 2
0.0	0.0

THETA EPS

	ANOM 67	POWL 67	ANOM 71	POWL 71
ANOM 67	0.0			
POWL 67	0.0	0.0		
ANOM 71	63.706	49.751	0.0	
POWL 71	49.829	37.257	0.0	0.0

THETA DELTA

	EDUC	SEI
EDUC	0.0	
SEI	0.0	0.0

MAXIMUM MODIFICATION INDEX IS   63.71 FOR ELEMENT (3, 1) OF THETA EPS

The largest modification index is 63.7 for element θ_{31} of $\underset{\sim}{\theta}_\varepsilon$, indicating a drop in χ^2 if θ_{31} is relaxed equal to at least 63.7. This can be verified by running the model again adding TE = SY on the MO card and adding TE(3,1) on the FR card. The χ^2 for this modified model is 6.33 with 5 degrees of freedom. The drop in χ^2 is 65.21 with one degree of freedom, which is much larger than the modification index. The model B fits quite well. The largest modification index, 1.591, now occurs for the element θ_{42} of $\underset{\sim}{\theta}_\varepsilon$, but this is not significant. Thus, in this example, the modification indices lead us to the model B which, as indicated above, is also reasonable on a priori grounds.

The results for Model B are given in Table 8.

The input for Model B is

```
STABILITY OF ALIENATION    MODEL B
DA NI=6 NO=932
CM
*
11.834 6.947 9.364 6.819 5.091 12.532
4.783 5.028 7.495 9.986 -3.839 -3.889
-3.841 -3.625 9.61 -21.899 -18.831
-21.748 -18.775 35.522 450.288
LA
(6A8)
 ANOM 67 POWL 67 ANOM 71 POWL 71    EDUC      SEI
MO NY=4 NX=2 NE=2 NK=1 BE=SD PS=DI TE=SY
FR LY 2 1 LY 4 2 LX 2 1 TE 3 1
ST 1 LY 1 1 LY 3 2 LX 1 1
OU SE TV RS EF VA MI
```

TABLE III.8

LISREL Estimates for the Model in Figure 4 B

(Standard Errors in Parenthesis)

Parameter	Initial Estimates	Maximum Likelihood Estimates
λ_1	1.00	1.03 (0.05)
λ_2	0.96	0.97 (0.05)
λ_3	4.98	5.16 (0.42)
β	0.59	0.62 (0.05)
γ_1	-0.57	-0.55 (0.05)
γ_2	-0.24	-0.21 (0.05)
ψ_{11}	4.60	4.71 (0.43)
ψ_{22}	3.77	3.87 (0.34)
ϕ	7.14	6.88 (0.66)
$\theta_{11}^{(\delta)}$	2.47	2.73 (0.52)
$\theta_{22}^{(\delta)}$	273.56	266.90 (18.19)
$\theta_{11}^{(\varepsilon)}$	4.91	5.07 (0.37)
$\theta_{22}^{(\varepsilon)}$	2.40	2.22 (0.32)
$\theta_{33}^{(\varepsilon)}$	4.75	4.81 (0.40)
$\theta_{44}^{(\varepsilon)}$	2.77	2.68 (0.33)
$\theta_{31}^{(\varepsilon)}$	1.74	1.89 (0.24)

The specification TE = SY on the MO card does the same
thing as if TE is default. The only difference is that
when TE = SY , the full lower half of $\underset{\sim}{\Theta}_\varepsilon$ is stored in
the computer. The off-diagonal elements of $\underset{\sim}{\Theta}_\varepsilon$ are still
fixed zeroes, but with TE = SY , any such element can be
declared free, as we have done with $\theta_{31}^{(\varepsilon)}$.

The TOTAL EFFECTS and the VARIANCES AND COVARIANCES for
Model B are displayed side by side on the next page. The
total effect of SES on Alienation 71 is almost equal to
the direct effect of SES on Alienation 67, although the
direct effect of SES on Alienation 71 is much smaller.
The effects of SES on Alienation are negative indicating
that Alienation decreases when SES increases. Also shown
in the section of TOTAL EFFECTS are the total effects of
SES on the observed y-measures and also the total effects
of η_1 and η_2 on these observed measures. Although,
according to the model, SES does not have any direct
effects on any observed y , there are negative indirect
effects via η_1 and η_2 . Similarly, although η_1
does not have any direct effect on y_3 and y_4 , η_1
affects y_3 and y_4 indirectly via η_2 .

The general form of the LISREL model involves four basic
variables: $\underset{\sim}{y}$, $\underset{\sim}{\eta}$, $\underset{\sim}{x}$ and $\underset{\sim}{\xi}$. By using the model equations
(I.1), (I.2) and (I.3) and the associated assumptions one
can deduce that the joint covariance matrix of $\underset{\sim}{y}$, $\underset{\sim}{\eta}$, $\underset{\sim}{x}$
and $\underset{\sim}{\xi}$ is

$$
\begin{array}{c}
 \\
\underset{\sim}{y} \\[6pt]
\underset{\sim}{\eta} \\[6pt]
\underset{\sim}{x} \\[6pt]
\underset{\sim}{\xi}
\end{array}
\left[
\begin{array}{cccc}
\underset{\sim}{y}' & \underset{\sim}{\eta}' & \underset{\sim}{x}' & \underset{\sim}{\xi}' \\[4pt]
\underset{\sim}{\Lambda}_y(\underset{\sim}{\Pi}\underset{\sim}{\Phi}\underset{\sim}{\Pi}' + \underset{\sim}{\Psi}*)\underset{\sim}{\Lambda}_y' + \underset{\sim}{\Theta}_\varepsilon & & & \\[10pt]
(\underset{\sim}{\Pi}\underset{\sim}{\Phi}\underset{\sim}{\Pi}' + \underset{\sim}{\Psi}*)\underset{\sim}{\Lambda}_y' & \underset{\sim}{\Pi}\underset{\sim}{\Phi}\underset{\sim}{\Pi}' + \underset{\sim}{\Psi}* & & \\[10pt]
\underset{\sim}{\Lambda}_x\underset{\sim}{\Phi}\underset{\sim}{\Pi}'\underset{\sim}{\Lambda}_y' & \underset{\sim}{\Lambda}_x\underset{\sim}{\Phi}\underset{\sim}{\Pi}' & \underset{\sim}{\Lambda}_x\underset{\sim}{\Phi}\underset{\sim}{\Lambda}_x' + \underset{\sim}{\Theta}_\delta & \\[10pt]
\underset{\sim}{\Phi}\underset{\sim}{\Pi}'\underset{\sim}{\Lambda}_y' & \underset{\sim}{\Phi}\underset{\sim}{\Pi}' & \underset{\sim}{\Phi}\underset{\sim}{\Lambda}_x' & \underset{\sim}{\Phi}
\end{array}
\right]
$$

where $\underset{\sim}{\Pi} = (\underset{\sim}{I} - \underset{\sim}{B})^{-1}\underset{\sim}{\Gamma}$ and $\underset{\sim}{\Psi}* = (\underset{\sim}{I} - \underset{\sim}{B})^{-1}\underset{\sim}{\Psi}(\underset{\sim}{I} - \underset{\sim}{B}')^{-1}$.

STABILITY OF ALIENATION   MODEL B

TOTAL EFFECTS

TOTAL EFFECTS OF KSI ON ETA

	KSI 1
ETA 1	-0.550
ETA 2	-0.551

TOTAL EFFECTS OF KSI ON Y

	KSI 1
ANOM 67	-0.550
POWL 67	-0.564
ANOM 71	-0.551
POWL 71	-0.535

TOTAL EFFECTS OF ETA ON ETA

	ETA 1	ETA 2
ETA 1	0.0	0.0
ETA 2	0.617	0.0

TOTAL EFFECTS OF ETA ON Y

	ETA 1	ETA 2
ANOM 67	1.000	0.0
POWL 67	1.027	0.0
ANOM 71	0.617	1.000
POWL 71	0.599	0.971

VARIANCES AND COVARIANCES

ETA - ETA

	ETA 1	ETA 2
ETA 1	6.785	
ETA 2	4.988	7.747

ETA - KSI

	KSI 1
ETA 1	-3.783
ETA 2	-3.790

Y - ETA

	ETA 1	ETA 2
ANOM 67	6.785	4.988
POWL 67	6.965	5.121
ANOM 71	4.988	7.747
POWL 71	4.843	7.522

Y - KSI

	KSI 1
ANOM 67	-3.783
POWL 67	-3.883
ANOM 71	-3.790
POWL 71	-3.680

X - ETA

	ETA 1	ETA 2
EDUC	-3.783	-3.790
SEI	-19.528	-19.566

X - KSI

	KSI 1
EDUC	6.880
SEI	35.522

As a byproduct of the analysis it is possible to get all
these estimated variances and covariances. This is obtained by putting VA on the MO card. The resulting section
of the printout, as shown on the right side (p. 66), contains all
parts of the above covariance matrix except the y-y, y-x
and x-x parts. These parts are obtained in the $\hat{\Sigma}$ matrix
which will be given if one writes RS on the OU card.

Computer Exercise 7: Role Behavior of Farm Managers

    *Warren, White & Fuller (1974) report on a study wherein
a random sample of 98 managers of farmer cooperatives operating in Iowa was selected with the objective of studying
managerial behavior.*

    *The role behavior of a manager in farmer cooperatives,
as measured by his Role Performance, was assumed to be linearly related to the four variables*

    x_1: *Knowledge of economic phases of management directed
        toward profit-making in a business and product know-
        ledge;*

    x_2: *Value Orientation: tendency to rationally evaluate
        means to an economic end;*

    x_3: *Role Satisfaction: gratification obtained by the
        manager from performing the managerial role;*

    x_4: *Past Training: amount of formal education.*

*To measure Knowledge, sets of questions were formulated by
specialists in the relevant fields of economics and fertili-*

zers and chemicals. The measure of rational Value Orien-
tation to economic ends was a set of 30 items administrated
to respondents by questionnaire on which the respondents were
asked to indicate the strength of their agreement or dis-
agreement. The respondents indicated the strength of satisfaction or dissatisfaction for each of 11 statements covering four areas of satisfaction: (1) managerial role itself,
(2) the position, (3) rewards and (4) performance of comple-
mentary role players. The amount of past training was the
total number of years of formal schooling divided by six.

Role Performance was measured with a set of 24 questions
covering the five functions of planning, organizing, controlling, coordinating and directing. The recorded verbal responses of managers on how they performed given tasks were
scored by judges on a scale of 1 to 99 on the basis of performance leading to successful management. Responses to
each question were randomly presented to judges and the raw
scores were transformed by obtaining the "Z" value for areas
of 0.01 to 0.99 from a cumulative normal distribution (a raw
score of 40 received transformed score of -0.253). For each
question, the mean of transformed scores of judges was calcu-
lated.

The covariance matrix of the five variables is

	y	x_1	x_2	x_3	x_4
y	0.0209				
x_1	0.0177	0.0520			
x_2	0.0245	0.0280	0.1212		
x_3	0.0046	0.0044	-0.0063	0.0901	
x_4	0.0187	0.0192	0.0353	-0.0066	0.0946

A.   *Use LISREL to compute the regression of y on x_1, x_2, x_3 and x_4 and obtain the standard errors of the regression coefficients.*

To estimate the effect of measurement error in the observed variables, Rock et. al. (1977) splitted each of the measures y, x_1, x_2 and x_3 randomly into two parallel halves. The full covariance matrix of all the split-halves is (the number of items in each split-half are given in parenthesis)

	y_1	y_2	x_{11}	x_{12}	x_{21}	x_{22}	x_{31}	x_{32}	x_4
y_1 (12)	.0271								
y_2 (12)	.0172	.0222							
x_{11}(13)	.0219	.0193	.0876						
x_{12}(13)	.0164	.0130	.0317	.0568					
x_{21}(15)	.0284	.0294	.0383	.0151	.1826				
x_{22}(15)	.0217	.0185	.0356	.0230	.0774	.1473			
x_{31} (5)	.0083	.0011	-.0001	.0055	-.0087	-.0069	.1137		
x_{32} (6)	.0074	.0015	.0035	.0089	-.0007	-.0088	.0722	.1024	
x_4	.0180	.0194	.0203	.0182	.0563	.0142	-.0056	-.0077	.0946

This can be used to estimate the true regression equation

$$\eta = \gamma_1 \xi_1 + \gamma_2 \xi_2 + \gamma_3 \xi_3 + \gamma_4 \xi_4 + \zeta$$

using the following measurement models

$$\begin{pmatrix} y_1 \\ \\ y_2 \end{pmatrix} = \begin{pmatrix} 1 \\ \\ 1 \end{pmatrix} \eta + \begin{pmatrix} \varepsilon_1 \\ \\ \varepsilon_2 \end{pmatrix}$$

$$\begin{pmatrix} x_{11} \\ x_{12} \\ x_{21} \\ x_{22} \\ x_{31} \\ x_{32} \\ x_4 \end{pmatrix} = \begin{bmatrix} 1 & 0 & 0 & 0 \\ 1 & 0 & 0 & 0 \\ 0 & 1 & 0 & 0 \\ 0 & 1 & 0 & 0 \\ 0 & 0 & 1 & 0 \\ 0 & 0 & 1.2 & 0 \\ 0 & 0 & 0 & 1 \end{bmatrix} \begin{pmatrix} \xi_1 \\ \xi_2 \\ \xi_3 \\ \xi_4 \end{pmatrix} + \begin{pmatrix} \delta_{11} \\ \delta_{12} \\ \delta_{21} \\ \delta_{22} \\ \delta_{31} \\ \delta_{32} \\ 0 \end{pmatrix}$$

B. *Use LISREL to obtain estimates of the γ's, their standard errors and all the other parameters. Use the LISREL estimates to obtain estimates of the reliabilities of y, x_1, x_2 and x_3.*

III.7 Example 6: A Simplex Model for Academic Performance

A simplex model is a type of covariance structure which often occurs in longitudinal studies when the same variable is measured repeatedly on the same people over several occasions. The simplex model is equivalent to the co-variance structure generated by a first-order non-stationary

autoregressive process. Guttman (1954) used the term
simplex also for variables which are not ordered through
time but by other criteria. One of his examples concerns
tests of verbal ability ordered according to increasing
complexity. The typical feature of a simplex correlation
structure is that the correlations decrease as one moves
away from the main diagonal.

Jöreskog (1970b) formulated various simplex models in
terms of the well-known Wiener and Markov stochastic pro-
cesses. A distinction was made between a perfect simplex
and a quasi-simplex. A perfect simplex is reasonable only
if the measurement errors in the test scores are negligible.
A quasi-simplex, on the other hand, allows for sizeable
errors of measurement.

Consider p fallible variables $y_1, y_2, \ldots, y_p$. The
unit of measurement in the true variables η_i may be
chosen to be the same as in the observed variables y_i .
The equations defining the model are then

$$y_i = \eta_i + \varepsilon_i , \quad i = 1, 2, \ldots, p, \qquad \text{(III.25)}$$

$$\eta_i = \beta_i \eta_{i-1} + \zeta_i , \quad i = 2, 3, \ldots, p, \qquad \text{(III.26)}$$

where the ε_i are uncorrelated among themselves and uncorrelated with all the η_i and where ζ_{i+1} is uncorrelated with η_i , $i = 2, 3, \ldots, p-1$. A path diagram of

the simplex model with $p = 4$ is given in Figure 5.

FIGURE III.5

A Simplex Model

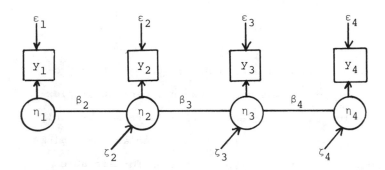

The parameters of the model are $\omega_1 = \text{Var}(\eta_1)$, $\psi_i = \text{Var}(\zeta_i)$, $i = 2, 3,$
..., p, $\theta_i = \text{Var}(\varepsilon_i)$, $i = 1, 2, \ldots, p$ and $\beta_2, \beta_3,$
..., β_p. Let $\omega_i = \text{Var}(\eta_i) = \beta_i^2 \omega_{i-1} + \psi_i$, $i = 2, 3,$
..., p. Then there is a one-to-one correspondence between
the parameters $\beta_2, \beta_3, \ldots, \beta_p, \omega_1, \psi_2, \psi_3, \ldots, \psi_p$ and
the parameters $\beta_2, \beta_3, \ldots, \beta_p, \omega_1, \omega_2, \ldots, \omega_p$. The
ω's are not parameters in the LISREL model, so in LISREL
the first set of parameters must be used. However, for
identification purposes it is more convenient to use the
second set of parameters. In terms of the ω's the covariance matrix of $y_1, y_2, \ldots, y_p$ is of the form, here illustrated with $p = 4$.

$$\underset{\sim}{\Sigma} = \begin{bmatrix} \omega_1 + \theta_1 & & & \\ \beta_2\omega_1 & \omega_2 + \theta_2 & & \\ \beta_2\beta_3\omega_1 & \beta_3\omega_2 & \omega_3 + \theta_3 & \\ \beta_2\beta_3\beta_4\omega_1 & \beta_3\beta_4\omega_2 & \beta_4\omega_3 & \omega_4 + \theta_4 \end{bmatrix} \qquad (III.27)$$

It is seen from (27) that although the product $\beta_2\omega_1 = \sigma_{21}$ is identified, β_2 and ω_1 are not separately identified. The product $\beta_2\omega_1$ is involved in the off-diagonal elements in the first column (and row) only. One can multiply β_2 by a constant and divide ω_1 by the same constant without changing the product. The change induced by ω_1 in σ_{11} can be absorbed in θ_1 in such a way that σ_{11} remains unchanged. Hence $\theta_1 = Var(\varepsilon_1)$ is not identified. For η_2 and η_3 we have

$$\omega_2 = \frac{\sigma_{32}\sigma_{21}}{\sigma_{31}} \quad ,$$

$$\omega_3 = \frac{\sigma_{43}\sigma_{32}}{\sigma_{42}} \quad ,$$

so that ω_2 and ω_3 , and hence also θ_2 and θ_3 , are identified. With ω_2 and ω_3 identified, β_3 and β_4 are identified by σ_{32} and σ_{43} . The middle coefficient β_3 is overidentified since

$$\beta_3 \omega_2 = \frac{\sigma_{31}\sigma_{42}}{\sigma_{41}} = \sigma_{32} \ .$$

Since both ω_4 and θ_4 are involved in σ_{44} only, these are not identified. Only their sum σ_{44} is.

This analysis of the identification problem shows that for the "inner" variables y_2 and y_3 , the parameters ω_2, ω_3, θ_2, θ_3 and β_3 are identified, whereas there is an indeterminacy associated with each of the "outer" variables y_1 and y_4 . To eliminate these indeterminacies one condition must be imposed on the parameters ω_1, θ_1 and β_2 , and another on the parameters ω_4 and θ_4 . In terms of the original LISREL parameters, β_2, $\psi_1 = \omega_1$, ψ_2, ψ_4, θ_1 and θ_4 are not identified whereas β_3, β_4, ψ_3, θ_2 and θ_3 are identified. One indeterminacy is associated with β_2, ψ_1, ψ_2 and θ_1 and another indeterminacy is associated with ψ_4 and θ_4 . The parameters β_2, ψ_1, ψ_2 and θ_1 are only determined by the three equations

$$\sigma_{11} = \psi_1 + \theta_1$$

$$\sigma_{21} = \beta_2 \psi_1$$

$$\omega_2 = \beta_2^2 \psi_1 + \psi_2 \ ,$$

where ω_2 is identified, and the parameters ψ_4 and θ_4 are only determined by the single equation

$$\sigma_{44} = \beta_4^2 \omega_3 + \psi_4 + \theta_4 ,$$

where ω_3 is identified. Perhaps the most natural way of eliminating the indeterminacies is to set $\theta_1 = \theta_2$ and $\theta_4 = \theta_3$.

Humphreys (1968) presented the correlation matrix shown in Table 9. The variables include eight semesters of grade-point averages, high school rank and a composite score on the American College Testing tests for approximately 1600 under-graduate students at the University of Illinois.

TABLE III.9

Correlations among Grade Point Averages, High School Rank and An Aptitude Test

	Y_0	Y_0'	Y_1	Y_2	Y_3	Y_4	Y_5	Y_6	Y_7	Y_8
Y_0	1.000									
Y_0'	.393	1.000								
Y_1	.387	.375	1.000							
Y_2	.341	.298	.556	1.000						
Y_3	.278	.237	.456	.490	1.000					
Y_4	.270	.255	.439	.445	.562	1.000				
Y_5	.240	.238	.415	.418	.496	.512	1.000			
Y_6	.256	.252	.399	.383	.456	.469	.551	1.000		
Y_7	.240	.219	.387	.364	.445	.442	.500	.544	1.000	
Y_8	.222	.173	.342	.339	.354	.416	.453	.482	.541	1.000

Note: y_0 is high school rank, y_0' ACT composite score, and y_1 through y_8 are eight semesters grade-point averages.

The quasi-simplex model (25) - (26) is a LISREL model of the form (I.11) - (I.12) with no x- or ξ-variables (sub-model type 3B) and with $\Lambda_y = I$ and

$$
B = \begin{bmatrix} 0 & 0 & 0 & 0 \\ \beta_2 & 0 & 0 & 0 \\ 0 & \beta_3 & 0 & 0 \\ 0 & 0 & \beta_4 & 0 \end{bmatrix}
$$

With this specification we have defined ζ_1 as η_1 so that $\psi_1 = \omega_1$.

We shall first use the variables $y_1, y_2, \ldots, y_8$ to illustrate what happens when one runs a model which is not identified. We have made three runs with the same data and model. In Run 1 we specified the model as if all the parameters were identified. The input for this run is given on the next page. In Run 2 we imposed the condition that $\theta_1 = \theta_2$ to eliminate the first indeterminacy and in Run 3 we imposed the condition $\theta_8 = \theta_7$, in addition, to eliminate the second indeterminacy also. The results are shown in Table 9. Run 1 gave the message that the parameter "TE 1 1 MAY NOT BE IDENTIFIED."

```
SIMPLEX MODEL FOR ACADEMIC PERFORMANCE EXAMPLE 6A RUN 1
DA NI=10 NO=1600
LA
(10A3)
 YOYO' Y1 Y2 Y3 Y4 Y5 Y6 Y7 Y8
KM SY
(10F4.3)
1000
 3931000
 387 3751000
 341 298 5561000
 278 237 456 4901000
 270 255 439 445 5621000
 240 238 415 418 496 5121000
 256 252 399 383 456 469 5511000
 240 219 387 364 445 442 500 5441000
 222 173 342 339 354 416 453 482 5411000
SE
3 4 5 6 7 8 9 10/
MO NY=8 NE=8 LY=ID BE=FU PS=DI
FR BE(2,1) BE(3,2) BE(4,3) BE(5,4) BE(6,5) C
BE(7,6) BE(8,7)
OU SS
```

In Run 2 the corresponding message was that the
parameter "TE 8 8 MAY NOT BE IDENTIFIED".   In Run 3
no such message was given indicating that the model is
identified. All three solutions in Table 9 have the same
x^2 goodness-of-fit measure and it is seen that all parameters which are identified come out with the same parameter estimate in all three runs. Only the non-identified
parameters vary over the three solutions. The values given
for the non-identified parameters are of course arbitrary
to some extent. However, these values are such that the
following three quantities are invariant over

TABLE III.10

Results for Simplex Model

Parameter Number	Parameter	Parameter "Estimates"		
		Run 1	Run 2	Run 3
1	β_2	0.73	0.98	0.98
2	β_3	0.84	0.84	0.84
3	β_4	0.96	0.96	0.96
4	β_5	0.91	0.91	0.91
5	β_6	0.93	0.93	0.93
6	β_7	0.94	0.94	0.94
7	β_8	0.89	0.89	0.89
8	ψ_1	0.76	0.57	0.57
9	ψ_2	0.16	0.03	0.03
10	ψ_3	0.17	0.17	0.17
11	ψ_4	0.03	0.03	0.03
12	ψ_5	0.12	0.12	0.12
13	ψ_6	0.07	0.07	0.07
14	ψ_7	0.10	0.10	0.10
15	ψ_8	0.26	0.26	0.13
16	θ_1	0.24	0.43	0.43
17	θ_2	0.43	0.43	0.43
18	θ_3	0.43	0.43	0.43
19	θ_4	0.44	0.44	0.44
20	θ_5	0.42	0.42	0.42
21	θ_6	0.42	0.42	0.42
22	θ_7	0.39	0.39	0.39
23	θ_8	0.26	0.26	0.39
	$\psi_1 + \theta_1$	1.00	1.00	1.00
	$\beta_2 \psi_1$	0.56	0.56	0.57
	$\psi_8 + \theta_8$	0.52	0.52	0.52

all solutions

$$\psi_1 + \theta_1$$

$$\beta_2 \psi_1$$

$$\psi_8 + \theta_8$$

These computer runs illustrate that LISREL can estimate models which are non-identified and that the program correctly identifies the last parameter involved in an indeterminacy.

The parameter SS on the OU card gives the standardized solution, and the parameter VA gives the correlation matrix of η. The intercorrelations among $\eta_2, \eta_3, \ldots, \eta_7$ are the same for all three solutions in Table 9. These are

	η_2	η_3	η_4	η_5	η_6	η_7
η_2	1.000					
η_3	0.838	1.000				
η_4	0.812	0.969	1.000			
η_5	0.724	0.865	0.892	1.000		
η_6	0.677	0.809	0.834	0.935	1.000	
η_7	0.619	0.740	0.763	0.855	0.914	1.000

Here every correlation ρ_{ij} with $|i-j| > 1$ is the product of the correlations just below the diagonal. For example, $\rho(\eta_5, \eta_2) = 0.838 \cdot 0.969 \cdot 0.892 = 0.724$. These correlations form a perfect Markov simplex. The goodness-of-fit measure is χ^2 = 23.91 with 15 degrees of freedom. This represents a reasonably good fit considering the large sample size. The reliabilities of the semester grades y_2, y_3, ..., y_7 can also be obtained directly from the solution in which the η's are standardized. The reliabilities are

y_2	y_3	y_4	$\dot{y}_5$	y_6	y_7
0.569	0.574	0.563	0.584	0.581	0.608

A test of the hypothesis that all reliabilities are equal gives χ^2 = 2.16 with 5 degrees of freedom, so that this hypothesis is not rejected by the data despite the large sample size.

Without identification conditions imposed, as in Run 1, the correlations $\rho(\eta_1, \eta_j)$, $j \neq 1$ and $\rho(\eta_i, \eta_8)$, $i \neq 8$ and the reliabilities of y_1 and y_8 are not identified. However, in view of the above test of equality of reliabilities it seems reasonable to assume that all reliabilities or equivalently all error variances in the standardized solution are equal for y_1 through y_8 . This assumption makes it possible to estimate the intercorrelations among all the η's.

Assuming that x_0 and x_0' are indicators of precollege academic achievement η_0 which is assumed to influence the true academic achievement in the first semester η_1 ,

one can estimate again the quasi-Markov simplex and show
how this use of x_0 and x_0' helps identify the parameters
of the model. The only parameters which are now not identified are ψ_8 and θ_8 . This gives a $\chi^2 = 36.92$ with 28
degrees of freedom. If we assume that the reliabilities
of all the semester grades are equal, all parameters are
identified and the goodness of fit becomes 45.22 with 34
degrees of freedom. The difference 8.30 with 6 degrees of
freedom provides another test of equality of the reliabilities. Finally a test of the hypothesis that the whole
process is stationary, i.e., that

$$\beta_2 = \beta_3 = \ldots = \beta_8$$

$$\theta_1 = \theta_2 = \ldots = \theta_8$$

gives $\chi^2 = 12.82$ with 11 degrees of freedom so that this
hypothesis cannot be rejected. There is good evidence that
the whole Markov process is stable over time.

III.8 Example 7: Peer Influences on Ambition

*Sociologists have often called attention to the way in which
one's peers -- e.g. best friends -- influence one's decisions
-- e.g. choice of occupation. They have recognized that the
relation must be reciprocal -- if my best friend influences
my choice, I must influence his. Duncan, Haller and Portes*

*(1971) present a simultaneous equation model of peer in-
fluences on occupational choice, using a sample of Michigan
high-school students paired with their best friends. The
authors interpret educational and occupational choice as
two indicators of a single latent variable "ambition", and
specify the choices. This model with simultaneity and
errors of measurement is displayed in Figure 6.*

This example was considered in detail in the LISREL IV
Manual pp 31-38. An error has been found in this example.
This error is that the two variables "best friend's occupational aspiration" and "best friend's educational aspiration" were interchanged, thereby causing the two η-vari-
ables to be in different metrics. Although the presentation of the example in the LISREL IV Manual is internally
consistent, the results of the analysis are not as good
as they should be.

LISREL Specification

Let

x_1 = respondent's parental aspiration

x_2 = respondent's intelligence

x_3 = respondent's socioeconomic status

x_4 = best friend's socioeconomic status

x_5 = best friend's intelligence

x_6 = best friend's parental aspiration

y_1 = respondent's occupational aspiration

FIGURE III.6

A Model of Duncan, Haller and Portes (1971)

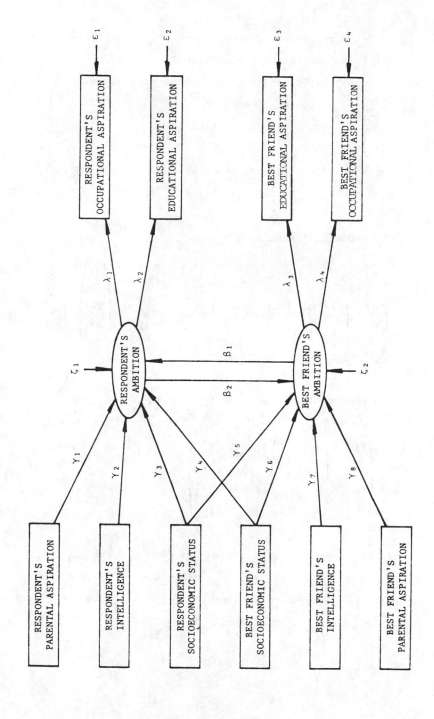

y_2 = respondent's educational aspiration

y_3 = best friend's educational aspiration

y_4 = best friend's occupational aspiration

η_1 = respondent's ambition

η_2 = best friend's ambition

In terms of our general model we take $\xi_i \equiv x_i$, i.e., in equation (I.3) we take $\underset{\sim}{\Lambda}_x (6 \times 6) = \underset{\sim}{I}$ and $\underset{\sim}{\delta} = \underset{\sim}{0}$ (FIXED X).

The structural equations are

$$
\begin{pmatrix} \eta_1 \\ \eta_2 \end{pmatrix} = \begin{pmatrix} 0 & \beta_1 \\ \beta_2 & 0 \end{pmatrix} \begin{pmatrix} \eta_1 \\ \eta_2 \end{pmatrix} + \begin{pmatrix} \gamma_1 & \gamma_2 & \gamma_3 & \gamma_4 & 0 & 0 \\ 0 & 0 & \gamma_5 & \gamma_6 & \gamma_7 & \gamma_8 \end{pmatrix} \begin{pmatrix} \xi_1 \\ \xi_2 \\ \xi_3 \\ \xi_4 \\ \xi_5 \\ \xi_6 \end{pmatrix} + \begin{pmatrix} \zeta_1 \\ \zeta_2 \end{pmatrix} \quad , \quad \text{(III.28)}
$$

and the equations relating the η's to the y's are

$$
\begin{pmatrix} y_1 \\ y_2 \\ y_3 \\ y_4 \end{pmatrix} = \begin{pmatrix} 1 & 0 \\ \lambda_2 & 0 \\ 0 & \lambda_3 \\ 0 & 1 \end{pmatrix} \begin{pmatrix} \eta_1 \\ \eta_2 \end{pmatrix} + \begin{pmatrix} \varepsilon_1 \\ \varepsilon_2 \\ \varepsilon_3 \\ \varepsilon_4 \end{pmatrix} \quad . \quad \text{(III.29)}
$$

In $\underset{\sim}{\Lambda}_y$ we have fixed the scales for η_1 and η_2 to be the same as in y_1 and y_4, respectively. Since $\underset{\sim}{\xi} \equiv \underset{\sim}{x}$ and there are no constraints on $\underset{\sim}{\Phi}$, $\underset{\sim}{\Phi} = \underset{\sim}{\Sigma}_{xx}$, which is estimated as $\underset{\sim}{S}_{xx}$. The matrix $\underset{\sim}{\Psi}(2 \times 2)$ is

$$\Psi = \begin{bmatrix} \psi_{11} & \\ & \\ \psi_{21} & \psi_{22} \end{bmatrix}$$

with $\psi_{ii} = \text{Var}(\zeta_i)$, $i = 1, 2$ and $\psi_{21} = \text{Cov}(\zeta_1, \zeta_2)$ and the matrix Θ_ε is diagonal with diagonal elements $\theta_{ii}^{(\varepsilon)} = \text{Var}(\varepsilon_i)$.

Since $\zeta = x$, the structural equations are equivalent to

$$\eta = B\eta + \Gamma x + \zeta$$

with reduced form

$$\eta = (I - B)^{-1}\Gamma x + (I - B)^{-1}\zeta . \qquad (III.30)$$

Furthermore, we have

$$y = \Lambda_y \eta + \varepsilon = \Lambda_y (I - B)^{-1}\Gamma x + \Lambda_y (I - B)^{-1}\zeta + \varepsilon = Px + z,$$
$$\qquad (III.31)$$

where

$$P = \Sigma_{yx}\Sigma_{xx}^{-1} = \Lambda_y (I - B)^{-1}\Gamma = \Lambda_y \Pi , \quad \text{say}$$

and

$$z = \Lambda_y (I - B)^{-1}\zeta + \varepsilon .$$

Identification

Since Ψ is unconstrained, it follows from (30) that there is a one to one correspondence between Ψ and the co-variance matrix of η, Ω say, where

$$\underset{\sim}{\Omega} = \begin{bmatrix} \omega_{11} & \\ \omega_{21} & \omega_{22} \end{bmatrix}$$

From the first part of (31) we have

$$\underset{\sim yy}{\Sigma} = \underset{\sim y}{\Lambda} \, \underset{\sim}{\Omega} \, \underset{\sim y}{\Lambda}' + \underset{\sim\varepsilon}{\Theta} = \begin{bmatrix} \omega_{11} + \theta_{11}^{(\varepsilon)} & & & \\ \lambda_2 \omega_{11} & \lambda_2^2 \omega_{11} + \theta_{22}^{(\varepsilon)} & & \\ \lambda_3 \omega_{21} & \lambda_2 \lambda_3 \omega_{21} & \lambda_3^2 \omega_{22} + \theta_{33}^{(\varepsilon)} & \\ \omega_{21} & \lambda_2 \omega_{21} & \lambda_3 \omega_{22} & \omega_{22} + \theta_{44}^{(\varepsilon)} \end{bmatrix}$$

Furthermore, we have

$$(\underset{\sim}{I} - \underset{\sim}{B})^{-1} = (1 - \beta_1 \beta_2)^{-1} \begin{bmatrix} 1 & \beta_1 \\ \beta_2 & 1 \end{bmatrix}$$

and

$$\underset{\sim}{\Pi} = (1 - \beta_1 \beta_2)^{-1} \begin{bmatrix} \gamma_1 & \gamma_2 & \gamma_3 + \beta_1 \gamma_5 & \gamma_4 + \beta_1 \gamma_6 & \beta_1 \gamma_7 & \beta_1 \gamma_8 \\ \beta_2 \gamma_1 & \beta_2 \gamma_2 & \gamma_5 + \beta_2 \gamma_3 & \gamma_6 + \beta_2 \gamma_4 & \gamma_7 & \gamma_8 \end{bmatrix}$$

The first and last rows of $\underset{\sim}{P}$ are identical to the first and second row of $\underset{\sim}{\Pi} = (\underset{\sim}{I}-\underset{\sim}{B})^{-1}\underset{\sim}{\Gamma}$, respectively. The second row of $\underset{\sim}{P}$ is λ_2 times the first row of $\underset{\sim}{\Pi}$ and the third row of $\underset{\sim}{P}$ is λ_3 times the second row of $\underset{\sim}{\Pi}$. Hence it is clear that λ_2 and λ_3 are identified and that

$$\lambda_2 = \frac{p_{2i}}{p_{1i}} \quad \text{and} \quad \lambda_3 = \frac{p_{3i}}{p_{4i}} \ , \quad i = 1, 2, \dots, 6 \ .$$

Since $\underset{\sim}{\Pi}$ consists of two rows of P, $\underset{\sim}{\Pi}$ is identified. From $\underset{\sim}{\Pi}$ it follows that $\gamma_1, \gamma_2, \gamma_7, \gamma_8, \beta_1$ and β_2 are determined as

$$\gamma_1 = \pi_{11}, \; \gamma_2 = \pi_{12}, \; \gamma_7 = \pi_{25}, \; \gamma_8 = \pi_{26}$$

$$\beta_1 = (\pi_{15}/\pi_{25}) = (\pi_{16}/\pi_{26}) \; ,$$

$$\beta_2 = (\pi_{21}/\pi_{11}) = (\pi_{22}/\pi_{12}) \; .$$

$\gamma_3, \gamma_4, \gamma_5$ and γ_6 are then determined by $\pi_{13}, \pi_{14}, \pi_{23}$ and π_{24}. With λ_2 and λ_3 determined we can now determine ω_{11}, ω_{12} and ω_{22} from the off-diagonal elements of $\underset{\sim}{\Sigma}_{yy}$. Finally, the $\theta_{ii}^{(\varepsilon)}$, $i = 1, 2, 3, 4$, can be determined from the diagonal of $\underset{\sim}{\Sigma}_{yy}$.

This analysis shows that all parameters are identified. Altogether there are 19 parameters (2 β´s, 8 γ´s, 3 ω´s, 2 λ´s, and 4 $\theta^{(\varepsilon)}$´s) if x is fixed. When x is random there will be an additional 21 parameters in $\underset{\sim}{\Phi} = \underset{\sim}{\Sigma}_{xx}$. In both cases the degrees of freedom will be 15.

Data

The correlation matrix based on N = 329 observations taken from Duncan, Haller & Portes (1971) is given in Table 11.

The overall goodness-of-fit measure is $\chi^2 = 26.70$ with 15 degrees of freedom. A test of the hypothesis $\psi_{21} = 0$ gives $\chi^2 = 0.19$ with 1 degree of freedom and a

TABLE III.11

Correlations for Background and Aspiration Measures for 329 Respondents and Their Best Friends.

Respondent									
Intelligence (x_2)									
Parental Aspiration (x_1)	.1839								
Family SES (x_3)	.2220	.0489							
Occupation Aspiration (y_1)	.4105	.2137	.3240						
Educational Aspiration (y_2)	.4043	.2742	.4047	.6247					
Best Friend									
Intelligence (x_5)	.3355	.0782	.2302	.2995	.2863				
Parental Aspiration (x_6)	.1021	.1147	.0931	.0760	.0702	.2087			
Family SES (x_4)	.1861	.0186	.2707	.2930	.2407	.2950	-.0438		
Occupational Aspiration (y_4)	.2598	.0839	.2786	.4216	.3275	.5007	.1988	.3607	
Educational Aspiration (y_3)	.2903	.1124	.3054	.3269	.3669	.5191	.2784	.4105	.6404

test of $\beta_1 = \beta_2$, given $\psi_{21} = 0$, gives $\chi^2 = 0.01$ with 1 degree of freedom. Hence, it is clear that these hypotheses cannot be rejected. The overall goodness-of-fit of the model with $\psi_{21} = 0$ and $\beta_1 = \beta_2$ is given by $\chi^2 = 26.90$ with 17 degrees of freedom. This has a p-level of 0.06.

The input for this model is shown on the next page. The initial estimates and the maximum likelihood estimates with their standard errors are given in Table 12. The standardized solution in which η_1 and η_2 are scaled to unit variance is also given in Table 12. It

```
PEER INFLUENCES ON AMBITION : MODEL A
DA NI=10 NO=329
LABEL UN=8
CM UN=8 RE
SELECTION
 4 5 10 9 2 1 3 8 6 7
MODEL NY=4 NE=2 NX=6 FIXEDX PS=DI BE=FU
FREE LY(2,1) LY(3,2) BE(1,2)
FI GA(5) - GA(8)
ST 1 LY 1 LY 8
EQ BE(1,2) BE(2,1)
OU SE TV EF SS
```

is seen in Table 12 that the corresponding parameters for
the respondent and his best friend are very close. There
are good reasons to suggest that the whole model should be
completely symmetric between the respondent and his best
friend so that not only $\beta_1 = \beta_2$ but also $\lambda_2 = \lambda_3$,
$\gamma_1 = \gamma_8$, $\gamma_2 = \gamma_7$, $\gamma_3 = \gamma_6$, $\gamma_4 = \gamma_5$, $\psi_{11} = \psi_{22}$,
$\theta_{11}^{(\varepsilon)} = \theta_{44}^{(\varepsilon)}$ and $\theta_{22}^{(\varepsilon)} = \theta_{33}^{(\varepsilon)}$. The overall χ^2 for this model
is 30.76 with 25 degrees of freedom with p=0.20. Thus, this model is
both more parsimonous and has a better fit than the other
models. The input for this model is given below.

```
PEER INFLUENCES ON AMBITION : MODEL D
DA NI=10 NO=329
LABEL UN=8
CM UN=8 RE
SELECTION
 4 5 10 9 2 1 3 8 6 7
MODEL NY=4 NE=2 NX=6 FIXEDX PS=DI BE=FU
FREE LY(2,1) BE(1,2)
FI GA(5) - GA(8)
ST 1 LY 1 LY 8
EQ BE(1,2) BE(2,1)
EQ LY 2 1 LY 3 2
EQ BE(1,2) BE(2,1)
EQ GA 1 1 GA 2 6
EQ GA 1 2 GA 2 5
EQ GA 1 3 GA 2 4
EQ GA 1 4 GA 2 3
EQ PS 1 PS 2
EQ TE 1 TE 4
EQ TE 2 TE 3
OU SE TV EF SS
```

TABLE III.12

Estimates for the Model in Figure 5

with $\psi_{21} = 0$ and $\beta_1 = \beta_2$.

The standard errors of the estimates are given in parenthesis.

Parameter	Initial Estimates	Unscaled Solution (ML)	Standardized Solution (ML)
λ_1	1.000*	1.0000*	0.767
λ_2	1.122	1.061 (0.089)	0.813
λ_3	1.120	1.074 (0.081)	0.828
λ_4	1.000*	1.000*	0.771
β_1	0.218	0.180 (0.039)	0.181
β_2	0.218	0.180 (0.039)	0.179
γ_1	0.156	0.164 (0.039)	0.213
γ_2	0.242	0.254 (0.042)	0.331
γ_3	0.208	0.221 (0.042)	0.288
γ_4	0.072	0.077 (0.041)	0.101
γ_5	0.058	0.068 (0.039)	0.089
γ_6	0.208	0.218 (0.039)	0.283
γ_7	0.314	0.331 (0.041)	0.429
γ_8	0.150	0.152 (0.036)	0.197
ψ_{11}	0.266	0.281 (0.046)	0.478
ψ_{22}	0.220	0.229 (0.039)	0.385
$\theta_{11}^{(\epsilon)}$	0.443	0.412 (0.051)	0.412
$\theta_{22}^{(\epsilon)}$	0.299	0.338 (0.052)	0.338
$\theta_{33}^{(\epsilon)}$	0.283	0.313 (0.046)	0.313
$\theta_{44}^{(\epsilon)}$	0.428	0.404 (0.046)	0.404

Asterisks denote parameter values fixed by scaling.

A final comment on this example concerns the total effects
and the test of stability of non-recursive models. The
TOTAL EFFECTS for Model A are given below.

PEER INFLUENCES ON AMBITION : MODEL A

TOTAL EFFECTS

TOTAL EFFECTS OF X ON ETA

	RESP PAS	RESP INT	RESP SS	BF SS	BF INT	BF PAS
ETA 1	0.169	0.262	0.241	0.121	0.062	0.028
ETA 2	0.030	0.047	0.112	0.240	0.342	0.157

TOTAL EFFECTS OF X ON Y

	RESP PAS	RESP INT	RESP SS	BF SS	BF INT	BF PAS
RESP OCC	0.169	0.262	0.241	0.121	0.062	0.028
RESP EDU	0.179	0.278	0.256	0.128	0.065	0.030
BF EDU	0.033	0.051	0.120	0.258	0.367	0.169
BF OCC	0.030	0.047	0.112	0.240	0.342	0.157

TOTAL EFFECTS OF ETA ON ETA

	ETA 1	ETA 2
ETA 1	0.034	0.186
ETA 2	0.186	0.034

LARGEST EIGENVALUE OF BETA*BETA-TRANSPOSED (STABILITY INDEX) IS   0.032

TOTAL EFFECTS OF ETA ON Y

	ETA 1	ETA 2
RESP OCC	1.034	0.186
RESP EDU	1.097	0.197
BF EDU	0.200	1.110
BF OCC	0.186	1.034

Although there are never direct effects of an η on itself, i.e., all diagonal elements of $\underset{\sim}{B}$ are zero, the
above results state that there is a total effect of each
η on itself. How can this be? This can only occur in
non-recursive models and can best be understood by defining a

cycle. A cycle is a causal chain going from one η , passing over some other η's and returning to the original η . In this example, where there are only two η's:

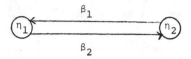

one cycle for η_1 consists of one path to η_2 and a return to η_1 . The effect of one cycle on η_1 is $\dot{\beta}_2 \beta_1$. After two cycles the effect will be $\beta_2^2 \beta_1^2$, after three cycles $\beta_2^3 \beta_1^3$, etc. The total effect on η_1 will be the sum of the infinite geometric series

$$\beta_1 \beta_2 + \beta_1^2 \beta_2^2 + \beta_1^3 \beta_2^3 + \ldots$$

which is $\beta_1 \beta_2 / (1 - \beta_1 \beta_2)$. In this case when $\beta_1 = \beta_2 = 0.18$, this is 0.034.

In general, the total effect of $\underset{\sim}{\eta}$ on itself is (c.f. Table III.4)

$$\underset{\sim}{B} + \underset{\sim}{B}^2 + \underset{\sim}{B}^3 + \ldots = (\underset{\sim}{I} - \underset{\sim}{B})^{-1} - \underset{\sim}{I} \quad , \tag{III.32}$$

provided the infinite series converges. Similarly, one finds that the total effect of $\underset{\sim}{\xi}$ on $\underset{\sim}{\eta}$ is (c.f. Table 4)

$$(\underset{\sim}{I} + \underset{\sim}{B} + \underset{\sim}{B}^2 + \underset{\sim}{B}^3 + \ldots)\underset{\sim}{\Gamma} = (\underset{\sim}{I} - \underset{\sim}{B})^{-1}\underset{\sim}{\Gamma} \quad . \tag{III.33}$$

A necessary and sufficient condition for convergence, i.e., for stability of the system, is that all the eigenvalues of

(I-B) are within the unit circle. The eigenvalues of (I-B) are
in general complex numbers which are somewhat difficult to
compute. However, a sufficient condition is that the largest
eigenvalue of (I-B)*(I-B)' is less than one. This is very easy
to verify, so we are using this test in the program.

Computer Exercise 8: Social Status and Social Participation

*Hodge and Treiman (1968) studied the relationship between
social status and social participation. For a sample of
530 women, they report data on x_1 = income, x_2 = occupation, x_3 = education, y_1 = church attendance, y_2 = member-
ships, y_3 = friends seen. All variables are expressed
in standardized form. The y's are viewed as independent
indicators of a latent variable η = social participation,
which is caused by the x's. Thus,*

$$\eta = \alpha_1 x_1 + \alpha_2 x_2 + \alpha_3 x_3 + \zeta ,$$

$$y_1 = \beta_1 \eta + \varepsilon_1, \quad y_2 = \beta_2 \eta + \varepsilon_2, \quad y_3 = \beta_3 \eta + \varepsilon_3 .$$

*From a substantive viewpoint, it may be helpful to view
the x's as determining $\xi = \alpha_1 x_1 + \alpha_2 x_2 + \alpha_3 x_3$ = social
status, which in turn determines $\eta = \xi + \varepsilon$ = social participation. Goldberger (1972) and Jöreskog and Goldberger
(1975) called this model a MIMIC (multiple-indicator, multiple*

cause) model. The correlations of the variables are

	x_1	x_2	x_3	y_1	y_2	y_3
x_1	1.000					
x_2	.304	1.000				
x_3	.305	.344	1.000			
y_1	.100	.156	.158	1.000		
y_2	.284	.192	.324	.360	1.000	
y_3	.176	.136	.226	.210	.265	1.000

Use LISREL to estimate this model and examine the fit of it. This simple MIMIC model may be generalized in various ways (see e.g. Robinson (1974, 1977)). Applications have been given by Chamberlain (1977) and Avery (1979), among others.

III.9 Example 8: A Hypothetical Model

To illustrate a fairly complex LISREL model we use a hypothetical model depicted in Figure 7. This model contains many of the features of the general model. There are 7 x-variables as indicators of 3 latent ξ-variables. Note that x_3 is a complex variable measuring both ξ_1 and ξ_2. There are 2 latent η-variables each with two y-indicators. The 5 latent variables are connected in a two-equation interdependent system. The model involves both errors in equations (the ζ's) and errors in variables (the ε's and δ's).

FIGURE III.7

A Hypothetical Model

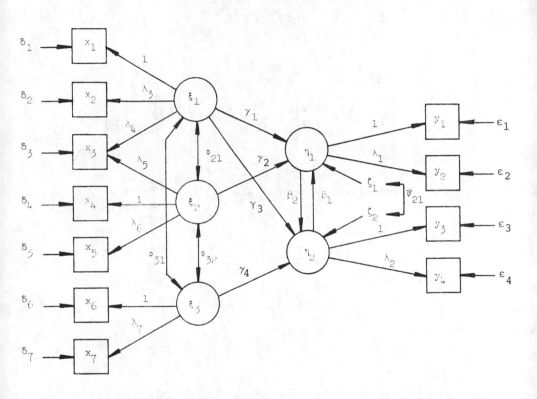

The structural equations are

$$\eta_1 = \beta_1 \eta_2 + \gamma_1 \xi_1 + \gamma_2 \xi_2 + \zeta_1$$

$$\eta_2 = \beta_2 \eta_1 + \gamma_3 \xi_1 + \gamma_4 \xi_3 + \zeta_2$$

or

$$\begin{pmatrix} \eta_1 \\ \eta_2 \end{pmatrix} = \begin{pmatrix} 0 & \beta_1 \\ \beta_2 & 0 \end{pmatrix} \begin{pmatrix} \eta_1 \\ \eta_2 \end{pmatrix} + \begin{pmatrix} \gamma_1 & \gamma_2 & 0 \\ \gamma_3 & 0 & \gamma_4 \end{pmatrix} \begin{pmatrix} \xi_1 \\ \xi_2 \\ \xi_3 \end{pmatrix} + \begin{pmatrix} \zeta_1 \\ \zeta_2 \end{pmatrix} .$$

The measurement model equations are

$$\begin{pmatrix} y_1 \\ y_2 \\ y_3 \\ y_4 \end{pmatrix} = \begin{pmatrix} 1 & 0 \\ \lambda_1 & 0 \\ 0 & 1 \\ 0 & \lambda_2 \end{pmatrix} \begin{pmatrix} \eta_1 \\ \eta_2 \end{pmatrix} + \begin{pmatrix} \varepsilon_1 \\ \varepsilon_2 \\ \varepsilon_3 \\ \varepsilon_4 \end{pmatrix} ,$$

and

$$\begin{pmatrix} x_1 \\ x_2 \\ x_3 \\ x_4 \\ x_5 \\ x_6 \\ x_7 \end{pmatrix} = \begin{pmatrix} 1 & 0 & 0 \\ \lambda_3 & 0 & 0 \\ \lambda_4 & \lambda_5 & 0 \\ 0 & 1 & 0 \\ 0 & \lambda_6 & 0 \\ 0 & 0 & 1 \\ 0 & 0 & \lambda_7 \end{pmatrix} \begin{pmatrix} \xi_1 \\ \xi_2 \\ \xi_3 \end{pmatrix} + \begin{pmatrix} \delta_1 \\ \delta_2 \\ \delta_3 \\ \delta_4 \\ \delta_5 \\ \delta_6 \\ \delta_7 \end{pmatrix} .$$

Here one λ in each column of $\underset{\sim y}{\Lambda}$ and $\underset{\sim x}{\Lambda}$ has been set equal to unity to fix the scales of measurement in the latent variables.

Data for this model were generated by assigning the following values

$$
\underset{\sim}{\Lambda} = \begin{bmatrix} 1.000 & 0.0 \\ 0.902 & 0.0 \\ 0.0 & 1.000 \\ 0.0 & 1.095 \end{bmatrix} ,
$$

$$
\underset{\sim x}{\Lambda} = \begin{bmatrix} 1.000 & 0.0 & 0.0 \\ 1.300 & 0.0 & 0.0 \\ 0.901 & 1.200 & 0.0 \\ 0.0 & 1.000 & 0.0 \\ 0.0 & 1.098 & 0.0 \\ 0.0 & 0.0 & 1.000 \\ 0.0 & 0.0 & 1.400 \end{bmatrix} ,
$$

$$
\underset{\sim}{B} = \begin{bmatrix} 0.000 & 0.493 \\ 0.595 & 0.000 \end{bmatrix} ,
$$

$$
\underset{\sim}{\Gamma} = \begin{bmatrix} 0.399 & 0.399 & 0.0 \\ -1.000 & 0.0 & 1.098 \end{bmatrix} ,
$$

$$
\underset{\sim}{\Phi} = \begin{bmatrix} 0.999 & & \\ 0.699 & 1.199 & \\ 0.601 & 0.300 & 1.399 \end{bmatrix} ,
$$

$$
\underset{\sim}{\Psi} = \begin{bmatrix} 0.506 & \\ 0.386 & 0.705 \end{bmatrix} ,
$$

$\Theta_{\underset{\sim}{\varepsilon}}$ = diag (0.272, 0.186, 0.128, 0.203) ,

$\Theta_{\underset{\sim}{\delta}}$ = diag (0.375, 0.265, 0.175, 0.272, 0.376, 0.276, 0.173) ,

to each of the parameter matrices. These generate a $\underset{\sim}{\Sigma}$
according to (I.4) where

$$
\underset{\sim yy}{\Sigma} =
\begin{bmatrix}
3.815 & & & \\
3.195 & 3.068 & & \\
3.890 & 3.508 & 5.773 & \\
4.259 & 3.842 & 6.182 & 6.973
\end{bmatrix}
$$

$$
\underset{\sim xy}{\Sigma} =
\begin{bmatrix}
0.764 & 0.690 & 0.176 & 0.193 \\
0.994 & 0.896 & 0.229 & 0.251 \\
1.690 & 1.525 & 0.347 & 0.380 \\
0.835 & 0.753 & 0.157 & 0.172 \\
0.917 & 0.827 & 0.173 & 0.189 \\
1.259 & 1.136 & 1.824 & 1.997 \\
1.763 & 1.591 & 2.554 & 2.797
\end{bmatrix}
$$

$$
\underset{\sim xx}{\Sigma} =
\begin{bmatrix}
1.374 & & & & & & \\
1.298 & 1.952 & & & & & \\
1.739 & 2.260 & 4.224 & & & & \\
0.700 & 0.909 & 2.069 & 1.471 & & & \\
0.768 & 0.998 & 2.272 & 1.317 & 1.822 & & \\
0.601 & 0.781 & 0.902 & 0.300 & 0.330 & 1.675 & \\
0.841 & 1.094 & 1.262 & 0.421 & 0.462 & 1.958 & 2.914
\end{bmatrix}
$$

It is possible to regard the matrix $\underset{\sim}{\Sigma}$ as a sample covariance matrix and analyze it according to the model that
generated it. This serves as a check that the program works
correctly and delivers consistent estimates. Indeed, as
a computer run will verify, all three methods of estimation give parameter estimates which are identical to the true parameter values that
were used to generate $\underset{\sim}{\Sigma}$ and all three solutions have a
perfect fit to the data as demonstrated, for example, by
the fact that χ^2 is zero. We shall not, however, be satis-
fied with this rather limited demonstration but also perform a small scale Monte Carlo experiment to check on the
sampling variability.

Using the matrix $\underset{\sim}{\Sigma}$ as the true population covariance
matrix, a random sample of 100 observations were generated,
having a multivariate normal distribution with mean vector
zero and covariance matrix $\underset{\sim}{\Sigma}$. The resulting sample covariance matrix was

$$
\underset{\sim}{S} = \begin{bmatrix}
3.204 & & & \\
2.722 & 2.629 & & \\
3.198 & 2.875 & 4.855 & \\
3.545 & 3.202 & 5.373 & 6.315
\end{bmatrix}
$$

$$
\underset{\sim}{S} = \begin{bmatrix}
0.329 & 0.371 & -0.357 & -0.471 \\
0.559 & 0.592 & -0.316 & -0.335 \\
1.006 & 1.019 & -0.489 & -0.591 \\
0.468 & 0.456 & -0.438 & -0.539 \\
0.502 & 0.539 & -0.363 & -0.425 \\
1.050 & 0.960 & 1.416 & 1.714 \\
1.260 & 1.154 & 1.923 & 2.309
\end{bmatrix}
$$

$$
\underset{\sim}{S} = \begin{bmatrix}
1.363 & & & & & & \\
1.271 & 1.960 & & & & & \\
1.742 & 2.276 & 3.803 & & & & \\
0.788 & 1.043 & 1.953 & 1.376 & & & \\
0.838 & 1.070 & 2.090 & 1.189 & 1.741 & & \\
0.474 & 0.694 & 0.655 & 0.071 & 0.104 & 1.422 & \\
0.686 & 0.907 & 0.917 & 0.136 & 0.162 & 1.688 & 2.684
\end{bmatrix}
$$

This matrix $\underset{\sim}{S}$ was analyzed with LISREL using the following
input.

```
HYPOTHETICAL MODEL
DA NI=11
LA
(11A2)
Y1Y2Y3Y4X1X2X3X4X5X6X7
CM SY
(16F5.3)
 3204
 2722 2629
 3198 2875 4855
 3545 3202 5373 6315
  329  371 -357 -471 1363
  559  592 -316 -335 1271 1960
 1006 1019 -489 -591 1742 2276 3803
  468  456 -438 -539  788 1043 1953 1376
  502  539 -363 -425  838 1070 2090 1189 1741
 1050  960 1416 1714  474  694  655   71  104 1422
 1260 1154 1923 2309  686  907  917  136  162 1688 2684
MO NY=4 NE=2 NX=7 NK=3 BE=FU
FR LY(2,1) LY(4,2) LX(2,1) LX(3,1) LX(3,2) LX(5,2) LX(7,3)
FR BE(1,2) BE(2,1)
FI GA(1,3) GA(2,2)
VA 1 LY(1,1) LY(3,2) LX(1,1) LX(4,2) LX(6,3)
OU ALL
```

This produced initial estimates, ML estimates and standard errors of the ML-estimates. The χ^2 goodness-of-fit measure was 29.10 with 33 degrees of freedom. A second analysis used the same input but with ULS added on the OU card. This produced ULS estimates. All three sets of parameter estimates are given in Table 13. These results seem very reasonable with regard to the asymptotic theory. It is seen that the ULS estimates are generally closer to the true values than the initial estimates though the difference is rather small. Also it is seen that the ML estimates are generally closer than the ULS estimates.

A final analysis was done to test the hypothesis $\gamma_1 = \gamma_2$. The overall χ^2 goodness-of-fit measure for this constrained model was 30.01 with 34 degrees of freedom. The χ^2 for testing the hypothesis is 0.91 with one degree of freedom. The hypothesis cannot be rejected.

TABLE III.13

Parameter Estimates for Hypothetical Model

Parameter	True Parameter Value	Initial Estimates	ULS-Estimates	ML-Estimates
λ_1	0.90	0.92	0.91	0.92 (0.04)
λ_2	1.10	1.14	1.14	1.14 (0.03)
λ_3	1.30	1.26	1.31	1.29 (0.11)
λ_4	0.90	0.83	1.10	0.92 (0.12)
λ_5	1.20	1.14	0.93	1.09 (0.12)
λ_6	1.10	1.08	1.05	1.08 (0.08)
λ_7	1.40	1.39	1.32	1.44 (0.09)
β_1	0.49	0.55	0.55	0.54 (0.06)
β_2	0.60	0.89	1.01	0.94 (0.18)
γ_1	0.40	0.18	0.24	0.21 (0.15)
γ_2	0.40	0.51	0.46	0.50 (0.15)
γ_3	-1.00	-1.18	-1.25	-1.22 (0.12)
γ_4	1.20	1.00	0.89	1.00 (0.15)

III.10   Example 9:   Principal Components of Fowl Bone
Measurements

Factor analysis is often confused with principal component analysis.   The two methods are similar to some extent
but have entirely different aims, see e.g. Jöreskog, 1979.
It should be emphasized that none of the LISREL models
considered so far have any relationship to principal component analysis.   This subsection, however, illustrates
that LISREL can be used to do principal component   analysis as well.

Wright (1954) gave the following correlation matrix for
six bone measurements of 276 white leghorn fowl.   These
anatomical measurements have a hierarchical pattern.   The
skull contributes two dimensions, while the two wing bones
numerus and ulna and the two leg bones femur and tibia
are also represented.

Skull Length	1.000					
Skull Breadth	0.584	1.000				
Humerus	0.615	0.576	1.000			
Ulna	0.601	0.530	0.940	1.000		
Femur	0.570	0.526	0.875	0.877	1.000	
Tibia	0.600	0.555	0.878	0.886	0.924	1.000

All the analyses reported in this section are based on the
LISREL submodel of type 1 (see Table I.2) with $\Phi = I$ and
$\Theta_\delta = 0$ and the use of the ULS method.   The only parameter
matrix really involved in the analysis is Λ_x .

To obtain the first principal component set NK = 1 and

let $\underset{\sim x}{\Lambda}$ be free. The input is as follows.

```
PRINCIPAL COMPONENTS OF FOWL BONE MEASUREMENTS RUN 1
DA NI=6 NO=276
CM UN=8
MO NX=6 NK=1 LX=FR PH=ID TD=ZE
ST 0.5 ALL
OU UL NS
```

The six λ-values are estimated as

    0.74   0.70   0.95   0.94   0.93   0.94

The sum of squares of these values is 4.57 which is the

largest characteristic root of the correlation matrix.

This first principal component may be interpreted as a

general average of all bone dimensions.

To obtain the second principal component one can proceed

in two alternative ways. One is to input the residual

matrix and do the same analysis again. The other alter-

native, which is a little more convenient, is to set NK = 2

and fix all the elements in the first column of $\underset{\sim x}{\Lambda}$ equal

to the values of the first principal component. The input

for such an analysis is

```
PRINCIPAL COMPONENTS OF FOWL BONE MEASUREMENTS RUN 2
DA NI=6 NO=276
CM UN=8
MO NX=6 NK=2 PH=ID TD=ZE
FR LX(1,2) LX(2,2) LX(3,2) LX(4,2) LX(5,2) LX(6,2)
MA LX
(20F4.3)
 743 300 698 300 948 300 940 300 929 300 941 300
OU UL NS
```

and the second principal component is estimated as

    0.45   0.59   -0.16   -0.21   -0.24   -0.19

with characteristic root equal to 0.71. This may be
interpreted as a contrast between skull size and wing and
leg length. Together the first two principal components
account for the variance 4.57 + 0.71 = 5.28 or 78 % of
the total variance in all the observed measurements.

It is also possible to estimate two components simultaneously. This can be done with the following input.

```
PRINCIPAL COMPONENTS OF FOWL BONE MEASUREMENTS RUN 3
DA NI=6 NO=276
CM UN=8
MO NX=6 NK=2 LX=FR PH=ID TD=ZE
ST 0.5 ALL
ST 0. LX(1,2)
OU UL NS
```

This model is underidentified, of course. Nevertheless,
the program is able to compute an arbitrary solution if
it is given a starting point where the two columns are
different. The two components "estimated" in this way are

    0.86   0.91   0.63   0.59   0.57   0.60
                                                          (III.34)
    0.12   -0.01   0.73   0.76   0.77   0.75

These components are uncorrelated (orthogonal) and together
they account for exactly the same amount of variance as the
first two principal components as may be verified by computing the total sum of squares. The two components in (34)

are just an arbitrary rotation of the first two principal components.

It is also possible to estimate components which have pre-
scribed correlations with the observed measurements. For
example, we may prescribe that the second component should
be uncorrelated with skull length and in a three-component solution we may prescribe, in addition, that the third component should be uncorrelated with both skull length and skull
breadth. The input for such an analysis is

```
PRINCIPAL COMPONENTS OF FOWL BONE MEASUREMENTS RUN 4
DA NI=6 NO=276
CM UN=8
MO NX=6 NK=3 LX=FR PH=ID TD=ZE
FI LX(1,2) LX(1,3) LX(2,3)
ST 0.5 ALL
OU UL NS
```

which gives the following parameter estimates.

	Component		
	First	Second	Third
Skull Length	1.000	0.	0.
Skull Breadth	0.58	0.81	0.
Humerus	0.62	0.27	0.69
Ulna	0.61	0.22	0.72
Femur	0.56	0.24	0.74
Tibia	0.60	0.26	0.71

These three components together account for the same amount
of variance as the first three principal components. They
are just a particular rotation of these.

<u>III.11 Example 10: Nine Psychological Variables:</u>
<u>A Confirmatory Factor Analysis.</u>

Holzinger and Swineford (1939) collected data on twentysix
psychological tests administered to 145 seventh and eighth
grade children in the Grant-White school in Chicago. Nine of
these tests were selected and it was hypothesized that these
measure three common factors: visual perception (P), verbal
ability (V) and speed (S) such that the first three variables
measures P, the next three measures V and the last three mea-
sures S. The nine selected variables and their intercorrela-
tions are given below.

	1	2	3	4	5	6	7	8	9
1. *Visual perception*	1.000								
2. *Cubes*	0.318	1.000							
3. *Lozenges*	0.436	0.419	1.000						
4. *Paragraph comprehension*	0.335	0.234	0.323	1.000					
5. *Sentence completion*	0.304	0.157	0.283	0.722	1.000				
6. *Word meaning*	0.326	0.195	0.350	0.714	0.685	1.000			
7. *Addition*	0.116	0.057	0.056	0.203	0.246	0.170	1.000		
8. *Counting dots*	0.314	0.145	0.229	0.095	0.181	0.113	0.585	1.000	
9. *Straight-curved capitals*	0.489	0.239	0.361	0.309	0.345	0.280	0.408	0.512	1.000

Test the stated hypothesis. If the hypothesis is rejected, suggest
an alternative model which fits the data better.

To do this problem we use the automatic model specification.
The input is given below, followed by the full output, which
is self-explanatory.

NINE PSYCHOLOGICAL VARIABLES — A CONFIRMATORY FACTOR ANALYSIS

INPUT FILE

```
NINE PSYCHOLOGICAL VARIABLES — A CONFIRMATORY FACTOR ANALYSIS
DA NI=9 NO=145 MA=KM
LA
'VIS-PERC' 'CUBES' 'LOZENGES' 'PAR-COMP' 'SEN-COMP' 'WORDMEAN' 'ADDITION'
'COUNTDOT' 'S-C-CAPS'
KM
1 .318 1 .436 .419 1 .335 .234 .323 1 .304 .157 .283 .722 1
.326 .195 .350 .714 .685 1
.116 .057 .056 .203 .246 .170 1
.314 .145 .229 .095 .181 .113 .585 1
.489 .239 .361 .309 .345 .280 .408 .512 1
MO NX=9 NK=3 PH=ST
LK
'VISUAL' 'VERBAL' 'SPEED'
PA LX
3(1 0 0) 3(0 1 0) 3(0 0 1)
PL LX(9,1)
OU SE TV MI RS TO AM
```

L I S R E L VI

BY

KARL G JORESKOG AND DAG SORBOM

NINE PSYCHOLOGICAL VARIABLES - A CONFIRMATORY FACTOR ANALYSIS

THE FOLLOWING LISREL CONTROL LINES HAVE BEEN READ :

```
DA NI=9 NO=145 MA=KM
LA
'VIS-PERC' 'CUBES' 'LOZENGES' 'PAR-COMP' 'SEN-COMP' 'WORDMEAN' 'ADDITION'
'COUNTDOT' 'S-C-CAPS'
KM
1 .318 1 .436 .419 1 .335 .234 .323 1 .304 .157 .283 .722 1
.326 .195 .350 .714 .685 1
.116 .057 .056 .203 .246 .170 1
.314 .145 .229 .095 .181 .113 .585 1
.489 .239 .361 .309 .345 .280 .408 .512 1
MO NX=9 NK=3 PH=ST
LK
'VISUAL' 'VERBAL' 'SPEED'
PA LX
3(1 0 0) 3(0 1 0) 3(0 0 1)
PL LX(9,1)
OU SE TV MI RS TO AM
```

NUMBER OF INPUT VARIABLES	9
NUMBER OF Y - VARIABLES	O
NUMBER OF X - VARIABLES	9
NUMBER OF ETA - VARIABLES	O
NUMBER OF KSI - VARIABLES	3
NUMBER OF OBSERVATIONS	145

OUTPUT REQUESTED

TECHNICAL OUTPUT	NO
STANDARD ERRORS	YES
T - VALUES	YES
CORRELATIONS OF ESTIMATES	NO
FITTED MOMENTS	YES
TOTAL EFFECTS	NO
VARIANCES AND COVARIANCES	NO
MODIFICATION INDICES	YES
FACTOR SCORES REGRESSIONS	NO
FIRST ORDER DERIVATIVES	NO
STANDARDIZED SOLUTION	NO
PARAMETER PLOTS	YES
AUTOMATIC MODIFICATION	YES

NINE PSYCHOLOGICAL VARIABLES - A CONFIRMATORY FACTOR ANALYSIS

CORRELATION MATRIX TO BE ANALYZED

	VIS-PERC	CUBES	LOZENGES	PAR-COMP	SEN-COMP	WORDMEAN
VIS-PERC	1.000					
CUBES	0.318	1.000				
LOZENGES	0.436	0.419	1.000			
PAR-COMP	0.335	0.234	0.323	1.000		
SEN-COMP	0.304	0.157	0.283	0.722	1.000	
WORDMEAN	0.326	0.195	0.350	0.714	0.685	1.000
ADDITION	0.116	0.057	0.056	0.203	0.246	0.170
COUNTDOT	0.314	0.145	0.229	0.095	0.181	0.113
S-C-CAPS	0.489	0.239	0.361	0.309	0.345	0.280

CORRELATION MATRIX TO BE ANALYZED

	ADDITION	COUNTDOT	S-C-CAPS
ADDITION	1.000		
COUNTDOT	0.585	1.000	
S-C-CAPS	0.408	0.512	1.000

DETERMINANT = 0.317744D-01

PARAMETER SPECIFICATIONS

LAMBDA X

	VISUAL	VERBAL	SPEED
VIS-PERC	1	0	0
CUBES	2	0	0
LOZENGES	3	0	0
PAR-COMP	0	4	0
SEN-COMP	0	5	0
WORDMEAN	0	6	0
ADDITION	0	0	7
COUNTDOT	0	0	8
S-C-CAPS	0	0	9

PHI

	VISUAL	VERBAL	SPEED
VISUAL	0		
VERBAL	10	0	
SPEED	11	12	0

THETA DELTA

VIS-PERC	CUBES	LOZENGES	PAR-COMP	SEN-COMP	WORDMEAN
13	14	15	16	17	18

THETA DELTA

ADDITION	COUNTDOT	S-C-CAPS
19	20	21

NINE PSYCHOLOGICAL VARIABLES - A CONFIRMATORY FACTOR ANALYSIS

INITIAL ESTIMATES (TSLS)

LAMBDA X

	VISUAL	VERBAL	SPEED
VIS-PERC	0.728	0.0	0.0
CUBES	0.478	0.0	0.0
LOZENGES	0.661	0.0	0.0
PAR-COMP	0.0	0.871	0.0
SEN-COMP	0.0	0.828	0.0
WORDMEAN	0.0	0.824	0.0
ADDITION	0.0	0.0	0.741
COUNTDOT	0.0	0.0	0.778
S-C-CAPS	0.0	0.0	0.614

PHI

	VISUAL	VERBAL	SPEED
VISUAL	1.000		
VERBAL	0.535	1.000	
SPEED	0.489	0.345	1.000

THETA DELTA

VIS-PERC	CUBES	LOZENGES	PAR-COMP	SEN-COMP	WORDMEAN
0.469	0.771	0.563	0.241	0.315	0.321

THETA DELTA

ADDITION	COUNTDOT	S-C-CAPS
0.451	0.395	0.623

SQUARED MULTIPLE CORRELATIONS FOR X - VARIABLES

VIS-PERC	CUBES	LOZENGES	PAR-COMP	SEN-COMP	WORDMEAN
0.531	0.229	0.437	0.759	0.685	0.679

SQUARED MULTIPLE CORRELATIONS FOR X - VARIABLES

ADDITION	COUNTDOT	S-C-CAPS
0.549	0.605	0.377

TOTAL COEFFICIENT OF DETERMINATION FOR X - VARIABLES IS 0.983

NINE PSYCHOLOGICAL VARIABLES - A CONFIRMATORY FACTOR ANALYSIS

LISREL ESTIMATES (MAXIMUM LIKELIHOOD)

LAMBDA X

	VISUAL	VERBAL	SPEED
VIS-PERC	0.673	0.0	0.0
CUBES	0.513	0.0	0.0
LOZENGES	0.684	0.0	0.0
PAR-COMP	0.0	0.867	0.0
SEN-COMP	0.0	0.830	0.0
WORDMEAN	0.0	0.826	0.0
ADDITION	0.0	0.0	0.662
COUNTDOT	0.0	0.0	0.797
S-C-CAPS	0.0	0.0	0.681

PHI

	VISUAL	VERBAL	SPEED
VISUAL	1.000		
VERBAL	0.543	1.000	
SPEED	0.511	0.320	1.000

THETA DELTA

VIS-PERC	CUBES	LOZENGES	PAR-COMP	SEN-COMP	WORDMEAN
0.548	0.737	0.532	0.248	0.311	0.318

THETA DELTA

ADDITION	COUNTDOT	S-C-CAPS
0.562	0.365	0.536

SQUARED MULTIPLE CORRELATIONS FOR X - VARIABLES

VIS-PERC	CUBES	LOZENGES	PAR-COMP	SEN-COMP	WORDMEAN
0.452	0.263	0.468	0.752	0.689	0.682

SQUARED MULTIPLE CORRELATIONS FOR X - VARIABLES

ADDITION	COUNTDOT	S-C-CAPS
0.438	0.635	0.464

TOTAL COEFFICIENT OF DETERMINATION FOR X - VARIABLES IS   0.982

MEASURES OF GOODNESS OF FIT FOR THE WHOLE MODEL :

CHI-SQUARE WITH 24 DEGREES OF FREEDOM IS   52.62 (PROB. LEVEL = 0.001)

GOODNESS OF FIT INDEX IS 0.928

ADJUSTED GOODNESS OF FIT INDEX IS 0.866

ROOT MEAN SQUARE RESIDUAL IS   0.075

NINE PSYCHOLOGICAL VARIABLES - A CONFIRMATORY FACTOR ANALYSIS

MODIFICATION INDICES

        LAMBDA X

	VISUAL	VERBAL	SPEED
VIS-PERC	0.0	0.265	3.947
CUBES	0.0	0.665	0.974
LOZENGES	0.0	0.032	1.357
PAR-COMP	0.004	0.0	0.683
SEN-COMP	0.342	0.0	2.050
WORDMEAN	0.275	0.0	0.308
ADDITION	10.859	0.148	0.0
COUNTDOT	2.609	9.869	0.0
S-C-CAPS	24.645	9.882	0.0

        PHI

	VISUAL	VERBAL	SPEED
VISUAL	0.0		
VERBAL	0.0	0.0	
SPEED	0.0	0.0	0.0

        THETA DELTA

VIS-PERC	CUBES	LOZENGES	PAR-COMP	SEN-COMP	WORDMEAN
0.0	0.0	0.0	0.0	0.0	0.0

        THETA DELTA

ADDITION	COUNTDOT	S-C-CAPS
0.0	0.0	0.0

        MAXIMUM MODIFICATION INDEX IS   24.65 FOR ELEMENT (9, 1) OF LAMBDA X

NINE PSYCHOLOGICAL VARIABLES - A CONFIRMATORY FACTOR ANALYSIS

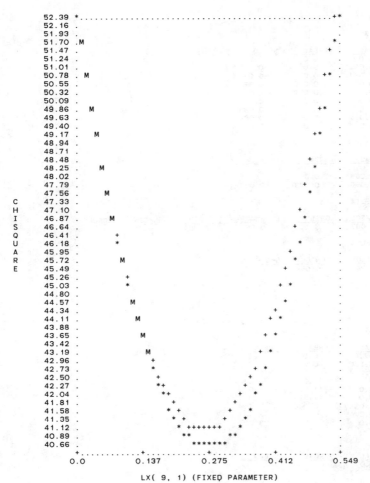

LX(9, 1) (FIXED PARAMETER)

+ = FITTING FUNCTION, * = QUADRATIC APPROXIMATION,

M = MULTIPLE POINTS

NINE PSYCHOLOGICAL VARIABLES - A CONFIRMATORY FACTOR ANALYSIS

STANDARD ERRORS

LAMBDA X

	VISUAL	VERBAL	SPEED
VIS-PERC	0.091	0.0	0.0
CUBES	0.092	0.0	0.0
LOZENGES	0.091	0.0	0.0
PAR-COMP	0.0	0.070	0.0
SEN-COMP	0.0	0.072	0.0
WORDMEAN	0.0	0.072	0.0
ADDITION	0.0	0.0	0.085
COUNTDOT	0.0	0.0	0.084
S-C-CAPS	0.0	0.0	0.085

PHI

	VISUAL	VERBAL	SPEED
VISUAL	0.0		
VERBAL	0.086	0.0	
SPEED	0.096	0.093	0.0

THETA DELTA

VIS-PERC	CUBES	LOZENGES	PAR-COMP	SEN-COMP	WORDMEAN
0.097	0.101	0.097	0.051	0.054	0.054

THETA DELTA

ADDITION	COUNTDOT	S-C-CAPS
0.087	0.089	0.087

T-VALUES

LAMBDA X

	VISUAL	VERBAL	SPEED
VIS-PERC	7.392	0.0	0.0
CUBES	5.550	0.0	0.0
LOZENGES	7.514	0.0	0.0
PAR-COMP	0.0	12.348	0.0
SEN-COMP	0.0	11.609	0.0
WORDMEAN	0.0	11.525	0.0
ADDITION	0.0	0.0	7.763
COUNTDOT	0.0	0.0	9.431
S-C-CAPS	0.0	0.0	8.007

PHI

	VISUAL	VERBAL	SPEED
VISUAL	0.0		
VERBAL	6.327	0.0	
SPEED	5.304	3.450	0.0

THETA DELTA

VIS-PERC	CUBES	LOZENGES	PAR-COMP	SEN-COMP	WORDMEAN
5.642	7.301	5.466	4.820	5.786	5.883

THETA DELTA

ADDITION	COUNTDOT	S-C-CAPS
6.448	4.096	6.184

NINE PSYCHOLOGICAL VARIABLES - A CONFIRMATORY FACTOR ANALYSIS

FITTED MOMENTS AND RESIDUALS

FITTED MOMENTS

	VIS-PERC	CUBES	LOZENGES	PAR-COMP	SEN-COMP	WORDMEAN
VIS-PERC	1.000					
CUBES	0.345	1.000				
LOZENGES	0.460	0.351	1.000			
PAR-COMP	0.317	0.242	0.322	1.000		
SEN-COMP	0.303	0.231	0.308	0.720	1.000	
WORDMEAN	0.302	0.230	0.307	0.716	0.685	1.000
ADDITION	0.228	0.174	0.231	0.184	0.176	0.175
COUNTDOT	0.274	0.209	0.279	0.221	0.212	0.211
S-C-CAPS	0.234	0.179	0.238	0.189	0.181	0.180

FITTED MOMENTS

	ADDITION	COUNTDOT	S-C-CAPS
ADDITION	1.000		
COUNTDOT	0.527	1.000	
S-C-CAPS	0.451	0.543	1.000

FITTED RESIDUALS

	VIS-PERC	CUBES	LOZENGES	PAR-COMP	SEN-COMP	WORDMEAN
VIS-PERC	0.000					
CUBES	-0.027	-0.000				
LOZENGES	-0.024	0.068	-0.000			
PAR-COMP	0.018	-0.008	0.001	0.000		
SEN-COMP	0.001	-0.074	-0.025	0.002	0.000	
WORDMEAN	0.024	-0.035	0.043	-0.002	-0.000	0.000
ADDITION	-0.112	-0.117	-0.175	0.019	0.070	-0.005
COUNTDOT	0.040	-0.064	-0.050	-0.126	-0.031	-0.098
S-C-CAPS	0.255	0.060	0.123	0.120	0.164	0.100

FITTED RESIDUALS

	ADDITION	COUNTDOT	S-C-CAPS
ADDITION	-0.000		
COUNTDOT	0.058	0.000	
S-C-CAPS	-0.043	-0.031	-0.000

NORMALIZED RESIDUALS

	VIS-PERC	CUBES	LOZENGES	PAR-COMP	SEN-COMP	WORDMEAN
VIS-PERC	0.000					
CUBES	-0.307	-0.000				
LOZENGES	-0.261	0.771	-0.000			
PAR-COMP	0.209	-0.089	0.010	0.000		
SEN-COMP	0.009	-0.869	-0.291	0.022	0.000	
WORDMEAN	0.280	-0.410	0.496	-0.019	-0.004	0.000
ADDITION	-1.305	-1.378	-2.050	0.226	0.828	-0.060
COUNTDOT	0.462	-0.752	-0.574	-1.481	-0.364	-1.149
S-C-CAPS	2.977	0.713	1.434	1.412	1.934	1.178

NORMALIZED RESIDUALS

	ADDITION	COUNTDOT	S-C-CAPS
ADDITION	-0.000		
COUNTDOT	0.614	0.000	
S-C-CAPS	-0.465	-0.324	-0.000

NINE PSYCHOLOGICAL VARIABLES - A CONFIRMATORY FACTOR ANALYSIS

QPLOT OF NORMALIZED RESIDUALS

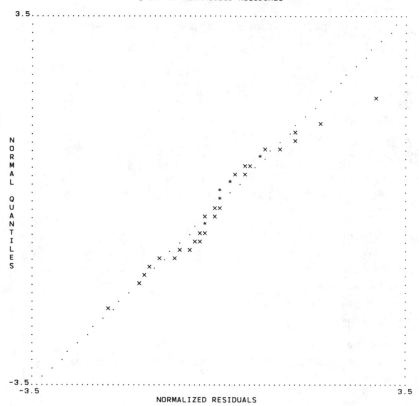

NINE PSYCHOLOGICAL VARIABLES - A CONFIRMATORY FACTOR ANALYSIS

MODIFIED MODEL WITH ELEMENT (9, 1) OF LAMBDA X   SET FREE

LISREL ESTIMATES (MAXIMUM LIKELIHOOD)

LAMBDA X

	VISUAL	VERBAL	SPEED
VIS-PERC	0.708	0.0	0.0
CUBES	0.483	0.0	0.0
LOZENGES	0.650	0.0	0.0
PAR-COMP	0.0	0.868	0.0
SEN-COMP	0.0	0.830	0.0
WORDMEAN	0.0	0.825	0.0
ADDITION	0.0	0.0	0.681
COUNTDOT	0.0	0.0	0.859
S-C-CAPS	0.457	0.0	0.419

PHI

	VISUAL	VERBAL	SPEED
VISUAL	1.000		
VERBAL	0.557	1.000	
SPEED	0.390	0.223	1.000

THETA DELTA

VIS-PERC	CUBES	LOZENGES	PAR-COMP	SEN-COMP	WORDMEAN
0.498	0.766	0.578	0.247	0.311	0.319

THETA DELTA

ADDITION	COUNTDOT	S-C-CAPS
0.536	0.262	0.467

SQUARED MULTIPLE CORRELATIONS FOR X - VARIABLES

VIS-PERC	CUBES	LOZENGES	PAR-COMP	SEN-COMP	WORDMEAN
0.502	0.234	0.422	0.753	0.689	0.681

SQUARED MULTIPLE CORRELATIONS FOR X - VARIABLES

ADDITION	COUNTDOT	S-C-CAPS
0.464	0.738	0.533

TOTAL COEFFICIENT OF DETERMINATION FOR X - VARIABLES IS 0.989

MEASURES OF GOODNESS OF FIT FOR THE WHOLE MODEL :

CHI-SQUARE WITH 23 DEGREES OF FREEDOM IS   29.01 (PROB. LEVEL = 0.180)

GOODNESS OF FIT INDEX IS 0.958

ADJUSTED GOODNESS OF FIT INDEX IS 0.917

ROOT MEAN SQUARE RESIDUAL IS   0.045

NINE PSYCHOLOGICAL VARIABLES - A CONFIRMATORY FACTOR ANALYSIS

MODIFICATION INDICES

     LAMBDA X

	VISUAL	VERBAL	SPEED
VIS-PERC	0.0	0.120	1.602
CUBES	0.0	0.351	0.546
LOZENGES	0.0	0.139	0.556
PAR-COMP	0.003	0.0	0.922
SEN-COMP	0.141	0.0	2.444
WORDMEAN	0.101	0.0	0.292
ADDITION	2.873	2.448	0.0
COUNTDOT	2.873	2.957	0.0
S-C-CAPS	0.0	0.278	0.0

     PHI

	VISUAL	VERBAL	SPEED
VISUAL	0.0		
VERBAL	0.0	0.0	
SPEED	0.0	0.0	0.0

     THETA DELTA

VIS-PERC	CUBES	LOZENGES	PAR-COMP	SEN-COMP	WORDMEAN
0.0	0.0	0.0	0.0	0.0	0.0

     THETA DELTA

ADDITION	COUNTDOT	S-C-CAPS
0.0	0.0	0.0

     MAXIMUM MODIFICATION INDEX IS   2.96 FOR ELEMENT (8, 2) OF LAMBDA X

NINE PSYCHOLOGICAL VARIABLES - A CONFIRMATORY FACTOR ANALYSIS

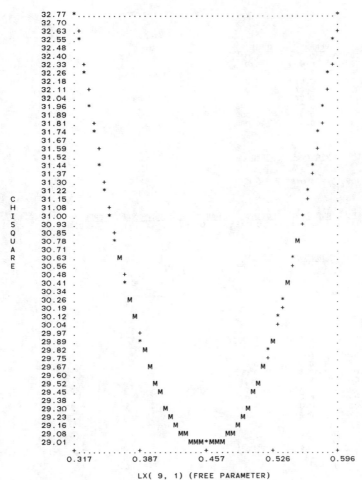

LX(9, 1) (FREE PARAMETER)

+ = FITTING FUNCTION, * = QUADRATIC APPROXIMATION,

M = MULTIPLE POINTS

NINE PSYCHOLOGICAL VARIABLES - A CONFIRMATORY FACTOR ANALYSIS

STANDARD ERRORS

LAMBDA X

	VISUAL	VERBAL	SPEED
VIS-PERC	0.087	0.0	0.0
CUBES	0.091	0.0	0.0
LOZENGES	0.087	0.0	0.0
PAR-COMP	0.0	0.070	0.0
SEN-COMP	0.0	0.071	0.0
WORDMEAN	0.0	0.072	0.0
ADDITION	0.0	0.0	0.089
COUNTDOT	0.0	0.0	0.092
S-C-CAPS	0.089	0.0	0.088

PHI

	VISUAL	VERBAL	SPEED
VISUAL	0.0		
VERBAL	0.081	0.0	
SPEED	0.105	0.096	0.0

THETA DELTA

VIS-PERC	CUBES	LOZENGES	PAR-COMP	SEN-COMP	WORDMEAN
0.090	0.101	0.091	0.051	0.054	0.054

THETA DELTA

ADDITION	COUNTDOT	S-C-CAPS
0.093	0.113	0.073

T-VALUES

LAMBDA X

	VISUAL	VERBAL	SPEED
VIS-PERC	8.158	0.0	0.0
CUBES	5.326	0.0	0.0
LOZENGES	7.430	0.0	0.0
PAR-COMP	0.0	12.371	0.0
SEN-COMP	0.0	11.609	0.0
WORDMEAN	0.0	11.514	0.0
ADDITION	0.0	0.0	7.679
COUNTDOT	0.0	0.0	9.372
S-C-CAPS	5.153	0.0	4.734

PHI

	VISUAL	VERBAL	SPEED
VISUAL	0.0		
VERBAL	6.868	0.0	
SPEED	3.727	2.322	0.0

THETA DELTA

VIS-PERC	CUBES	LOZENGES	PAR-COMP	SEN-COMP	WORDMEAN
5.527	7.617	6.339	4.809	5.800	5.908

THETA DELTA

ADDITION	COUNTDOT	S-C-CAPS
5.758	2.312	6.424

NINE PSYCHOLOGICAL VARIABLES - A CONFIRMATORY FACTOR ANALYSIS

FITTED MOMENTS AND RESIDUALS

FITTED MOMENTS

	VIS-PERC	CUBES	LOZENGES	PAR-COMP	SEN-COMP	WORDMEAN
VIS-PERC	1.000					
CUBES	0.342	1.000				
LOZENGES	0.460	0.314	1.000			
PAR-COMP	0.343	0.234	0.314	1.000		
SEN-COMP	0.328	0.224	0.301	0.720	1.000	
WORDMEAN	0.326	0.222	0.299	0.716	0.685	1.000
ADDITION	0.188	0.128	0.172	0.132	0.126	0.125
COUNTDOT	0.237	0.162	0.218	0.166	0.159	0.158
S-C-CAPS	0.439	0.300	0.403	0.302	0.289	0.287

FITTED MOMENTS

	ADDITION	COUNTDOT	S-C-CAPS
ADDITION	1.000		
COUNTDOT	0.585	1.000	
S-C-CAPS	0.406	0.513	1.000

FITTED RESIDUALS

	VIS-PERC	CUBES	LOZENGES	PAR-COMP	SEN-COMP	WORDMEAN
VIS-PERC	0.000					
CUBES	-0.024	-0.000				
LOZENGES	-0.024	0.105	-0.000			
PAR-COMP	-0.008	0.000	0.009	0.000		
SEN-COMP	-0.024	-0.067	-0.018	0.002	0.000	
WORDMEAN	0.000	-0.027	0.051	-0.002	0.000	0.000
ADDITION	-0.072	-0.071	-0.116	0.071	0.120	0.045
COUNTDOT	0.077	-0.017	0.011	-0.071	0.022	-0.045
S-C-CAPS	0.050	-0.061	-0.042	0.007	0.056	-0.007

FITTED RESIDUALS

	ADDITION	COUNTDOT	S-C-CAPS
ADDITION	0.000		
COUNTDOT	0.000	-0.000	
S-C-CAPS	0.002	-0.001	-0.000

NORMALIZED RESIDUALS

	VIS-PERC	CUBES	LOZENGES	PAR-COMP	SEN-COMP	WORDMEAN
VIS-PERC	0.000					
CUBES	-0.276	-0.000				
LOZENGES	-0.264	1.201	-0.000			
PAR-COMP	-0.087	0.002	0.098	0.000		
SEN-COMP	-0.269	-0.780	-0.203	0.017	0.000	
WORDMEAN	0.003	-0.320	0.588	-0.020	0.003	0.000
ADDITION	-0.848	-0.848	-1.377	0.848	1.429	0.533
COUNTDOT	0.898	-0.199	0.134	-0.843	0.261	-0.534
S-C-CAPS	0.550	-0.697	-0.466	0.081	0.648	-0.081

NORMALIZED RESIDUALS

	ADDITION	COUNTDOT	S-C-CAPS
ADDITION	0.000		
COUNTDOT	0.000	-0.000	
S-C-CAPS	0.019	-0.008	-0.000

NINE PSYCHOLOGICAL VARIABLES - A CONFIRMATORY FACTOR ANALYSIS

QPLOT OF NORMALIZED RESIDUALS

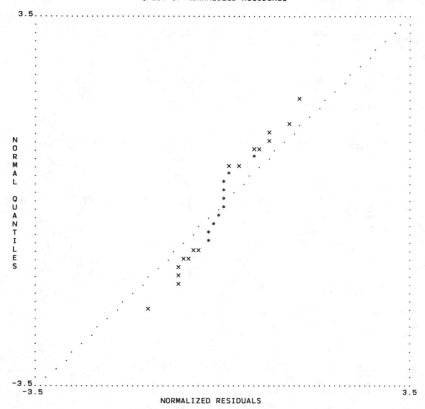

THE PROBLEM REQUIRED   946 DOUBLE PRECISION WORDS, THE CPU-TIME WAS   2.94 SECONDS

CHAPTER IV

ANALYSIS OF DISCRETE VARIABLES

IV.1 Continuous vs Discrete Variables

In the previous chapters we have assumed that the observed
variables to be analyzed by the LISREL computer program
are quantitative variables in the sense that they represent
measurements which are, at least approximately, on an
interval scale. If such variables are approximately normally
distributed, in addition, the use of maximum likelihood
estimates and their associated standard errors and χ^2
goodness-of-fit measure may be justified. If the distribution of the observed variables are moderately non-symmetric,
skewed or peaked, the ML method may still be used to fit
the model to the data but one should not rely on standard
errors and χ^2-values, as these are rather sensitive to departures from normality. If the observed variables are
highly non-normally distributed it is probably best to avoid
the ML estimates and use only initial estimates and/or ULS
estimates.

In many cases, especially when data are collected through
questionnaires, the variables are only ordinal, i.e.,
responses are classified into different ordered categories.

Sometimes some variables may be only nominal, such as sex, ethnicity, urban/rural etc. Nominal, i.e., coded dummy variables, and ordinal variables may be used in LISREL if they are fixed x-variables. Example 7 in Chapter III is an example of this. LISREL is then concerned only with the conditional distribution of $\underset{\sim}{y}$ for given $\underset{\sim}{x}$ and if this distribution is approximately multinormal, even the ML method may be used. If there are nominal variables among the y-variables and/or nominal x-variables which are not considered fixed, these are best treated as separate groups for which the methods of the next chapter can be used. This chapter will be concerned with the case when there are ordinal variables among the y-variables and/or ordinal x-variables which are not fixed.

An ordinal variable z (z may be either a y- or a x-variable in LISREL sense) may be regarded as a crude measurement of an underlying unobserved or unobservable continuous variable z^* . For example, a four-point ordinal scale may be conceived as

If $z^* \leq \alpha_1$, z is scored 1

If $\alpha_1 < z^* \leq \alpha_2$, z is scored 2

If $\alpha_2 < z^* \leq \alpha_3$, z is scored 3

If $\alpha_3 < z^*$, z is scored 4 ,

where $\alpha_1 < \alpha_2 < \alpha_3$ are threshold values for z^* . It is often assumed that z^* has a standard normal distribution

in which case the thresholds can be determined from the
inverse of the normal distribution function.

Suppose z_1 and z_2 are two ordinal variables with underlying continuous variables z_1^* and z_2^*, respectively.
Assuming that z_1^* and z_2^* have a bivariate normal distribution, their correlation is called *the polychoric correlation coefficient*. A special case of this is *the tetrachoric
correlation coefficient* when both z_1 and z_2 are dichotomous. Now, suppose further that z_3 is a continuous variable measured on an interval scale. The correlation between
z_1^* and z_3 is called *the polyserial correlation coefficient* assuming that z_1^* and z_3 have a bivariate normal
distribution.

When the observed variables in LISREL are all ordinal or
are of mixed scale types (ordinal and interval), the use
of ordinary product moment correlations is not recommended.
Instead it is suggested that estimates of polychoric and
polyserial correlations be computed and that a matrix of
such correlations be analyzed by the ULS method. If the
number of y-variables is small, an exact treatment of the
problem may be obtained by an approach which has been
worked out for the dichotomous case by Muthén (1978, 1979, 1981). When
the number of y-variables is large, this approach
will be very heavy or unfeasible and the approach given
here is likely to serve as a satisfactory compromise.

IV.2 Handling of Raw Data

LISREL provides options for dealing with raw data. These include
the handling of missing observations and possibilities for
computing polychoric and poly-serial correlations from discrete
data. These options are governed by the following parameters
which may be given on the RA card when reading raw data:

XM = missing data value, i.e., any real number representing a missing observation. It is assumed that the
same value is used to represent a missing observation for all variables. When XM is not given on
the RA card, the program assumes that there are no
missing observations in the data matrix.

MV = maximum number of distinct values in any discrete (ordinal)
variable. *MV must not exceed 9.* Default is MV = 0,
which implies that all variables are treated as continuous (interval) variables, see below.

The meaning of these two parameters is best explained by
describing what the program does. When both XM and MV are
default,the program uses the raw data to compute a moment
matrix, a covariance matrix or a correlation matrix depending
on the value of the parameter MA on the DA card (see Section
II.3).   Otherwise, if MV is given, each column of the data matrix,i.e.,
each variable, is scanned. If there are more than MV distinct
values in a column this variable is treated as a continuous
variable and the mean and standard deviation of this variable

are computed ignoring missing **values, if any. If MV = 0, all**
variables will be treated as continuous and missing data will be
deleted <u>listwise</u>. MV = 1 also treats all variables as continuous,
but there will be <u>pairwise</u> deletion of missing data. Otherwise,
if MV $\geqslant$ 2, missing data will be deleted <u>pairwise</u> and variables
with less than MV distinct values are treated as discrete: the
corresponding frequencies are recorded and used to compute
threshold values for a standard normal distribution as follows.
If a variable has $k \leqslant$ MV distinct values with n_1, n_2, ..., n_k of
each, $k - 1$ threshold values a_1, a_2, ..., a_{k-1} are computed as

$$a_i = \phi^{-1} \left(\sum_{j=1}^{i} n_j/n \right) , \quad i = 1, 2, \ldots , k-1,$$

where $\phi^{-1}(p)$ is the inverse of the standard normal distribution function and $n = n_1 + n_2 + \ldots + n_k$.

When all variables have been scanned in this way, all
pairs of variables are scanned. For each pair of variables
one of the following three alternatives will occur:

(i)   Both variables are continuous (interval). Then the product
      moment correlation is computed using all observations
      with no missing data for these variables.

(ii) Both variables are discrete (ordinal). Then a contingency
      table is computed and used to estimate the polychoric
      correlation assuming an underlying bivariate normal
      distribution, see Olsson (1979).

(iii)   One variable is discrete (ordinal) and the other is continuous
        (interval). Then the program finds the values of the continuous
        variable corresponding to each value of the discrete
        variable and uses these to estimate the polyserial
        correlation assuming again a bivariate normal
        distribution, see Olsson, Drasgow and Dorans (1981).

In cases (ii) and (iii) the program uses a simple search
and interpolation procedure to maximize the likelihood of
the bivariate normal distribution.

The end product of the entire procedure is a correlation
matrix for all input variables, where each correlation
has been estimated separately. There is no guarantee
that such a correlation matrix is positive definite.
Experience indicates that such a matrix sometimes fails
to be positive definite. When a non-positive definite
matrix is to be used to estimate a LISREL model, the ML
method cannot be used; the ULS method must be used instead.
Furthermore, even if the matrix of correlations is positive
definite, these correlations are unlikely to behave like
ordinary sample moments even asymptotically. So even if
one uses the ML method for fitting the model, one should
not use standard errors and χ^2 goodness-of-fit measures.

In addition to the two parameters XM and MV on the RA
card, two other parameters PP and PT may be given on the

RA card to specify the amount of printed output from this procedure. The default is no output. When PP is given, one gets one page of results for each pair of variables. When also PT is given one gets a technical output describing the behaviour of the iterations under the minimization of the negative of the likelihood function. The printed output will now be described by means of an example based on generated data.

IV.3 Example 11: Artificial Data of Mixed Scale Types

Two hundred observations were generated from a multivariate normal distribution with mean vector zero and covariance matrix

$$
\Sigma =
\begin{bmatrix}
1.000 \\
0.720 & 1.000 \\
0.378 & 0.336 & 1.000 \\
0.324 & 0.288 & 0.420 & 1.000 \\
0.270 & 0.240 & 0.350 & 0.300 & 1.000 \\
0.270 & 0.240 & 0.126 & 0.108 & 0.090 & 1.000
\end{bmatrix}
\qquad \text{(IV.1)}
$$

This Σ has been constructed to satisfy exactly a factor analysis model with two correlated factors and a clear simple structure, see Jöreskog (1979a). The following threshold values $\alpha_1, \alpha_2, \ldots, \alpha_k$ were assigned to variables 2, 3, 4 and 6:

Variable 2: $k = 2$ $\alpha_1 = -0.25$

Variable 3: $k = 3$ $\alpha_1 = -0.5,\ \alpha_2 = 0.5$

Variable 4: $k = 5$ $\alpha_1 = -1.5,\ \alpha_2 = -0.5,\ \alpha_3 = 0.5,\ \alpha_4 = 1.5$

Variable 6: $k = 7$ $\alpha_1 = -2,\ \alpha_2 = -1,\ \alpha_3 = -0.5,\ \alpha_4 = 0,$

$$\alpha_5 = 0.75,\ \alpha_6 = 1.5$$

These variables were then discretized as follows:

If $x \leq \alpha_1$ *the value* 0 *was assigned to the observation* x

If $\alpha_i < x \leq \alpha_{i+1}$, *the value* i *was assigned to the observation* x, $i = 1, 2, \ldots, k-1$.

If $\alpha_k < x$, *the value* k *was assigned to the observation* x.

The variables 1 and 5 were unchanged. Finally, exactly 120 (20%) values equal to 99 were randomly assigned over the whole data matrix to represent missing observations. The first 30 observations of the data matrix generated in this way are given on the next page.

The data matrix of order 200 x 6 were analyzed using this RA card

    RAW UN=8 XM=99. MV=7 PP PT

The raw data were read from a file on unit 8.

The resulting output consists of 15 pages, one for each pair of variables. We present only the following pairs here (5,1), (6,3) and (6,5), illustrating the three cases (i), (ii) and (iii), respectively. The printout on these pages are self explanatory.

```
(1X,D12.0,5D13.0)              INPUT DATA FOR ARTIFICIAL DATA
 -0.23458E+01  0.0            0.0            0.99000E+02 -0.12742E+01  0.30000E+01
 -0.15132E+01  0.99000E+02    0.20000E+01    0.99000E+02 -0.53270E+00  0.10000E+01
  0.17620E+01  0.10000E+01    0.20000E+01    0.30000E+01 -0.29295E+00  0.40000E+01
 -0.13840E+01  0.0            0.0            0.0          -0.91350E+00  0.99000E+02
  0.99000E+02  0.99000E+02    0.10000E+01    0.99000E+02  0.35375E-01  0.30000E+01
 -0.77501E+00  0.0            0.0            0.99000E+02  0.74470E+00  0.10000E+01
 -0.27780E+01  0.10000E+01    0.99000E+02    0.10000E+01 -0.13830E+00  0.50000E+01
  0.22000E+00  0.10000E+01    0.10000E+01    0.10000E+01 -0.10200E+01  0.20000E+01
  0.99000E+02  0.10000E+01    0.20000E+01    0.20000E+01  0.19865E+00  0.40000E+01
  0.80095E+00  0.10000E+01    0.0            0.30000E+01  0.12419E+01  0.40000E+01
 -0.40102E+00  0.10000E+01    0.0            0.99000E+02  0.93007E+00  0.20000E+01
  0.99000E+02  0.0            0.20000E+01    0.20000E+01 -0.96735E-01  0.60000E+01
 -0.12803E+01  0.0            0.10000E+01    0.10000E+01 -0.55317E+00  0.40000E+01
  0.99000E+02  0.10000E+01    0.0            0.0          -0.10007E+01  0.10000E+01
 -0.90109E+00  0.0            0.0            0.20000E+01 -0.84819E+00  0.40000E+01
  0.11048E+01  0.10000E+01    0.20000E+01    0.30000E+01 -0.13117E+01  0.20000E+01
  0.10536E+01  0.10000E+01    0.20000E+01    0.40000E+01  0.99000E+02  0.40000E+01
 -0.28295E+00  0.0            0.10000E+01    0.20000E+01 -0.59472E+00  0.10000E+01
 -0.56024E+00  0.10000E+01    0.20000E+01    0.30000E+01  0.72145E+00  0.30000E+01
  0.15734E+01  0.10000E+01    0.20000E+01    0.10000E+01  0.18618E+01  0.30000E+01
 -0.32847E+00  0.0            0.10000E+01    0.20000E+01  0.15690E+00  0.0
  0.99000E+02  0.0            0.10000E+01    0.10000E+01  0.10716E+01  0.60000E+01
 -0.36802E+00  0.0            0.20000E+01    0.20000E+01  0.99000E+02  0.60000E+01
 -0.65146E+00  0.10000E+01    0.20000E+01    0.30000E+01  0.51073E+00  0.40000E+01
  0.67161E+00  0.10000E+01    0.0            0.10000E+01  0.99000E+02  0.40000E+01
  0.11218E+01  0.10000E+01    0.20000E+01    0.99000E+02 -0.25063E-01  0.30000E+01
  0.52972E+00  0.10000E+01    0.0            0.10000E+01 -0.37657E-01  0.60000E+01
 -0.71247E+00  0.0            0.99000E+02    0.20000E+01 -0.52636E+00  0.20000E+01
 -0.52019E+00  0.10000E+01    0.0            0.10000E+01  0.31565E+00  0.40000E+01
 -0.84125E+00  0.0            0.20000E+01    0.30000E+01  0.19846E+01  0.99000E+02
```

COMPUTING CORRELATION BETWEEN VARIABLES   VAR 5 AND   VAR 1

VARIABLE   VAR 5 HAS MORE THAN   7 VALUES AND IS TREATED AS A CONTINUOUS VARIABLE

NUMBER OF MISSING VALUES (CODE = 99.0000)   12

MEAN FOR VARIABLE   VAR 5   0.092

STANDARD DEVIATION FOR VARIABLE   VAR 5   0.964

VARIABLE   VAR 1 HAS MORE THAN   7 VALUES AND IS TREATED AS A CONTINUOUS VARIABLE

NUMBER OF MISSING VALUES (CODE = 99.0000)   30

MEAN FOR VARIABLE   VAR 1   -0.036

STANDARD DEVIATION FOR VARIABLE   VAR 1   1.055

 PRODUCT MOMENT CORRELATION IS   0.138

COMPUTING CORRELATION BETWEEN VARIABLES   VAR 6 AND   VAR 3

VARIABLE   VAR 6 HAS   7 VALUES AND IS TREATED AS A DISCRETE VARIABLE

NUMBER OF MISSING VALUES (CODE = 99.0000)   14

MARGINAL FREQUENCES FOR VARIABLE   VAR 6
   CATEGORY   1   2   3   4   5   6   7
   FREQUENCY   2   24   28   41   52   24   15

ESTIMATED THRESHOLD VALUES FOR VARIABLE   VAR 6

-2.30   -1.08   -0.55   0.03   0.81   1.40

VARIABLE   VAR 3 HAS   3 VALUES AND IS TREATED AS A DISCRETE VARIABLE

NUMBER OF MISSING VALUES (CODE = 99.0000)   25

MARGINAL FREQUENCES FOR VARIABLE   VAR 3
   CATEGORY   1   2   3
   FREQUENCY   60   58   57

ESTIMATED THRESHOLD VALUES FOR VARIABLE   VAR 3

-0.40   0.45

CONTINGENCY TABLE   (ROWS =   VAR 6 COLS =   VAR 3)

	1	2	3	MISSING
1	0	1	1	0
2	9	6	6	3
3	5	10	3	10
4	13	12	13	3
5	15	13	19	5
6	7	10	3	4
7	7	3	5	0
MISSING	4	3	7	0

TECHNICAL OUTPUT FROM MINIMIZATION

CORRELATION	FUNCTION	SLOPE
0.0	0.78677677D+01	0.30982972D+01
-0.2900	0.12499625D+02	-0.38361078D+02
-0.0277	0.78286063D+01	-0.26995093D+00
-0.0255	0.78283072D+01	0.21241567D-03

POLYCHORIC CORRELATION IS -0.025

COMPUTING CORRELATION BETWEEN VARIABLES   VAR 6 AND   VAR 5

VARIABLE   VAR 6 HAS   7 VALUES AND IS TREATED AS A DISCRETE VARIABLE

NUMBER OF MISSING VALUES (CODE = 99.0000)   14

MARGINAL FREQUENCES FOR VARIABLE   VAR 6
```
   CATEGORY      1     2     3     4     5     6     7
   FREQUENCY     2    24    28    41    52    24    15
```

ESTIMATED THRESHOLD VALUES FOR VARIABLE   VAR 6

-2.30   -1.08   -0.55   0.03   0.81   1.40

VARIABLE   VAR 5 HAS MORE THAN   7 VALUES AND IS TREATED AS A CONTINUOUS VARIABLE

NUMBER OF MISSING VALUES (CODE = 99.0000)   12

MEAN FOR VARIABLE   VAR 5   0.092

STANDARD DEVIATION FOR VARIABLE   VAR 5   0.964

TECHNICAL OUTPUT FROM MINIMIZATION

```
CORRELATION      FUNCTION           SLOPE

0.0              0.30323977D+03    -0.78908594D+01
0.2900           0.30771068D+03     0.44196765D+02
0.0587           0.30302731D+03     0.66875740D+00
0.0541           0.30302580D+03    -0.2644410OD-02
```

   POLYSERIAL CORRELATION IS   0.054

The raw data matrix may be analyzed to estimate the correlation matrix and this may be analyzed according to a
LISREL model in a single run using the following LISREL
control cards

```
ARTIFICIAL DATA
DA NI=6 NO=200
RA UN=8 XM=99 MV=7 PP PT
MO NX=6 NK=2 PH=ST
FR LX 1 1 LX 2 1 LX 3 2 LX 4 2 LX 5 2 LX 6 1
OU SE TV
```

The model is the same as the population model used to
generate $\underset{\sim}{\Sigma}$ in (1), see Jöreskog (1979a). The polychoric
correlation matrix turned out to be positive definite in
this case so that maximum likelihood estimation is possible. The maximum likelihood estimates and the true parameter values are given in Table 1. The estimates are
remarkably close considering the brutal treatment which
the data was given.

It is also possible to analyze the raw data to estimate
the correlation matrix only without having a LISREL model.
To do this just omit the MO card and all cards following it
except the OU card. The computation of polychoric and polyserial correlations from raw data is a rather time-consuming
process especially when the number of variables and/or number
of observations is large. One will not know in advance whether
the estimated correlation matrix will be positive definite
or not and therefore one does not know whether the ML method

can be used or not. If the matrix of correlations is to
be estimated and analyzed in the same run, the safest way
is to use ULS instead of ML. In any case it is adviseable
to save the estimated correlation matrix on a file so that
it can be used as input for another LISREL run. The estimated correlation matrix can be saved on a file by writing
MA=n on the OU card, where n is a unit number.

TABLE IV.1

ML-Estimates and True Parameters for Parameters

Estimated from Polychoric and Polyserial Correlations

Parameter	True Value	ML-Estimate
λ_{11}	0.9	0.80
λ_{21}	0.8	0.85
λ_{32}	0.7	0.68
λ_{42}	0.6	0.55
λ_{52}	0.5	0.48
λ_{61}	0.3	0.23
ϕ_{21}	0.6	0.56
θ_{11}	0.19	0.37
θ_{22}	0.36	0.28
θ_{33}	0.51	0.53
θ_{44}	0.64	0.70
0_{55}	0.75	0.77
θ_{66}	0.91	0.95

IV.4 Example 12: Attitudes of Morality and Equality

*Approximately 2000 Swedish school children in grade 9 were
asked questions about their attitudes regarding social
issues in family, school and society. Among the questions
asked were the following eight items (in free translation
from Swedish)(Hasselrot and Lernberg, 1980).*

For me questions about ...

1. *human rights*

2. *equal conditions for all people*

3. *racial problems*

4. *equal value of all people*

5. *euthanasia*

6. *crime and punishment*

7. *conscientious objectors*

8. *guilt and bad conscience*

are   unimportant   not important   important   very important

*We are interested in investigating to what extent it is
reasonable to assume that the first four items measure one
latent variable "attitudes towards equality between people"
and the last four items measure another latent variable
"attitudes towards morality". If such a measurement model
is reasonable, we would like to know how highly correlated
the latent variables are and which items are most reliable.*

Table 2 gives the relative frequencies, in percent, of all
responses for each item, as computed from all the data.

TABLE IV.2

Response Frequencies on Eight Items Concerning
Morality and Equality of People

Item	Unimportant	Not important	Important	Very Important
1	1	8	34	58
2	3	13	42	42
3	5	17	38	40
4	3	12	37	48
5	4	13	41	42
6	2	12	53	33
7	13	30	36	21
8	5	19	49	27

It is seen that the distributions are skewed in the sense
that most of the responses are in the two "important" categories.

A subsample of 200 observations were used for the present
analysis. The responses to the eight items were scored
1, 2, 3 and 4, where 4 = very important. The data matrix
consists of 200 rows and 8 columns. Only five out of all
1600 responses were missing. These were scored zero. The

data was analyzed in one single run by first computing

the matrix of polychoric correlations and then analyzing

this using ULS according to a LISREL submodel of type 1,

see Table I.2. The input for this run was

```
ATTITUDES OF MORALITY AND EQUALITY
DA NI=8 NO=200
RA UN=8 MV=4 XM=0.
SE
1 2 4 5 3 6 7 8
MO NX=8 NK=2 PH=ST
FR LX 1 1 LX 2 1 LX 3 1 LX 4 1
FR LX 5 2 LX 6 2 LX 7 2 LX 8 2
OU RS UL TO
```

This illustrates the use of the parameter TO to obtain

80 column format on the printout.

The matrix of estimated polychoric correlations came out

as follows

```
ATTTITUDES OF MORALITY AND EQUALITY
        CORRELATION MATRIX TO BE ANALYZED
```

	VAR 1	VAR 2	VAR 4	VAR 5	VAR 3	VAR 6
VAR 1	1.000					
VAR 2	0.419	1.000				
VAR 4	0.373	0.635	1.000			
VAR 5	0.443	0.706	0.692	1.000		
VAR 3	0.221	0.203	0.284	0.317	1.000	
VAR 6	0.215	0.236	0.423	0.218	0.282	1.000
VAR 7	0.189	0.292	0.340	0.224	0.312	0.312
VAR 8	0.094	0.315	0.322	0.341	0.239	0.207

```
        CORRELATION MATRIX TO BE ANALYZED
```

	VAR 7	VAR 8
VAR 7	1.000	
VAR 8	0.201	1.000

```
NOTE : THIS MATRIX IS A MATRIX OF POLYCHORIC AND/OR POLYSERIAL CORRELATIONS
```

The ULS solution is given on the next page.

These results show that items 2, 3, and 4 have reason-
ably large reliabilities for measuring "attitudes towards
equality" whereas all the four items 5, 6, 7 and 8 have
very small reliabilities for measuring "attitudes towards
morality". Nevertheless the model seems to have a fairly
good fit as judged by the GFI and the RMR. The fit can
be examined more closely by looking at the RESIDUALS given
on page 19. Most of the residuals are small. Only one residual is larger than 0.09. This is considered a sufficiently good
fit for most purposes. One should probably not rely on
the normalized residuals in this case since these are
based on a formula for the asymptotic variances of the
elements of $\underset{\sim}{S}$ which is probably not valid in this case.

ATTTITUDES OF MORALITY AND EQUALITY

LISREL ESTIMATES (UNWEIGHTED LEAST SQUARES)

LAMBDA X

	KSI 1	KSI 2
VAR 1	0.501	0.0
VAR 2	0.786	0.0
VAR 4	0.844	0.0
VAR 5	0.838	0.0
VAR 3	0.0	0.511
VAR 6	0.0	0.526
VAR 7	0.0	0.519
VAR 8	0.0	0.485

PHI

	KSI 1	KSI 2
KSI 1	1.000	
KSI 2	0.699	1.000

THETA DELTA

VAR 1	VAR 2	VAR 4	VAR 5	VAR 3	VAR 6
0.749	0.382	0.288	0.298	0.739	0.723

THETA DELTA

VAR 7	VAR 8
0.731	0.765

SQUARED MULTIPLE CORRELATIONS FOR X - VARIABLES

VAR 1	VAR 2	VAR 4	VAR 5	VAR 3	VAR 6
0.251	0.618	0.712	0.702	0.261	0.277

SQUARED MULTIPLE CORRELATIONS FOR X - VARIABLES

VAR 7	VAR 8
0.269	0.235

TOTAL COEFFICIENT OF DETERMINATION FOR X - VARIABLES IS   0.912

MEASURES OF GOODNESS OF FIT FOR THE WHOLE MODEL :

GOODNESS OF FIT INDEX IS 0.991

ADJUSTED GOODNESS OF FIT INDEX IS 0.983

ROOT MEAN SQUARE RESIDUAL IS   0.044

ATTTITUDES OF MORALITY AND EQUALITY

FITTED MOMENTS AND RESIDUALS

FITTED MOMENTS

	VAR 1	VAR 2	VAR 4	VAR 5	VAR 3	VAR 6
VAR 1	1.000					
VAR 2	0.394	1.000				
VAR 4	0.423	0.664	1.000			
VAR 5	0.420	0.659	0.707	1.000		
VAR 3	0.179	0.281	0.301	0.299	1.000	
VAR 6	0.184	0.289	0.310	0.308	0.269	1.000
VAR 7	0.182	0.285	0.306	0.304	0.265	0.273
VAR 8	0.170	0.266	0.286	0.284	0.247	0.255

FITTED MOMENTS

	VAR 7	VAR 8
VAR 7	1.000	
VAR 8	0.251	1.000

FITTED RESIDUALS

	VAR 1	VAR 2	VAR 4	VAR 5	VAR 3	VAR 6
VAR 1	-0.000					
VAR 2	0.024	-0.000				
VAR 4	-0.050	-0.028	-0.000			
VAR 5	0.023	0.048	-0.015	0.000		
VAR 3	0.042	-0.078	-0.017	0.018	-0.000	
VAR 6	0.031	-0.053	0.113	-0.090	0.013	-0.000
VAR 7	0.008	0.007	0.034	-0.080	0.047	0.039
VAR 8	-0.075	0.049	0.036	0.058	-0.008	-0.048

FITTED RESIDUALS

	VAR 7	VAR 8
VAR 7	-0.000	
VAR 8	-0.050	-0.000

NORMALIZED RESIDUALS

	VAR 1	VAR 2	VAR 4	VAR 5	VAR 3	VAR 6
VAR 1	-0.000					
VAR 2	0.322	-0.000				
VAR 4	-0.648	-0.332	-0.000			
VAR 5	0.300	0.562	-0.177	-0.000		
VAR 3	0.579	-1.058	-0.226	0.240	-0.000	
VAR 6	0.430	-0.715	1.522	-1.209	0.182	-0.000
VAR 7	0.106	0.089	0.457	-1.077	0.645	0.535
VAR 8	-1.048	0.663	0.491	0.783	-0.110	-0.654

NORMALIZED RESIDUALS

	VAR 7	VAR 8
VAR 7	-0.000	
VAR 8	-0.688	-0.000

CHAPTER V

MULTI-SAMPLE ANALYSIS

V.1 Analysis Based on Covariance Matrices

The LISREL model (I.1) - (I.3)   can be used to analyze
data from several groups simultaneously according to LISREL
models for each group with some or all parameters constrained
to be equal over groups. Examples of such simultaneous analysis have been given by Jöreskog (1971), McGaw & Jöreskog
(1971), Sörbom (1974, 1975, 1978, 1981), Jöreskog & Sörbom
(1981a-b) and Sörbom & Jöreskog (1981).

Consider a set of G populations. These may be different nations, states or regions, culturally or socioeconomi-
cally different groups, groups of individuals selected on the
basis of some known or unknown selection variables, groups
receiving different treatments, etc. In fact, they may be
any set of mutually exclusive groups of individuals which are
clearly defined. It is assumed that a number of variables
have been measured on a number of individuals from each population. This approach is particularly useful in comparing
a number of treatment and control groups regardless of whether
individuals have been assigned to the groups randomly or not.

It is assumed that a LISREL model of the form (I.1), (I.2)
and (I.3) holds in each group. The model for group g is de-
fined by the parameter matrices $\underset{\sim}{\Lambda}_y^{(g)}$, $\underset{\sim}{\Lambda}_x^{(g)}$, $\underset{\sim}{B}^{(g)}$, $\underset{\sim}{\Gamma}^{(g)}$,

$\phi^{(g)}$, $\psi^{(g)}$, $\Theta^{(g)}$ where the superscript (g) refers to the g:th group, g = 1, 2, ..., G. Each of these matrices may contain fixed, free and constrained parameters as before. If there are no constraints between groups, each group can be analyzed separately. However, if there are constraints between groups, the data from all groups must be analyzed simultaneously to get efficient estimates of the parameters.

Multi-sample LISREL analysis can be used to test equality of covariance or correlation matrices of the observed variables. To test the equality of covariance matrices of x, one specifies $\Lambda_x^{(g)} = I$ and $\Theta_\delta^{(g)} = 0$ for all groups and tests the hypothesis that $\phi^{(1)} = \phi^{(2)} = \ldots = \phi^{(G)}$. To test the equality of correlation matrices of x, one specifies that $\Theta_\delta^{(g)} = 0$ for all groups, that $\Lambda_x^{(g)} = D_\sigma^{(g)}$, where $D_\sigma^{(g)}$ is a diagonal matrix of standard deviations of x for the g:th group, and tests that $\phi^{(1)} = \phi^{(2)} = \ldots = \phi^{(G)}$, all ϕ - matrices having ones in the diagonal.

One can also test various forms of less strong equalities. For example, with measurement models of the forms (2) and (3), if the measurement properties of the observed variables are the same in all groups one would postulate that

$$\Lambda_y^{(1)} = \Lambda_y^{(2)} = \ldots = \Lambda_y^{(G)} \quad,$$

$$\Lambda_x^{(1)} = \Lambda_x^{(2)} = \ldots = \Lambda_x^{(G)}$$

and perhaps also that

$$\Theta_{\sim\epsilon}^{(1)} = \Theta_{\sim\epsilon}^{(2)} = \ldots = \Theta_{\sim\epsilon}^{(G)} \quad ,$$

$$\Theta_{\sim\delta}^{(1)} = \Theta_{\sim\delta}^{(2)} = \ldots = \Theta_{\sim\delta}^{(G)} \quad .$$

The possible differences between groups would then be represented by differences in the distributions of the latent variables, i.e., by $\phi_{\sim}^{(g)}$ and $\psi_{\sim}^{(g)}$. By postulating

$$B_{\sim}^{(1)} = B_{\sim}^{(2)} = \ldots = B_{\sim}^{(G)} \quad ,$$

$$\Gamma_{\sim}^{(1)} = \Gamma_{\sim}^{(2)} = \ldots = \Gamma_{\sim}^{(G)}$$

one can test the hypotheses that also the structural relations are invariant over groups.

In general, any degree of invariance can be tested, from the one extreme where all parameters are assumed to be invariant over groups to the other extreme when there are no constraints between groups.

To estimate all the models simultaneously, LISREL minimizes the fitting function

$$F = \sum_{g=1}^{G} (N_g/N) F_g (\Sigma_{\sim g}, S_{\sim g}) \quad , \tag{V.1}$$

where

$$F_g = \log|\Sigma_{\sim g}| + \text{tr}(S_{\sim g}\Sigma_{\sim g}^{-1}) - \log|S_{\sim g}| - (p + q) \text{ for ML} \tag{V.2}$$

and

$$F_g = \frac{1}{2} \text{tr} (S_{\sim g} - \Sigma_{\sim g})^2 \qquad \text{for ULS.} \qquad (V.3)$$

Here N_g is the sample size in group g and $N = N_1 + N_2 + + \ldots + N_G$ and $S_{\sim g}$ and $\Sigma_{\sim g}$ are the sample and population moment matrices for group g. When $G = 1$, (V.1) reduces to the fitting function defined in I.10.

Initial estimates are computed as before, for each group separately, ignoring all equality constraints between groups.

The χ^2 goodness-of-fit measure is defined as before. This measures the fit of all LISREL models in all groups, including all constraints, to the data from all groups. The degrees of freedom are

$$d = (1/2) G (p + q) (p + q + 1) - t,$$

where t is the total number of independent parameters estimated in all groups. Thus, in a multi-sample analysis, only one χ^2 goodness-of-fit measure is given, whereas the GFI and RMR measures are given for each group.

V.2 Input Data for Multi-sample Analysis

The input data for each group are stacked after each
other. The data for each group are set up as described
in Chapter II, with the following additional rules

1. NGroups must be defined on the DA card for the first
   group.

2. For each group g , g = 2, 3, ..., G , every input
   parameter which has the same value as in the previous
   group may be omitted, except for UNit.

3. Pattern matrices and non-zero fixed values as well
   as starting values are defined as before.
   A matrix element such as BE(4,3) , with
   one or two indices, refers to the element in the
   current group. To refer to an element in another group
   one must use three indices where the first one refers
   to the group number. For example, BE(2,4,3) refers
   to β_{43} in $\underset{\sim}{B}^{(2)}$.

4. To define equality constraints between groups, one
   specifies the constrained elements as free for the
   first group, and equality constraints in each of the
   other groups. For example, if β_{43} is to be invariant
   over groups, one specifies
   in group 1: FR BE(4,3)
   in group 2: EQ BE(1,4,3) BE(4,3)
   in group 3: EQ BE(1,4,3) BE(4,3)   etc.

5. If a matrix is specified as ID or ZE in group 1, it must not be specified as DI, FU or SY in subsequent groups.

6. In addition to the matrix specifications described in II.6, the following specifications are possible on the MO card for groups 2, 3, ..., NG .

   SP means that the matrix has the <u>same pattern</u> of fixed and free elements as the corresponding matrix in the previous group

   SS means that the matrix will be given the <u>same starting values</u> as the corresponding matrix in the previous group

   PS means same pattern and starting values as the corresponding matrix in the previous group

   IN means that the matrix is invariant over groups, i.e., each free element is specified to be equal over groups, and the same starting values as given to group 1 are set in groups 2, 3, ..., NG by the program.

We shall illustrate LISREL input by means of a detailed example.

V.3 Example 13: Testing Equality of Factor Structures

*Sörbom (1976) gave the covariance matrices in Table 1.
These are based on scores on the ETS Sequential Test of
Educational Progress (STEP) for two groups of boys who
took the test in both grade 5 and grade 7. The two groups
were defined according to whether or not they were in the
academic curriculum in grade twelve.*

A. *Test the hypothesis* H_Σ: $\Sigma^{(1)} = \Sigma^{(2)}$

B. *Assuming that a measurement (factor analysis) model of
the form $x = \Lambda_x \xi + \delta$ holds in both groups, test the
hypothesis that there are two correlated common factors
in both groups with a factor pattern of the form*

$$\Lambda_x = \begin{bmatrix} x & 0 \\ x & 0 \\ 0 & x \\ 0 & x \end{bmatrix}$$

C. *Assuming B, test the hypothesis* H_Λ: $\Lambda_x^{(1)} = \Lambda_x^{(2)}$

D. *Assuming C, test the hypothesis* $H_{\Lambda\Theta}$: $\Theta_\delta^{(1)} = \Theta_\delta^{(2)}$

E. *Assuming D, test the hypothesis* $H_{\Lambda\Phi\Theta}$: $\Phi^{(1)} = \Phi^{(2)}$

TABLE V.1

Covariance Matrices for STEP Reading and Writing for Academic and Non-academic Boys (Sörbom, 1976)

Boys Academic (N = 373)

STEP Reading, Grade 5	281.349			
STEP Writing, Grade 5	184.219	182.821		
STEP Reading, Grade 7	216.739	171.699	283.289	
STEP Writing, Grade 7	198.376	153.201	208.837	246.069

Boys Non-academic (N = 249)

STEP Reading, Grade 5	174.485			
STEP Writing, Grade 5	134.468	161.869		
STEP Reading, Grade 7	129.840	118.836	228.449	
STEP Writing, Grade 7	102.194	97.797	136.058	180.460

All five problems A-E can be solved by using a LISREL model with only x-variables, i.e.,

$$\underset{\sim}{x} = \underset{\sim x}{\Lambda}\underset{\sim}{\xi} + \underset{\sim}{\delta} \ .$$

As already explained in V.1, in problem A we set $\underset{\sim x}{\Lambda}^{(1)} = \underset{\sim x}{\Lambda}^{(2)} = \underset{\sim}{I}$ and $\underset{\sim \delta}{\Theta}^{(1)} = \underset{\sim \delta}{\Theta}^{(2)} = \underset{\sim}{0}$. This means that $\underset{\sim}{x} = \underset{\sim}{\xi}$ and that $\underset{\sim}{\Sigma}^{(g)} = \underset{\sim}{\Phi}^{(g)}$ for $g = 1,2$. The hypothesis $\underset{\sim}{\Sigma}^{(1)} = \underset{\sim}{\Sigma}^{(2)}$ is therefore the same as $\underset{\sim}{\Phi}^{(1)} = \underset{\sim}{\Phi}^{(2)}$. The input is extremely simple as shown on the next page.

```
TESTING EQUALITY OF FACTOR STRUCTURES HYPOTHESIS A (GROUP A)
DA NG=2 NI=4 NO=373
LA UN=8
CM UN=8
MO NX=4 NK=4 LX=ID TD=ZE
OU
TESTING EQUALITY OF FACTOR STRUCTURES HYPOTHESIS A (GROUP N-A)
DA NO=249
LA UN=8
CM UN=8 RE
MO PH=IN
OU
```

In group 1, $\underset{\sim}{\Phi}$ is free by default. In group 2, $\underset{\sim}{\Phi}$ is
declared invariant (PH = IN). Note that on the MO card
for the second group, the parameters NX, NK, LX and TD
need not be given since they are the same as for group 1.
The labels and the covariance matrices are read from a
file on unit 8 which is rewound after it is read so that
it can be read again in problem B.

In problem B we assume a common factor analysis model
with two common factors and leave $\underset{\sim}{\Phi}(2 \times 2)$ to be a free
covariance matrix in both groups. To fix the scale for
the two factors ξ_1 and ξ_2 we fix the elements λ_{11}
and λ_{32} of $\underset{\sim}{\Lambda}_x$ equal to one for both groups. The other
elements λ_{21} and λ_{42} and the diagonal elements of $\underset{\sim}{\Theta}_\delta$
are free in both groups. The hypothesis in problem B
does not impose any equality constraints on parameters;
it only states that the number of factors is the same for
both groups. The input for the problem B is

```
TESTING EQUALITY OF FACTOR STRUCTURES HYPOTHESIS B (GROUP A)
DA NI=4 NO=373 NG=2
LA UN=8
CM UN=8
MO NX=4 NK=2
FR LX 2 1 LX 4 2
ST 1 LX 1 1 LX 3 2
OU
TESTING EQUALITY OF FACTOR STRUCTURES HYPOTHESIS B (GROUP N-A)
DA NO=249
LA UN=8
CM UN=8 RE
MO LX=PS
OU
```

The matrices $\Phi^{(1)}$ and $\Phi^{(2)}$ are both free by default. The matrices $\underset{\sim}{\Theta}_\delta^{(1)}$ and $\underset{\sim}{\Theta}_\delta^{(2)}$ are diagonal and free, also by default. The elements λ_{21} and λ_{42} are declared free in group one. Starting values for these are estimated by the program using the method described in I.4. In group 2 $\underset{\sim}{\Lambda}_x$ is specified to have the same pattern and the same starting values as for group 1 (LX = PS).

In problems C, D and E the input for group 1 are all the same as in problem B. In problem C, the input for group 2 differs from that of problem B only in that $\underset{\sim}{\Lambda}_x$ is declared invariant, i.e., LX = IN instead of only LX = PS. In problem D, TD = IN in addition and in problem E, PH = IN in addition. The input for problems C, D and E are given on the next page.

TESTING EQUALITY OF FACTOR STRUCTURES HYPOTHESIS C (GROUP A)


```
TESTING EQUALITY OF FACTOR STRUCTURES HYPOTHESIS C (GROUP A)
DA NI=4 NO=373 NG=2
LA UN=8
CM UN=8
MO NX=4 NK=2
FR LX 2 1 LX 4 2
ST 1 LX 1 1 LX 3 2
OU
TESTING EQUALITY OF FACTOR STRUCTURES HYPOTHESIS C (GROUP N-A)
DA NO=249
LA UN=8
CM UN=8 RE
MO LX=IN
OU
TESTING EQUALITY OF FACTOR STRUCTURES HYPOTHESIS D (GROUP A)
DA NI=4 NO=373 NG=2
LA UN=8
CM UN=8
MO NX=4 NK=2
FR LX 2 1 LX 4 2
ST 1 LX 1 1 LX 3 2
OU
TESTING EQUALITY OF FACTOR STRUCTURES HYPOTHESIS D (GROUP N-A)
DA NO=249
LA UN=8
CM UN=8 RE
MO LX=IN TD=IN
OU
TESTING EQUALITY OF FACTOR STRUCTURES HYPOTHESIS E (GROUP A)
DA NI=4 NO=373 NG=2
LA UN=8
CM UN=8
MO NX=4 NK=2
FR LX 2 1 LX 4 2
ST 1 LX 1 1 LX 3 2
OU
TESTING EQUALITY OF FACTOR STRUCTURES HYPOTHESIS E (GROUP N-A)
DA NO=249
LA UN=8
CM UN=8 RE
MO LX=IN PH=IN TD=IN
OU
```

In the printout from a multi-sample analysis all requested parts of the printout are given for each group. For the maximum likelihood solution the GOODNESS-OF-FIT INDEX and the ROOT MEAN SQUARE RESIDUAL are given for each group but the χ^2

measure is only given for the last group. This χ^2 is a measure of the overall fit of all models in all groups.

The results of the tests are given in Table 2. The most reasonable hypothesis to retain is H_Λ. The two groups have an invariant factor pattern but there is some evidence that they differ in error variances and in factor covariance matrices.

TABLE V.2

Summary of Results for Example 8

Problem	Hypothesis	χ^2	Degrees of Freedom	P-value	Decision
A	H_Σ	38.08	10	0.000	Rejected
B	$H_{n=2}$	1.53	2	0.466	Accepted
C	H_Λ	8.79	4	0.067	Accepted
D	$H_{\Lambda\Theta}$	21.55	8	0.006	Rejected
E	$H_{\Lambda\Phi\Theta}$	38.22	11	0.000	Rejected

Computer Exercise 9: Testing Psychometric Assumptions Within and Between Groups

The tables on the next page give the observed covariance matrices for two random samples ($N_1 = 865$, $N_2 = 900$, respectively) of candidates who took the Scholastic Aptitude Test in January 1971. The four measures are, in order: $x_1 =$ a 40-item verbal aptitude section, $x_2 =$ a separately timed 50-item verbal aptitude section, $x_3 =$ a 35-item math aptitude section, and $x_4 =$ a separately timed 25-item math aptitude section (Werts et al, 1976).

Covariance Matrix for Group 1

Item	x_1	x_2	x_3	x_4
x_1 = a 40-item verbal aptitude section	63.382			
x_2 = a separately time 50-item verbal aptitude section	70.984	110.237		
x_3 = a 35-item math aptitude section	41.710	52.747	60.584	
x_4 = a separately timed 25-item math aptitude section	30.218	37.489	36.392	32.295

Covariance Matrix for Group 2

Item	x_1	x_2	x_3	x_4
x_1 = a 40-item verbal aptitude section	67.898			
x_2 = a separately timed 50-item verbal aptitude section	72.301	107.330		
x_3 = a 35-item math aptitude section	40.549	55.347	63.203	
x_4 = a separately timed 25-item math aptitude section	28.976	38.896	39.261	35.403

A.   Test the hypothesis of equal correlation matrices between groups.

B.   For each group separately and for both groups simultaneously estimate the disattenuated correlation between verbal and mathematical aptitude and determine a 99 % confidence interval for this correlation.

C.   Using the data for group 1, test the hypothesis that the partial correlation $\rho_{23.14} = 0.7$.

Each problem should be done separately disregarding the results in the other problems. All test should be made at the 1 % level.

V.4   The LISREL-Model with Structured Means

.   In chapter I the LISREL model was defined by (I.1), (I.2) and (I.3) in which all random variables were assumed to have zero means. This assumption will now be relaxed and it will be shown how the LISREL computer program can also be used to estimate the same three equations even if they include constant intercept terms. This is possible if we introduce a fixed variable whose observations are all equal to one and analyze the sample moment matrix instead of the sample co-variance matrix.

The LISREL model is now defined by the following three equations corresponding to (I.1), (I.2) and (I.3), respectively:

$$\underset{\sim}{\eta} = \underset{\sim}{\alpha} + B\underset{\sim}{\eta} + \Gamma\underset{\sim}{\xi} + \underset{\sim}{\zeta} \quad , \tag{V.4}$$

$$\underset{\sim}{y} = \underset{\sim}{\nu}_y + \Lambda_y\underset{\sim}{\eta} + \underset{\sim}{\varepsilon} \quad , \tag{V.5}$$

$$\underset{\sim}{x} = \underset{\sim}{\nu}_x + \Lambda_x\underset{\sim}{\xi} + \underset{\sim}{\delta} \quad , \tag{V.6}$$

where $\underset{\sim}{\alpha}, \underset{\sim}{\nu}_y$ and $\underset{\sim}{\nu}_x$ are vectors of constant intercept terms. As before, we assume that $\underset{\sim}{\zeta}$ is uncorrelated with $\underset{\sim}{\xi}$, $\underset{\sim}{\varepsilon}$ is uncorrelated with $\underset{\sim}{\eta}$ and that $\underset{\sim}{\delta}$ is uncorrelated with $\underset{\sim}{\xi}$. However, it will not be necessary to assume that $\underset{\sim}{\varepsilon}$ is uncorrelated with $\underset{\sim}{\delta}$ as we did in Section I.2. We also assume, as before, that $E(\underset{\sim}{\zeta}) = 0$, $E(\underset{\sim}{\varepsilon}) = 0$ and $E(\underset{\sim}{\delta}) = 0$, but it is not assumed that $E(\underset{\sim}{\xi})$ and $E(\underset{\sim}{\eta})$ are zero (E is the expected value operator). The mean of $\underset{\sim}{\xi}$, $E(\underset{\sim}{\xi})$ will be a parameter denoted by $\underset{\sim}{\kappa}$. The mean of $\underset{\sim}{\eta}$, $E(\underset{\sim}{\eta})$ is obtained by taking the expectation of (4):

$$E(\underset{\sim}{\eta}) = (\underset{\sim}{I} - \underset{\sim}{B})^{-1}(\underset{\sim}{\alpha} + \underset{\sim}{\Gamma}\underset{\sim}{\kappa}) \tag{V.7}$$

By taking the expectations of (5) and (6) we find the mean
vectors of the observed variables to be

$$E(\underset{\sim}{y}) = \underset{\sim}{\nu}_y + \underset{\sim}{\Lambda}_y(\underset{\sim}{I} - \underset{\sim}{B})^{-1}(\underset{\sim}{\alpha} + \underset{\sim}{\Gamma}\underset{\sim}{\kappa}) , \tag{V.8}$$

$$E(\underset{\sim}{x}) = \underset{\sim}{\nu}_x + \underset{\sim}{\Lambda}_x\underset{\sim}{\kappa} . \tag{V.9}$$

In general, in a single population, all the mean parameters
$\underset{\sim}{\nu}_y$, $\underset{\sim}{\nu}_x$, $\underset{\sim}{\alpha}$ and $\underset{\sim}{\kappa}$ will not be identified without further
conditions imposed. However, in simultaneous analysis of
data from several groups, simple conditions (see e.g. Jöreskog & Sörbom , 1980) can be imposed to make all the mean
parameters identified. We shall not be concerned with identification here but merely confine ourselves to show how the
model (4) - (6) can be written in the form of (I.1), (I.2)
and (I.3).

The LISREL specification of (4)-·(6) is as follows. We treat y
and $\underset{\sim}{x}$ as y-variables and $\underset{\sim}{\eta}$ and $\underset{\sim}{\xi}$ as η-variables in the
LISREL sense. In addition, we use a single fixed x-variable
equal to 1. This variable is also used as the last η-variable
and as a single ξ-variable. We can then write the model (4)
- (6) in the form of (I.1) - (I.3) as

$$\begin{pmatrix} \underset{\sim}{\eta} \\ \underset{\sim}{\xi} \\ 1 \end{pmatrix} = \begin{pmatrix} \underset{\sim}{B} & \underset{\sim}{\Gamma} & \underset{\sim}{0} \\ \underset{\sim}{0} & \underset{\sim}{0} & \underset{\sim}{0} \\ \underset{\sim}{0}' & \underset{\sim}{0}' & 0 \end{pmatrix} \begin{pmatrix} \underset{\sim}{\eta} \\ \underset{\sim}{\xi} \\ 1 \end{pmatrix} + \begin{pmatrix} \underset{\sim}{\alpha} \\ \underset{\sim}{\kappa} \\ 1 \end{pmatrix} 1 + \begin{pmatrix} \underset{\sim}{\zeta} \\ \underset{\sim}{\xi} - \underset{\sim}{\kappa} \\ 0 \end{pmatrix} , \tag{V.10}$$

$$
\begin{pmatrix} y \\ \sim \\ x \\ \sim \end{pmatrix} = \begin{bmatrix} \Lambda_y & 0 & \nu_y \\ \sim & \sim & \sim \\ 0 & \Lambda_x & \nu_x \\ & \sim & \sim \end{bmatrix} \begin{pmatrix} \eta \\ \sim \\ \xi \\ \sim \\ 1 \end{pmatrix} + \begin{pmatrix} \varepsilon \\ \sim \\ \delta \\ \sim \end{pmatrix} \tag{V.11}
$$

$$
1 = 1 \ (\text{FIXEDX}) \tag{V.12}
$$

Note that the mean parameter vectors α and κ appear in the Γ-matrix in LISREL and ν_y and ν_x appear in the last column of Λ_y in LISREL.

In order to perform this kind of analysis one must analyze the matrix of moments about zero rather than the covariance matrix. One must also include the variable 1 among the input variables. This is a fixed x-variable; all the other variables in the model should be treated as y-variables.

There are three ways one can provide the information necessary for the program to compute the moment matrix:

(i)   read in the raw data including the variable 1, or

(ii)   read in the moment matrix including one variable having a one in the diagonal and the means of all the other variables as off diagonal elements, or

(iii)   read in a covariance matrix (or a correlation matrix plus standard deviations) including one row of only zeroes plus a vector of means including the mean 1 of the variable 1.

Analysis of the moment matrix is requested by putting MA = MM on the DA card.

The analysis of mean structures will now be illustrated by means of a detailed example. The identification of the mean parameters will also be discussed in terms of this example.

V.5 Example 14: Head Start Summer Program

Sörbom (1981) reanalyzed some data from the Head Start summer program previously reanalyzed by Magidson (1977). Sörbom used data on 303 white children consisting of a Head Start sample (N = 148) and a matched Control sample (N = 155). The correlations, standard deviations and means are given in Table 3. The children were matched on sex and kindergarten attendance but no attempt had been made to match on social status variables. The variables used in Sörbom's reanalysis were

x_1 = *Mother's education*

x_2 = *Father's education*

x_3 = *Father's occupation*

x_4 = *Family income*

y_1 = *Score on the Metropolitan Readiness Test*

y_2 = *Score on the Illinois Test of Psycholinguistic Abilities*

A. *Test whether x_1, x_2, x_3 and x_4 can be regarded as indicators of a single construct, ξ = "Socio-economic status", for both groups. Is the measurement model the same for both groups? Is there a difference in the mean of ξ between groups?*

TABLE V.3

Correlations, Standard Deviations and Means for the Head Start Data.

Head Start Group

	Correlations						Standard deviations	Means
x_1	1.000						1.332	3.520
x_2	.441	1.000					1.281	3.081
x_3	.220	.203	1.000				1.075	2.088
x_4	.304	.182	.377	1.000			2.648	5.358
y_1	.274	.265	.208	.084	1.000		3.764	19.672
y_2	.270	.122	.251	.198	.664	1.000	2.677	9.562

Control Group

	Correlations						Standard deviations	Means
x_1	1.000						1.360	3.839
x_2	.484	1.000					1.195	3.290
x_3	.224	.342	1.000				1.193	2.600
x_4	.268	.215	.387	1.000			3.239	6.435
y_1	.230	.215	.196	.115	1.000		3.900	20.415
y_2	.265	.297	.234	.162	.635	1.000	2.719	10.070

B. Assuming that y_1 and y_2 can be used as indicators of another construct η = "cognitive ability", test whether the same measurement model applies to both groups. Test the hypothesis of no difference in the mean of η between groups.

C. Estimate the structural equation

$$\eta = \alpha + \beta \xi + \zeta.$$

Is β the same for the two groups? Test the hypothesis $\alpha = 0$. Interpret the results.

Consider the model in Figure 1 for the four social status indicators x_1, x_2, x_3, and x_4. The model assumes that the x-variables can be accounted for by a single common factor ξ

$$x_i^{(g)} = \nu_i + \lambda_i \xi^{(g)} + \delta_i^{(g)}, \qquad i = 1, 2, 3, 4. \qquad (V.13)$$

The superscript, g, is running over the two groups, $g = 1$ for Head Start children and $g = 2$ for Control children. There is no superscript for ν and λ, since we are using the same observed variables in the two groups. Our main interest is here in the mean κ of ξ. Assuming $E(\delta_i^{(g)}) = 0$ we find

$$E(x_i^{(g)}) = \nu_i + \lambda_i \kappa.$$

If we add a constant, c say, to κ this can be compensated for by subtracting $\lambda_i c$ from ν_i. This means that κ and ν_i cannot be identified simultaneously or phrased in other words: there is no definite origin for the construct ξ. All we can do is to estimate differences among groups, i.e., we can specify the mean of ξ to be zero in the Control group, and then κ is the mean difference in social status between the two groups.

The LISREL specification for problem A is

$$\begin{pmatrix} x_1 \\ x_2 \\ x_3 \\ x_4 \end{pmatrix} = \begin{pmatrix} 1 & \nu_1 \\ \lambda_2 & \nu_2 \\ \lambda_3 & \nu_3 \\ \lambda_4 & \nu_4 \end{pmatrix} \begin{pmatrix} \xi \\ 1 \end{pmatrix} + \begin{pmatrix} \delta_1 \\ \delta_2 \\ \delta_3 \\ \delta_4 \end{pmatrix}, \qquad (V.14)$$

$$\begin{pmatrix} \xi \\ 1 \end{pmatrix} = \begin{pmatrix} \kappa \\ 1 \end{pmatrix} 1 + \begin{pmatrix} \xi - \kappa \\ 0 \end{pmatrix} \qquad\qquad (V.15)$$

i.e., we specify $\underset{\sim}{B} = \underset{\sim}{0}$ in both groups, $\underset{\sim}{\Lambda}_y$ to be invariant, $\underset{\sim}{\Gamma}' = (\kappa, 1)$, with $\kappa = 0$ for controls, $\underset{\sim}{\Psi} = \mathrm{diag}\,(\sigma_\xi^2, 0)$, with σ_ξ^2 free for both groups and $\underset{\sim}{\Theta}_\varepsilon$ a symmetric matrix with θ_{ii}, $i = 1, 2, 3, 4$ free for both groups.

The input for problem A is given on the next page.

```
HEAD START SUMMER PROGRAM : EXPERIMENTALS : HYPOTHESIS A
DA NI=7 NOBS=149 MA=MM NG=2
CM UN=8
ME UN=8
LA UN=8
SE
1 2 3 4 7 /
MO NY=4 NE=2 NX=1 TE=SY FI LY=FR PS=DI
FI LY 1 PS 2 GA 2
ST 1 GA 2 PS 1
MA LY
*
1 3.52 .872 3.081 .92 2.088 2 5.358
OU MI
HEAD START SUMMER PROGRAM : CONTROLS : HYPOTHESIS A
DA NOBS=156
CM UN=8
ME UN=8
LA UN=8 RE
SE
1 2 3 4 7 /
MO LY=IN PS=PS TE=PS GA=FI
ST 1 GA 2
OU
```

The automatic starting values for $\underset{\sim}{\Lambda}_y$ do not work in this case because of the intercept terms ν_i. Starting values must be given for the whole $\underset{\sim}{\Lambda}_y$-matrix. However, for given $\underset{\sim}{\Lambda}_y$ the program will generate starting values for all the remaining parameters, i.e., steps 3 and 4 of the starting value procedure of section I.11 still works. For the second group,

FIGURE V.1

Head Start Example:

The Initial Measurement Model for Social Status.

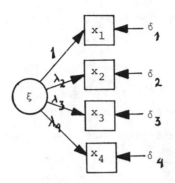

FIGURE V.2

Head Start Example:

The Model for Cognitive Ability.

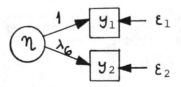

i.e., the control group, no starting values need to be given since $\underset{\sim}{\Lambda}_y$ is specified to be invariant and the other parameter matrices have the same pattern and the same starting values as for the first group, i.e., the experimentals.

For problem A we get an overall χ^2-measure of goodness-of-fit of the model equal to 35.9 with 10 degrees of freedom, indicating that the fit of the model is not very good. An examination of the modification indices reveals that there might be a correlation between the errors δ_1 and δ_2, i.e., when the correlation among the observed variables caused by the construct ξ has been accounted for, there seems to be a correlation left between x_1 and x_2. This correlation can be interpreted as an indication that parents' education levels correlate more than can be explained by social status. By adding the covariance θ_{21} we get a model with an acceptable fit, χ^2 with 8 degrees of freedom equals 6.5. The difference in degrees of freedom from the previous model is 2, since we have added two parameters, namely the covariances $\theta_{21}^{(1)}$ and $\theta_{21}^{(2)}$ in the two groups. The estimates and their estimated standard errors are given in Table 4. It is seen that the groups differ significantly in social status, the difference is 0.340 with a standard error equal to 0.096. λ_1 has been fixed to 1 in order to specify the scale of ξ.

As criterion Magidson (1977) used two cognitive ability tests, the Metropolitan Readiness Test (MRT) and the Illinois Test of Psycholinguistic Abilities (ITPA). Magidson made separate analyses for the two tests, but here, as suggested by Bentler & Woodward (1978), we will use the two tests to define the construct cognitive ability. The model is depicted in

Figure 2 and the data for the groups are given as variables y_1 and y_2 for MRT and ITPA, respectively in Table 3. This model is the same as before , except that there are only two y-variables. As a matter of fact, the model has no degrees of freedom, so one can compute the estimates simply by equating the first and second order moments implied by the model to their observed counterparts. The estimates and their estimated standard errors are listed in Table 5. It is seen that also in cognitive ability the Head Start group is inferior to the Control group in the sense that the estimated mean difference is negative (-0.743). However, the difference is not significant, having a standard error equal to 0.439.

The input for problem B is similar to problem A so it is not given here.

For problem C we use the combined model as depicted in Figure 3 where the main focus is on the structural equation

$$\eta^{(g)} = \alpha^{(g)} + \beta^{(g)} \xi^{(g)} + \zeta^{(g)} \ .$$

Here ξ is "social status" and η is "cognitive ability". Just as we could not previously find an absolute origin for ξ there is no way to find an absolute origin for η either. All we can do is to compare groups and look at differences. For example, we could fix α in the Control group to be zero, and then α in the Head Start group could be interpreted as the effect of the Head Start program when social status has been controlled for.

TABLE V.4

Head Start Example:

Estimates for the Measurement Model for Social Status with Standard Error Estimates within Parentheses.

	Head Start Group	Control Group
ν_1	3.849 (0.092)	
ν_2	3.326 (0.081)	
ν_3	2.578 (0.090)	
ν_4	6.464 (0.235)	
λ_2	0.862 (0.162)	
λ_3	1.382 (0.288)	
λ_4	3.309 (0.681)	
θ_{11}	1.484 (0.188)	1.543 (0.198)
θ_{22}	1.465 (0.182)	1.149 (0.148)
θ_{33}	0.711 (0.136)	0.787 (0.162)
θ_{44}	4.263 (0.791)	6.882 (1.117)
θ_{21}	0.532 (0.142)	0.498 (0.133)
κ	-0.340 (0.096)	0.0
σ_ξ^2	0.241 (0.091)	0.328 (0.119)

Note: The ν and λ values are shown centered between the two group columns in the source.

TABLE V.5

Head Start Example:

Estimates for the Model of Cognitive Ability with
Standard Error Estimates within Parentheses.

	Head Start Group	Control Group
ν_1	20.415 (0.311)	
ν_2	10.070 (0.217)	
λ_6	0.684 (0.342)	
θ_{11}	4.350 (4.976)	5.330 (5.026)
θ_{22}	2.570 (2.333)	2.771 (2.354)
$E(\eta)$	-0.743 (0.437)	0.0
σ_η^2	9.729 (5.077)	9.787 (5.111)

FIGURE V.3

Head Start Example:

The Combined Model

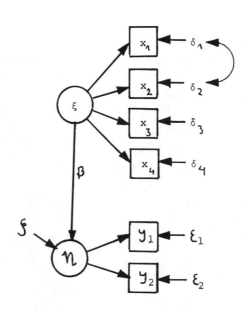

For problem C the LISREL specification is

$$
\begin{pmatrix} y_1 \\ y_2 \\ x_1 \\ x_2 \\ x_3 \\ x_4 \end{pmatrix}
=
\begin{pmatrix} 1 & 0 & \nu_1 \\ \lambda_6 & 0 & \nu_2 \\ 0 & 1 & \nu_3 \\ 0 & \lambda_2 & \nu_4 \\ 0 & \lambda_3 & \nu_5 \\ 0 & \lambda_4 & \nu_6 \end{pmatrix}
\begin{pmatrix} \eta \\ \xi \\ 1 \end{pmatrix}
+
\begin{pmatrix} \varepsilon_1 \\ \varepsilon_2 \\ \delta_1 \\ \delta_2 \\ \delta_3 \\ \delta_4 \end{pmatrix}
$$

$$
\begin{pmatrix} \eta \\ \xi \\ 1 \end{pmatrix}
=
\begin{pmatrix} 0 & \beta & 0 \\ 0 & 0 & 0 \\ 0 & 0 & 0 \end{pmatrix}
\begin{pmatrix} \eta \\ \xi \\ 1 \end{pmatrix}
+
\begin{pmatrix} \alpha \\ \kappa \\ 1 \end{pmatrix} 1
+
\begin{pmatrix} \zeta \\ \xi - \kappa \\ 0 \end{pmatrix} \quad ,
$$

i.e., we specify Λ_y to be invariant, $\Gamma' = (\alpha, \kappa, 1)$ with $\kappa = \alpha = 0$ for controls, $\Psi = \text{diag}(\sigma_\zeta^2, \sigma_\xi^2, 0)$ with σ_ξ^2 and σ_ζ^2 free for both groups and Θ_ε symmetric with θ_{21} and θ_{ii}, $i = 1, 2, \ldots, 6$ free for both groups. The input for problem C is

```
HEAD START SUMMER PROGRAM : EXPERIMENTALS : HYPOTHESIS C
DA NI=7 NOBS=149 MA=MM NG=2
CM UN=8
ME UN=8
LA UN=8
MO NY=6 FI NX=1 NE=3 TE=SY PS=DI BE=FU GA=FI
FR LY 2 1 LY 3 1 LY 4 1 LY 6 2 LY 1 3 LY 2 3 LY 3 3 C
LY 4 3 LY 5 3 LY 6 3 BE 2 1
FR TE 2 1 GA 1 GA 2
FI PS 3
MA LY
*
1 0 3.8 .8 0 3.3 1.2 0 2.5 2.7 0 6.4 0 1 20.4 0 .8 10.1
MA TE
*
1.4 .5 1.4 0 0 .7 0 0 0 4.6 0 0 0 0 6.2 0 0 0 0 0 1.5
ST 1 GA 3
ST 2.14 BE 2 1
OU
HEAD START SUMMER PROGRAM : CONTROLS : HYPOTHESIS C
DA NO=156
CM UN=8
ME UN=8
LA UN=8
MO LY=IN BE=PS PS=PS TE=PS
ST 1 GA 3
OU
```

The χ^2 for the combined model equals 27.53 with 22 degrees of freedom so the fit of the model is acceptable. An examination of the β parameters in the two groups shows that they are probably equal, since $\hat{\beta}^{(1)} = 2.295$ and $\hat{\beta}^{(2)} = 2.026$ with estimated standard errors equal to 0.742 and 0.626, respectively. Thus, the final model is a model with the β's constrained to be equal. The χ^2 for this model is 27.64 with 23 degrees of freedom. The difference in χ^2 for the last two models can be used as a test of the hypothesis that the β's are equal. χ^2 with 1 degree of freedom is 0.11 and thus we can treat the β's as equal. Then it is meaningful to talk about α as a measure of the effect of Head Start. The estimates of the model are given in Table 6. There seems to be no significant effect for the Head Start program when controlling for social status, although the inclusion of social class has changed the negative effect to be positive. The estimate of α is 0.182 with a standard error equal to 0.376.

In the more general case, when there are more than two groups and/or more than one dependent variable, one can test the hypothesis of no effect by re-estimation of the model with the restriction $\alpha^{(i)} = 0$ added, and then compare the χ^2's. In the above case we obtain χ^2 equal to 27.88 with 24 degrees of freedom. Thus the test of no effect results in a χ^2 with 1 degree of freedom equal to 0.24, which in this case is the same as the square of the estimate of α divided by its standard error.

TABLE V.6

Head Start Example:

Estimates for the Combined Model with Standard Error Estimates within Parentheses.

	Head Start Group				Control Group	
ν_3			3.869	(0.093)		
ν_4			3.339	(0.082)		
ν_5			2.573	(0.089)		
ν_6			6.422	(0.226)		
ν_1			20.357	(0.284)		
ν_2			10.085	(0.215)		
λ_2			0.850	(0.143)		
λ_3			1.208	(0.221)		
λ_4			2.762	(0.514)		
λ_6			0.850	(0.140)		
θ_{33}	1.410	(0.184)			1.459	(0.193)
θ_{44}	1.434	(0.180)			1.082	(0.143)
θ_{55}	0.709	(0.124)			0.834	(0.146)
θ_{66}	4.577	(0.729)			7.387	(1.049)
θ_{11}	6.268	(1.515)			7.281	(1.580)
θ_{22}	1.456	(0.975)			1.636	(0.991)
θ_{21}	0.482	(0.139)			0.423	(0.128)
β			2.135	(0.548)		
α	0.183	(0.375)			0.0	
σ^2_ξ	0.312	(0.105)			0.402	(0.130)
σ^2_ζ	6.316	(1.463)			6.151	(1.453)
κ	-0.382	(0.103)			0.0	

Example 15: Testing Equality of Means and Covariances

*The following data from Klugel et al (1977) measuring objective
and subjective social status may be used to test the hypotheses
A and B below.*

*Correlations, means and standard deviations for indicators of objective class
and subjective class.*
Correlations for whites below diagonal and for blacks above diagonal.
N(whites) = 432; N(blacks) = 368

Variables	x_1	x_2	x_3	x_4	x_5	x_6	x_7	Mean (s.d.)
x_1 education		404	268	216	233	211	207	1.274 (1.106)
x_2 occupation	495		220	277	183	270	157	23.467 (16.224)
x_3 income	398	292		268	424	325	282	4.041 (2.097)
x_4 s.c. occupation	218	282	184		550	574	482	1.288 (0.747)
x_5 s.c. income	299	166	383	386		647	517	1.129 (0.814)
x_6 s.c. life-style	272	161	321	396	553		647	1.235 (0.786)
x_7 s.c. influence	269	169	191	382	456	534		1.318 (0.859)
Mean (s.d.)	1.655 (1.203)	36.698 (21.277)	5.040 (2.198)	1.543 (0.640)	1.548 (0.670)	1.542 (0.623)	1.601 (0.647	

Hypotheses

A. *The covariance matrices for whites and blacks are equal.*

B. *The mean vectors for whites and blacks are equal.*

We make one single run to test both hypotheses. (There are
many other ways in which the tests can be made.) The input is
given below. The input reads the data from a file on unit 8.
This file follows the input file below. The output follows
this input file.

INPUT FILE

```
OBJECTIVE AND SUBJECTIVE SOCIAL STATUS.   HYPOTHESIS A.   WHITES
DA NI=7 NO=432 NG=2 MA=AM
LA UN=8
KM UN=8
ME UN=8
SD UN=8
MO NY=7 NX=1
OU TO
OBJECTIVE AND SUBJECTIVE SOCIAL STATUS.   HYPOTHESIS A.   BLACKS
DA NO=368
LA UN=8
KM UN=8
ME UN=8
SD UN=8 RE
MO PS=IN
OU
OBJECTIVE AND SUBJECTIVE SOCIAL STATUS.   HYPOTHESIS B.   WHITES
DA NI=7 NO=432 NG=2 MA=AM
LA UN=8
KM UN=8
ME UN=8
SD UN=8
MO NY=7 NX=1
OU TO
OBJECTIVE AND SUBJECTIVE SOCIAL STATUS.   HYPOTHESIS B.  BLACKS
DA NO=368
LA UN=8
KM UN=8
ME UN=8
SD UN=8
MO GA=IN
OU
```

DATA FILE

```
'EDUCAT:N' 'OCCUPATN' 'INCOME' 'S-C OCCU' 'S-C INCO' 'S-C LIFE' 'S-C INFL'
1 .495 1 .398 .292 1 .218 .282 .184 1 .299 .166 .383 .386 1
.272 .161 .321 .396 .553 1
.269 .169 .191 .382 .456 .534 1
1.655 36.698 5.040 1.543 1.548 1.542 1.601
1.203 21.277 2.198 0.640 0.670 0.623 0.647
'EDUCAT:N' 'OCCUPATN' 'INCOME' 'S-C OCCU' 'S-C INCO' 'S-C LIFE' 'S-C INFL'
1 .404 1 .268 .220 1 .216 .277 .268 1 .233 .183 .424 .550 1
.211 .270 .325 .574 .647 1
.207 .157 .282 .482 .517 .647 1
1.274 23.467 4.041 1.288 1.129 1.235 1.318
1.106 16.244 2.097 0.747 0.814 0.786 0.859
```

L I S R E L   VI

BY

KARL G JORESKOG AND DAG SORBOM

OBJECTIVE AND SUBJECTIVE SOCIAL STATUS. HYPOTHESIS A.   WHITES

THE FOLLOWING LISREL CONTROL LINES HAVE BEEN READ :

```
DA NI=7 NO=432 NG=2 MA=AM
LA UN=8
'EDUCAT:N' 'OCCUPATN' 'INCOME' 'S-C OCCU' 'S-C INCO' 'S-C LIFE' 'S-C INFL'
KM UN=8
1 .495 1 .398 .292 1 .218 .282 .184 1 .299 .166 .383 .386 1
.272 .161 .321 .396 .553 1
.269 .169 .191 .382 .456 .534 1
ME UN=8
1.655 36.698 5.040 1.543 1.548 1.542 1.601
SD UN=8
1.203 21.277 2.198 0.640 0.670 0.623 0.647
MO NY=7 NX=1
OU TO
```

NUMBER OF INPUT VARIABLES 7

NUMBER OF Y - VARIABLES   7

NUMBER OF X - VARIABLES   1

NUMBER OF ETA - VARIABLES 7

NUMBER OF KSI - VARIABLES 1

NUMBER OF OBSERVATIONS   432

NUMBER OF GROUPS   2

OUTPUT REQUESTED

TECHNICAL OUTPUT	NO
STANDARD ERRORS	NO
T - VALUES	NO
CORRELATIONS OF ESTIMATES	NO
FITTED MOMENTS	NO
TOTAL EFFECTS	NO
VARIANCES AND COVARIANCES	NO
MODIFICATION INDICES	NO
FACTOR SCORES REGRESSIONS	NO
FIRST ORDER DERIVATIVES	NO
STANDARDIZED SOLUTION	NO
PARAMETER PLOTS	NO
AUTOMATIC MODIFICATION	NO

OBJECTIVE AND SUBJECTIVE SOCIAL STATUS. HYPOTHESIS A. WHITES

MOMENT MATRIX TO BE ANALYZED

	EDUCAT:N	OCCUPATN	INCOME	S-C OCCU	S-C INCO	S-C LIFE
EDUCAT:N	4.183					
OCCUPATN	73.376	1798.406				
INCOME	9.391	198.582	30.222			
S-C OCCU	2.721	60.456	8.035	2.790		
S-C INCO	2.802	59.169	8.365	2.554	2.844	
S-C LIFE	2.755	58.718	8.210	2.537	2.617	2.765
S-C INFL	2.859	61.075	8.340	2.628	2.676	2.683
CONST.	1.655	36.698	5.040	1.543	1.548	1.542

MOMENT MATRIX TO BE ANALYZED

	S-C INFL	CONST.
S-C INFL	2.981	
CONST.	1.601	1.000

DETERMINANT = 0.159481D+02

L I S R E L VI

BY

KARL G JORESKOG AND DAG SORBOM

OBJECTIVE AND SUBJECTIVE SOCIAL STATUS. HYPOTHESIS A. BLACKS

THE FOLLOWING LISREL CONTROL LINES HAVE BEEN READ :

```
DA NO=368
LA UN=8
'EDUCAT:N' 'OCCUPATN' 'INCOME' 'S-C OCCU' 'S-C INCO' 'S-C LIFE' 'S-C INFL'
KM UN=8
1 .404 1 .268 .220 1 .216 .277 .268 1 .233 .183 .424 .550 1
.211 .270 .325 .574 .647 1
.207 .157 .282 .482 .517 .647 1
ME UN=8
1.274 23.467 4.041 1.288 1.129 1.235 1.318
SD UN=8 RE
1.106 16.244 2.097 0.747 0.814 0.786 0.859
MO PS=IN
OU
```

NUMBER OF INPUT VARIABLES   7

NUMBER OF Y - VARIABLES   7

NUMBER OF X - VARIABLES   1

NUMBER OF ETA - VARIABLES   7

NUMBER OF KSI - VARIABLES   1

NUMBER OF OBSERVATIONS   368

NUMBER OF GROUPS   2

OUTPUT REQUESTED

TECHNICAL OUTPUT	NO
STANDARD ERRORS	NO
T - VALUES	NO
CORRELATIONS OF ESTIMATES	NO
FITTED MOMENTS	NO
TOTAL EFFECTS	NO
VARIANCES AND COVARIANCES	NO
MODIFICATION INDICES	NO
FACTOR SCORES REGRESSIONS	NO
FIRST ORDER DERIVATIVES	NO
STANDARDIZED SOLUTION	NO
PARAMETER PLOTS	NO
AUTOMATIC MODIFICATION	NO

OBJECTIVE AND SUBJECTIVE SOCIAL STATUS.   HYPOTHESIS A.   BLACKS

MOMENT MATRIX TO BE ANALYZED

	EDUCAT:N	OCCUPATN	INCOME	S-C OCCU	S-C INCO	S-C LIFE
EDUCAT:N	2.843					
OCCUPATN	37.135	813.851				
INCOME	5.768	102.304	20.715			
S-C OCCU	1.819	33.578	5.623	2.215		
S-C INCO	1.648	28.907	5.284	1.788	1.935	
S-C LIFE	1.756	32.420	5.525	1.927	1.807	2.141
S-C INFL	1.875	33.114	5.833	2.006	1.849	2.063
CONST.	1.274	23.467	4.041	1.288	1.129	1.235

MOMENT MATRIX TO BE ANALYZED

	S-C INFL	CONST.
S-C INFL	2.473	
CONST.	1.318	1.000

DETERMINANT = 0.263046D+02

OBJECTIVE AND SUBJECTIVE SOCIAL STATUS. HYPOTHESIS A. WHITES

PARAMETER SPECIFICATIONS

GAMMA

	CONST.
EDUCAT:N	1
OCCUPATN	2
INCOME	3
S-C OCCU	4
S-C INCO	5
S-C LIFE	6
S-C INFL	7

PHI

	CONST.
CONST.	0

PSI

	EDUCAT:N	OCCUPATN	INCOME	S-C OCCU	S-C INCO	S-C LIFE
EDUCAT:N	8					
OCCUPATN	9	10				
INCOME	11	12	13			
S-C OCCU	14	15	16	17		
S-C INCO	18	19	20	21	22	
S-C LIFE	23	24	25	26	27	28
S-C INFL	29	30	31	32	33	34

PSI

	S-C INFL
S-C INFL	35

PARAMETER SPECIFICATIONS

GAMMA

	CONST.
EDUCAT:N	36
OCCUPATN	37
INCOME	38
S-C OCCU	39
S-C INCO	40
S-C LIFE	41
S-C INFL	42

PHI

	CONST.
CONST.	0

PSI

	EDUCAT:N	OCCUPATN	INCOME	S-C OCCU	S-C INCO	S-C LIFE
EDUCAT:N	8					
OCCUPATN	9	10				
INCOME	11	12	13			
S-C OCCU	14	15	16	17		
S-C INCO	18	19	20	21	22	
S-C LIFE	23	24	25	26	27	28
S-C INFL	29	30	31	32	33	34

PSI

	S-C INFL
S-C INFL	35

OBJECTIVE AND SUBJECTIVE SOCIAL STATUS.   HYPOTHESIS A.   WHITES

INITIAL ESTIMATES (TSLS)

GAMMA

	CONST.
EDUCAT:N	1.655
OCCUPATN	36.698
INCOME	5.040
S-C OCCU	1.543
S-C INCO	1.548
S-C LIFE	1.542
S-C INFL	1.601

PHI

	CONST.
CONST.	1.000

PSI

	EDUCAT:N	OCCUPATN	INCOME	S-C OCCU	S-C INCO	S-C LIFE
EDUCAT:N	1.220					
OCCUPATN	7.238	263.151				
INCOME	0.620	7.474	4.385			
S-C OCCU	0.178	3.352	0.419	0.556		
S-C INCO	0.209	2.413	0.722	0.334	0.661	
S-C LIFE	0.183	3.438	0.534	0.336	0.413	0.616
S-C INFL	0.196	2.185	0.507	0.308	0.361	0.436

PSI

	S-C INFL
S-C INFL	0.736

OBJECTIVE AND SUBJECTIVE SOCIAL STATUS.   HYPOTHESIS A.   BLACKS

INITIAL ESTIMATES (TSLS)

GAMMA

	CONST.
EDUCAT:N	1.274
OCCUPATN	23.467
INCOME	4.041
S-C OCCU	1.288
S-C INCO	1.129
S-C LIFE	1.235
S-C INFL	1.318

PHI

	CONST.
CONST.	1.000

PSI

	EDUCAT:N	OCCUPATN	INCOME	S-C OCCU	S-C INCO	S-C LIFE
EDUCAT:N	1.220					
OCCUPATN	7.238	263.151				
INCOME	0.620	7.474	4.385			
S-C OCCU	0.178	3.352	0.419	0.556		
S-C INCO	0.209	2.413	0.722	0.334	0.661	
S-C LIFE	0.183	3.438	0.534	0.336	0.413	0.616
S-C INFL	0.196	2.185	0.507	0.308	0.361	0.436

PSI

	S-C INFL
S-C INFL	0.736

OBJECTIVE AND SUBJECTIVE SOCIAL STATUS. HYPOTHESIS A. WHITES

LISREL ESTIMATES (MAXIMUM LIKELIHOOD)

GAMMA

	CONST.
EDUCAT:N	1.655
OCCUPATN	36.698
INCOME	5.040
S-C OCCU	1.543
S-C INCO	1.548
S-C LIFE	1.542
S-C INFL	1.601

PHI

	CONST.
CONST.	1.000

PSI

	EDUCAT:N	OCCUPATN	INCOME	S-C OCCU	S-C INCO	S-C LIFE
EDUCAT:N	1.341					
OCCUPATN	10.156	364.966				
INCOME	0.852	10.796	4.620			
S-C OCCU	0.172	3.611	0.332	0.477		
S-C INCO	0.226	2.385	0.636	0.243	0.546	
S-C LIFE	0.194	2.731	0.483	0.240	0.314	0.492
S-C INFL	0.203	2.258	0.379	0.227	0.272	0.316

PSI

	S-C INFL
S-C INFL	0.564

MEASURES OF GOODNESS OF FIT FOR THE WHOLE MODEL :

GOODNESS OF FIT INDEX IS 0.972

ROOT MEAN SQUARE RESIDUAL IS   14.464

OBJECTIVE AND SUBJECTIVE SOCIAL STATUS. HYPOTHESIS A. BLACKS

LISREL ESTIMATES (MAXIMUM LIKELIHOOD)

GAMMA

	CONST.
EDUCAT:N	1.274
OCCUPATN	23.467
INCOME	4.041
S-C OCCU	1.288
S-C INCO	1.129
S-C LIFE	1.235
S-C INFL	1.318

PHI

	CONST.
CONST.	1.000

PSI

	EDUCAT:N	OCCUPATN	INCOME	S-C OCCU	S-C INCO	S-C LIFE
EDUCAT:N	1.341					
OCCUPATN	10.156	364.966				
INCOME	0.852	10.796	4.620			
S-C OCCU	0.172	3.611	0.332	0.477		
S-C INCO	0.226	2.385	0.636	0.243	0.546	
S-C LIFE	0.194	2.731	0.483	0.240	0.314	0.492
S-C INFL	0.203	2.258	0.379	0.227	0.272	0.316

PSI

	S-C INFL
S-C INFL	0.564

MEASURES OF GOODNESS OF FIT FOR THE WHOLE MODEL :

CHI-SQUARE WITH 28 DEGREES OF FREEDOM IS   104.94 (PROB. LEVEL = 0.000)

GOODNESS OF FIT INDEX IS 0.966

ROOT MEAN SQUARE RESIDUAL IS   16.986

THE PROBLEM REQUIRED 1997 DOUBLE PRECISION WORDS, THE CPU-TIME WAS   0.55 SECONDS

L I S R E L   VI

BY

KARL G JORESKOG AND DAG SORBOM

OBJECTIVE AND SUBJECTIVE SOCIAL STATUS. HYPOTHESIS B. WHITES

THE FOLLOWING LISREL CONTROL LINES HAVE BEEN READ :


```
DA NI=7 NO=432 NG=2 MA=AM
LA UN=8
'EDUCAT:N' 'OCCUPATN' 'INCOME' 'S-C OCCU' 'S-C INCO' 'S-C LIFE' 'S-C INFL'
KM UN=8
1 .495 1 .398 .292 1 .218 .282 .184 1 .299 .166 .383 .386 1
.272 .161 .321 .396 .553 1
.269 .169 .191 .382 .456 .534 1
ME UN=8
1.655 36.698 5.040 1.543 1.548 1.542 1.601
SD UN=8
1.203 21.277 2.198 0.640 0.670 0.623 0.647
MO NY=7 NX=1
OU TO
```


NUMBER OF INPUT VARIABLES	7
NUMBER OF Y - VARIABLES	7
NUMBER OF X - VARIABLES	1
NUMBER OF ETA - VARIABLES	7
NUMBER OF KSI - VARIABLES	1
NUMBER OF OBSERVATIONS	432
NUMBER OF GROUPS	2

OUTPUT REQUESTED

TECHNICAL OUTPUT	NO
STANDARD ERRORS	NO
T - VALUES	NO
CORRELATIONS OF ESTIMATES	NO
FITTED MOMENTS	NO
TOTAL EFFECTS	NO
VARIANCES AND COVARIANCES	NO
MODIFICATION INDICES	NO
FACTOR SCORES REGRESSIONS	NO
FIRST ORDER DERIVATIVES	NO
STANDARDIZED SOLUTION	NO
PARAMETER PLOTS	NO
AUTOMATIC MODIFICATION	NO

OBJECTIVE AND SUBJECTIVE SOCIAL STATUS.   HYPOTHESIS B.   WHITES

MOMENT MATRIX TO BE ANALYZED

	EDUCAT:N	OCCUPATN	INCOME	S-C OCCU	S-C INCO	S-C LIFE
EDUCAT:N	4.183					
OCCUPATN	73.376	1798.406				
INCOME	9.391	198.582	30.222			
S-C OCCU	2.721	60.456	8.035	2.790		
S-C INCO	2.802	59.169	8.365	2.554	2.844	
S-C LIFE	2.755	58.718	8.210	2.537	2.617	2.765
S-C INFL	2.859	61.075	8.340	2.628	2.676	2.683
CONST.	1.655	36.698	5.040	1.543	1.548	1.542

MOMENT MATRIX TO BE ANALYZED

	S-C INFL	CONST.
S-C INFL	2.981	
CONST.	1.601	1.000

DETERMINANT = O.159481D+02

OBJECTIVE AND SUBJECTIVE SOCIAL STATUS.   HYPOTHESIS B. BLACKS

THE FOLLOWING LISREL CONTROL LINES HAVE BEEN READ :

```
DA NO=368
LA UN=8
'EDUCAT:N' 'OCCUPATN' 'INCOME' 'S-C OCCU' 'S-C INCO' 'S-C LIFE' 'S-C INFL'
KM UN=8
1 .404 1 .268 .220 1 .216 .277 .268 1 .233 .183 .424 .550 1
.211 .270 .325 .574 .647 1
.207 .157 .282 .482 .517 .647 1
ME UN=8
1.274 23.467 4.041 1.288 1.129 1.235 1.318
SD UN=8
1.106 16.244 2.097 0.747 0.814 0.786 0.859
MO GA=IN
OU
```

OUTPUT REQUESTED

NUMBER OF INPUT VARIABLES	7	TECHNICAL OUTPUT	NO
NUMBER OF Y - VARIABLES	7	STANDARD ERRORS	NO
NUMBER OF X - VARIABLES	1	T - VALUES	NO
NUMBER OF ETA - VARIABLES	7	CORRELATIONS OF ESTIMATES	NO
NUMBER OF KSI - VARIABLES	1	FITTED MOMENTS	NO
NUMBER OF OBSERVATIONS	368	TOTAL EFFECTS	NO
NUMBER OF GROUPS	2	VARIANCES AND COVARIANCES	NO
		MODIFICATION INDICES	NO
		FACTOR SCORES REGRESSIONS	NO
		FIRST ORDER DERIVATIVES	NO
		STANDARDIZED SOLUTION	NO
		PARAMETER PLOTS	NO
		AUTOMATIC MODIFICATION	NO

OBJECTIVE AND SUBJECTIVE SOCIAL STATUS.   HYPOTHESIS B. BLACKS

MOMENT MATRIX TO BE ANALYZED

	EDUCAT:N	OCCUPATN	INCOME	S-C OCCU	S-C INCO	S-C LIFE
EDUCAT:N	2.843					
OCCUPATN	37.135	813.851				
INCOME	5.768	102.304	20.715			
S-C OCCU	1.819	33.578	5.623	2.215		
S-C INCO	1.648	28.907	5.284	1.788	1.935	
S-C LIFE	1.756	32.420	5.525	1.927	1.807	2.141
S-C INFL	1.875	33.114	5.833	2.006	1.849	2.063
CONST.	1.274	23.467	4.041	1.288	1.129	1.235

MOMENT MATRIX TO BE ANALYZED

	S-C INFL	CONST.
S-C INFL	2.473	
CONST.	1.318	1.000

DETERMINANT = 0.263046D+02

OBJECTIVE AND SUBJECTIVE SOCIAL STATUS.   HYPOTHESIS B.   WHITES

PARAMETER SPECIFICATIONS

GAMMA

	CONST.
EDUCAT:N	1
OCCUPATN	2
INCOME	3
S-C OCCU	4
S-C INCO	5
S-C LIFE	6
S-C INFL	7

PHI

	CONST.
CONST.	0

PSI

	EDUCAT:N	OCCUPATN	INCOME	S-C OCCU	S-C INCO	S-C LIFE
EDUCAT:N	8					
OCCUPATN	9	10				
INCOME	11	12	13			
S-C OCCU	14	15	16	17		
S-C INCO	18	19	20	21	22	
S-C LIFE	23	24	25	26	27	28
S-C INFL	29	30	31	32	33	34

PSI

	S-C INFL
S-C INFL	35

OBJECTIVE AND SUBJECTIVE SOCIAL STATUS. HYPOTHESIS B. BLACKS

PARAMETER SPECIFICATIONS

GAMMA

	CONST.
EDUCAT:N	1
OCCUPATN	2
INCOME	3
S-C OCCU	4
S-C INCO	5
S-C LIFE	6
S-C INFL	7

PHI

	CONST.
CONST.	0

PSI

	EDUCAT:N	OCCUPATN	INCOME	S-C OCCU	S-C INCO	S-C LIFE
EDUCAT:N	36					
OCCUPATN	37	38				
INCOME	39	40	41			
S-C OCCU	42	43	44	45		
S-C INCO	46	47	48	49	50	
S-C LIFE	51	52	53	54	55	56
S-C INFL	57	58	59	60	61	62

PSI

	S-C INFL
S-C INFL	63

OBJECTIVE AND SUBJECTIVE SOCIAL STATUS. HYPOTHESIS B. WHITES

INITIAL ESTIMATES (TSLS)

GAMMA

	CONST.
EDUCAT:N	1.274
OCCUPATN	23.467
INCOME	4.041
S-C OCCU	1.288
S-C INCO	1.129
S-C LIFE	1.235
S-C INFL	1.318

PHI

	CONST.
CONST.	1.000

PSI

	EDUCAT:N	OCCUPATN	INCOME	S-C OCCU	S-C INCO	S-C LIFE
EDUCAT:N	1.444					
OCCUPATN	12.641	451.663				
INCOME	1.050	13.624	4.820			
S-C OCCU	0.167	3.831	0.258	0.409		
S-C INCO	0.240	2.361	0.563	0.165	0.448	
S-C LIFE	0.203	2.129	0.439	0.158	0.230	0.387
S-C INFL	0.209	2.321	0.271	0.158	0.197	0.215

PSI

	S-C INFL
S-C INFL	0.418

OBJECTIVE AND SUBJECTIVE SOCIAL STATUS. HYPOTHESIS B. BLACKS

INITIAL ESTIMATES (TSLS)

GAMMA

	CONST.
EDUCAT:N	1.274
OCCUPATN	23.467
INCOME	4.041
S-C OCCU	1.288
S-C INCO	1.129
S-C LIFE	1.235
S-C INFL	1.318

PHI

	CONST.
CONST.	1.000

PSI

	EDUCAT:N	OCCUPATN	INCOME	S-C OCCU	S-C INCO	S-C LIFE
EDUCAT:N	1.220					
OCCUPATN	7.238	263.151				
INCOME	0.620	7.474	4.385			
S-C OCCU	0.178	3.352	0.419	0.556		
S-C INCO	0.209	2.413	0.722	0.334	0.661	
S-C LIFE	0.183	3.438	0.534	0.336	0.413	0.616
S-C INFL	0.196	2.185	0.507	0.308	0.361	0.436

PSI

	S-C INFL
S-C INFL	0.736

OBJECTIVE AND SUBJECTIVE SOCIAL STATUS. HYPOTHESIS B. WHITES

LISREL ESTIMATES (MAXIMUM LIKELIHOOD)

GAMMA

	CONST.
EDUCAT:N	1.428
OCCUPATN	29.107
INCOME	4.562
S-C OCCU	1.449
S-C INCO	1.392
S-C LIFE	1.443
S-C INFL	1.504

PHI

	CONST.
CONST.	1.000

PSI

	EDUCAT:N	OCCUPATN	INCOME	S-C OCCU	S-C INCO	S-C LIFE
EDUCAT:N	1.495					
OCCUPATN	14.360	509.287				
INCOME	1.158	17.256	5.049			
S-C OCCU	0.189	4.542	0.303	0.417		
S-C INCO	0.276	3.547	0.637	0.180	0.472	
S-C LIFE	0.226	2.880	0.486	0.167	0.246	0.397
S-C INFL	0.231	3.061	0.318	0.167	0.212	0.224

PSI

	S-C INFL
S-C INFL	0.427

MEASURES OF GOODNESS OF FIT FOR THE WHOLE MODEL :

GOODNESS OF FIT INDEX IS 0.966

ROOT MEAN SQUARE RESIDUAL IS   74.316

OBJECTIVE AND SUBJECTIVE SOCIAL STATUS.   HYPOTHESIS B. BLACKS

LISREL ESTIMATES (MAXIMUM LIKELIHOOD)

GAMMA

	CONST.
EDUCAT:N	1.428
OCCUPATN	29.107
INCOME	4.562
S-C OCCU	1.449
S-C INCO	1.392
S-C LIFE	1.443
S-C INFL	1.504

PHI

	CONST.
CONST.	1.000

PSI

	EDUCAT:N	OCCUPATN	INCOME	S-C OCCU	S-C INCO	S-C LIFE
EDUCAT:N	1.244					
OCCUPATN	8.110	294.958				
INCOME	0.700	10.410	4.656			
S-C OCCU	0.203	4.262	0.503	0.583		
S-C INCO	0.250	3.895	0.859	0.376	0.730	
S-C LIFE	0.215	4.612	0.643	0.370	0.468	0.659
S-C INFL	0.225	3.231	0.603	0.338	0.409	0.474

PSI

	S-C INFL
S-C INFL	0.770

MEASURES OF GOODNESS OF FIT FOR THE WHOLE MODEL :

CHI-SQUARE WITH   7 DEGREES OF FREEDOM IS   133.60 (PROB. LEVEL = 0.0)

GOODNESS OF FIT INDEX IS 0.960

ROOT MEAN SQUARE RESIDUAL IS   55.405

THE PROBLEM REQUIRED 3236 DOUBLE PRECISION WORDS. THE CPU-TIME WAS   0.96 SECONDS

REFERENCES

Aigner, D.J. and Goldberger, A.S., Eds. (1977) *Latent variables in socio-economic models*. Amsterdam: North-Holland.

Aitkin, A.C. (1934-35) On least squares and the linear combination of observations. **Proceedings of the Royal Society of Edinburgh, 55, 42-48**

Algina, J. (1980) A note on identification in the oblique and orthogonal factor analysis model. *Psychometrika, 45, 393-396.*

Alwin, D.F. and Hauser, R.M. (1975) The decomposition of effects in path analysis. *American Sociological Review, 40, 37-47.*

Anderson, T.W. and Rubin, H. (1956) Statistical inference in factor analysis. *Proceedings of the Third Berkeley Symposium on Mathematical Statistics and Probability, 5, 111-150.*

Avery, R.B. (1979) Modeling monetary policy as an unobserved variable. *Journal of Econometrics, 10, 291-312.*

Bentler, P.M. (1980) Multivariate analysis with latent variables: Causal models. *Annual Review of Psychology, 31, 419-456.*

Bentler, P.M. and Woodward, J.A. (1978) A Head Start reevaluation: Positive effects are not yet demonstrable. *Evaluation Quarterly, 2, 493-510.*

Bielby, W.T. and Hauser, R.M. (1977) Structural equation models. *Annual Review of Sociology, 3, 137-161.*

Blalock, H.M., Jr., Ed. (1971) *Causal models in the social sciences*. Chicago: Aldine.

Blalock, H.M., Jr., Ed. (1974) *Measurement in the social sciences*. Chicago: Aldine.

Blau, P. and Duncan, O.D. (1967) *The American occupational structure*. New York: Wiley.

Bohrnstedt, G.W. (1969) Observations on the measurement of change. In E.F. Borgatta (Ed.): *Sociological Methodology*. San Francisco: Jossey-Bass, 113-133.

Browne, M.W. (1970) Analysis of covariance structure. Paper presented at the annual conference of the South African Statistical Association.

Caslyn, J.R. and Kenny, D.A. (1977) Self-concept of ability and perceived evaluation of others: Cause or effect of academic achievement? *Journal of Educational Psychology, 69, 136-145.*

Chamberlain, G. (1977) An instrumental variable interpretation of identification in variance-components and MIMIC models. In P. Taubman (Ed.): *The determinants of socio-economic success within and between families*. Amsterdam: North-Holland.

Duncan, O.D. (1969) Some linear models for two-wave, two-variable panel analysis. *Psychological Bulletin, 72, 177-182.*

Duncan, O.D. (1972) Unmeasured variables in linear models for panel analysis. In H.L. Costner (Ed.): *Sociological Methodology 1972*. San Francisco: Jossey-Bass, 36-82.

Duncan, O.D. (1975) *Introduction to structural equation models*. New York: Academic Press.

Duncan, O.D., Haller, A.O. and Portes, A. (1968) Peer influence on aspiration: A reinterpretation. *American Journal of Sociology, 74*, 119-137.

Dunn, J.E. (1973) A note on a sufficiency condition for uniqueness of a restricted factor matrix. *Psychometrika, 38*, 141-143.

Finn, J.D. (1974) *A general model for multivariate analysis*. New York: Holt, Reinhart, and Winston.

Geraci, V.J. (1976) Identification of simultaneous equation models with measurement error. *Journal of Econometrics, 4*, 263-283.

Gnadadesikan, R. (1977) *Methods for statistical data analysis of multivariate observations*. New York: Wiley.

Goldberger, A.S. (1964) *Econometric theory*. New York: Wiley.

Goldberger, A.S. (1972) Structural equation methods in the social sciences. *Econometrica, 40*, 979-1001.

Goldberger, A.S. and Duncan, O.D., Eds. (1973) *Structural equation models in the social sciences*. New York: Seminar Press.

Graff, J. and Schmidt, P. (1981) A general model for decomposition of effects. In K.G. Jöreskog and H. Wold (Eds.): *Systems under direct observation: Causality, structure, and prediction*. Amsterdam: North-Holland.

Guttman, L.A. (1954) A new approach to factor analysis: The radex. In P.F. Lazarsfeld (Ed.): *Mathematical thinking in the social sciences*. New York: Columbia University Press.

Hasselrot, T. and Lernberg, L.O., Eds. (1980) *Tonåringen och livet*. Vällingby, Sweden: Liber Förlag. (In Swedish)

Heise, D.R. (1969) Separating reliability and stability in test-retest correlation. *American Sociological Review, 34*, 93-101.

Heise, D.R. (1970) Causal inference from panel data. In E.F. Borgatta and G.W. Bohrnstedt (Eds.): *Sociological Methodology 1970*. San Francisco: Jossey-Bass, 3-27.

Heise, D.R. (1975) *Causal analysis*. New York: Wiley.

Hodge, R.W. and Treiman, D.J. (1968) Social participation and social status. *American Sociological Review, 33*, 723-740.

Howe, H.G. (1955) Some contributions to factor analysis. Report ORNL-1919. Oak Ridge, Tennessee: Oak Ridge National Laboratory.

Humphreys, L.G. (1968) The fleeting nature of college academic success. *Journal of Educational Psychology*, 59, 375-380.

Hägglund, G. (1980) Factor analysis by instrumental variables methods: A comparison of three estimation procedures. Research Report 80-2. University of Uppsala, Department of Statistics.

Hägglund, G. (1981) Factor analysis by instrumental variables methods: Least squares justification and standard errors. Research Report 81-1. University of Uppsala, Department of Statistics.

Jennrich, R.I. (1978) Rotational equivalence of factor loading matrices with specified values. *Psychometrika*, 43, 421-426.

Jöreskog, K.G. (1967) Some contributions to maximum likelihood factor analysis. *Psychometrika*, 32, 443-482.

Jöreskog, K.G. (1969) A general approach to confirmatory factor analysis. *Psychometrika*, 34, 183-202.

Jöreskog, K.G. (1970a) A general method for analysis of covariance structures. *Biometrika*, 57, 239-251.

Jöreskog, K.G. (1970b) Estimation and testing of simplex models. *British Journal of Mathematical and Statistical Psychology*, 23, 121-145.

Jöreskog, K.G. (1971) Simultaneous factor analysis in several populations. *Psychometrika*, 36, 409-426.

Joreskog, K.G. and Goldberger, A.S. (1972) Factor analysis by generalized least squares. Psychometrika, 37(3), 243-260

Jöreskog, K.G. (1973a) A general method for estimating a linear structural equation system. In A.S. Goldberger and O.D. Duncan (Eds.): *Structural equation models in the social sciences*. New York: Seminar Press, 85-112.

Jöreskog, K.G. (1973b) Analysis of covariance structures. In P.R. Krishnaiah (Ed.): *Multivariate Analysis - III*. New York: Academic Press, 263-285.

Jöreskog, K.G. (1974) Analyzing psychological data by structural analysis of covariance matrices. In R.C. Atkinson, D.H. Krantz, R.D. Luce, and P. Suppes (Eds.): *Contemporary developments in mathematical psychology - Volume II*. San Francisco: W.H. Freeman, 1-56.

Jöreskog, K.G. (1977) Structural equation models in the social sciences: Specification, estimation, and testing. In P.R. Krishnaiah (Ed.): *Applications of statistics*. Amsterdam: North-Holland, 265-287.

Jöreskog, K.G. (1978) Structural analysis of covariance and correlation matrices. *Psychometrika*, 43, 443-477.

Jöreskog, K.G. (1979a) Basic ideas of factor and component analysis. In K.G. Jöreskog and D. Sörbom: *Advances in factor analysis and structural equation models*. Cambridge, Mass.: Abt Books, 5-20.

Jöreskog, K.G. (1979b) Statistical estimation of structural models in longitudi-
nal developmental investigations. In J.R. Nesselroade and P.B. Baltes
(Eds.): *Longitudinal research in the study of behavior and development.*
New York: Academic Press.

Jöreskog, K.G. (1981a) Analysis of covariance structures. *Scandinavian Journal
of Statistics, 8,* 65-92.

Jöreskog, K.G. (1981b) Basic issues in the application of LISREL. *DATA, 1,* 1-6.

Jöreskog, K.G. and Goldberger, A.S. (1975) Estimation of a model with multiple
indicators and multiple causes of a single latent variable. *Journal of the
American Statistical Association, 70,* 631-639.

Jöreskog, K.G. and Sörbom, D. (1976) Statistical models and methods for test-
retest situations. In D.N.M. deGruijter and L.J.Th. van der Kamp (Eds.):
Advances in psychological and educational measurement. New York: Wiley,
285-325.

Jöreskog, K.G. and Sörbom, D. (1977) Statistical models and methods for analysis
of longitudinal data. In D.J. Aigner and A.S. Goldberger (Eds.): *Latent
variables in socio-economic models.* Amsterdam: North-Holland, 285-325.

Jöreskog, K.G. and Sörbom, D. (1979) *Advances in factor analysis and structural
equation models.* Cambridge, Mass.: Abt Books.

Jöreskog. K.G. and Sörbom, D. (1980) Simultaneous analysis of longitudinal data
from several cohorts. Research Report 80-5. University of Uppsala, Department of Statistics.

Kenny, D.A. (1979) *Correlation and causality.* New York: Wiley.

Kerchoff, A.C. (1974) *Ambition and Attainment.* Rose Monograph Series.

Klein, L.R. (1950) *Economic fluctuations in the United States 1921-1941.* Cowles
Commission Monograph No. 11. New York: Wiley.

Lawley, D.N. and Maxwell, A.E. (1971) *Factor analysis as a statistical method,*
(second edition). London: Butterworths.

Lord, F.M. (1957) A significance test for the hypothesis that two variables
measure the same trait except for errors of measurement. *Psychometrika,
22,* 207-220.

Lutz, R.J. (1975) An experimental investigation of causal relations among
cognitions, affect, and behavioral intention. *Journal of Consumer
Research, 3,* 197-208.

Magidson, J. (1977) Toward a causal model approach for adjusting pre-existing
differences in the non-equivalent control group situation. *Evaluation
Quarterly, 1,* 399-420.

McGaw, B. and Jöreskog, K.G. (1971) Factorial invariance of ability measures in groups differing in intelligence and socio-economic status. *British Journal of Mathematical and Statistical Psychology, 24*, 154-168.

Muthen, B. (1978) Contributions to factor analysis of dichotomous variables. *Psychometrika, 43*, 551-560.

Muthen, B. (1979) A structural brobit model with latent variables. *Journal of the American Statistical Association, 74*, 807-811.

Muthen, B. (1981) Some categorical response models with continuous latent variables. In K.G. Jöreskog and H. Wold (Eds.): *Systems under indirect observation: Causality, structure, and prediction.* Amsterdam: North-Holland.

Olsson, U. (1979) Maximum likelihood estimation of the polychoric correlation coefficient. *Psychometrika, 44*, 443-460.

Olsson, U., Drasgow, F. and Dorans, N.J. (1981) The polyserial correlation coefficient. Manuscript submitted for publication.

Robinson, P.M. (1974) Identification, estimation, and large-sample theory for regressions containing unobservable variables. *International Economic Review, 15*, 680-692.

Rock, D.A., Werts, C.E., Linn, R.L., and Jöreskog, K.G. (1977) A maximum likelihood solution to the errors in variables and errors in equations model. *Journal of Multivariate Behavioral Research, 12*, 187-197.

Sewell, W.H., Haller, A.O., and Ohlendorf, G.W. (1970) The educational and early occupational attainment process: Revisions and replications. *American Sociological Review, 35*, 1014-1027.

Sörbom, D. (1974) A general method for studying differences in factor means and factor structures between groups. *British Journal of Mathematical and Statistical Psychology, 27*, 229-239.

Sörbom, D. (1975) Detection of correlated errors in longitudinal data. *British Journal of Mathematical and Statistical Psychology, 28*, 138-151.

Sörbom, D. (1976) A statistical model for the measurement of change in true scores. In D.N.M. de Gruijter and J.L.Th. van der Kamp (Eds.): *Advances in psychological and educational measurement.* New York: Wiley, 159-169.

Sörbom, D. (1978) An alternative to the methodology for analysis of covariance. *Psychometrika, 43*, 381-396.

Sörbom, D. (1981) Structural equation models with structured means. In K.G. Jöreskog and H. Wold (Eds.): *Systems under indirect observation: Causality, structure, and prediction.* Amsterdam: North-Holland.

Sörbom, D. and Jöreskog, K.G. (1981) The use of structural equation models in evaluation research. Research Report 81-6. University of Uppsala, Department of Statistics.

Sörbom, D. and Jöreskog, K.G. (1982a) Recent developments in LISREL: Automatic starting values. Under preparation.

Sörbom, D. and Jöreskog, K.G. (1982b) Recent developments in LISREL: Modification indices. Under preparation.

Theil, H. (1971) *Principles of econometrics*. New York: Wiley.

Warren, R.D., White, J.K., and Fuller, W.A. (1974) An error in variables analysis of managerial role performance. *Journal of the American Statistical Association, 69*, 886-893.

Werts, C.E., Rock, D.A., Linn, R.L., and Jöreskog, K.G. (1976) A comparison of correlations, variances, covariances, and regression weights with or without measurement errors. *Psychological Bulletin, 83*, 1007-1013.

Wheaton, B., Muthen, B., Alwin, D., and Summers, G. (1977) Assessing reliability and stability in panel models. In D.R. Heise (Ed.): *Sociological Methodology 1977*. San Francisco: Jossey-Bass, 84-136.

Wiley, D.E. (1973) The identification problem for structural equation models with unmeasured variables. In A.S. Goldberger and O.D. Duncan (Eds.): *Structural models in the social sciences*. New York: Seminar Press, 69-83.

Wright, S. (1954) The interpretation of multivariate systems. In O. Kemthorne et al. (Eds.): *Statistics and mathematics in biology*. Ames, Iowa: Iowa State University, 11-23.

SUBJECT INDEX

SCIENTIFIC SOFTWARE INC.
P.O. BOX 536
MOORESVILLE (USA)
IN 46158-0536

SUPPLEMENT TO LISREL VI MANUAL

How LISREL VI treats missing values
and ordinal variables,
by Karl Joreskog and Dag Sorbom.
6 June 1984

[The following information clarifies and
supplements Sections II.4.4 and IV.2.]

The treatment of missing values and/or ordinal variables is controlled by the two parameters XM and MV on the RA card.

The XM-parameter is a numerical value designated by the user to represent a missing observation. The XM-value must be the same for all variables. The MV-parameter is used by the program to classify each variable as contiuous (interval or ratio scale) or ordinal (ordered categorical). MV is the maximum number of distinct non-missing values present in an ordinal variable. The MV-parameter can be assigned an integer value 0, 1, 2 ..., 9. The value O (zero) is the default. When MV is zero or default, all variables are treated as continuous and AM, MM, CM, or KM are computed depending on the value of MA specified on the DA card.

When MV=0 or default, in LISREL Version VI.4 or earlier:
The program assumes there are no missing values in the raw data. If an XM-value is specified and if such XM-values are present in the raw data, the program will use these values as actual observations (cases). Hence, to treat XM-values as missing observations, one must specify MV 1. (See below.)

When MV=0 or default, in LISREL Version VI.5 or larger:
Listwise deletion will be used; i.e., if an XM-value is specified and if XM-values are present in the raw data, observations (cases) with one or more XM-values will be ignored. The program computes the total number of observations (cases) without XM-values, substitutes this value for the value of NO specified on the DA card, and uses this new value in subsequent computations. The new value of NO will be given on the printout.

When MV=1. All versions of LISREL VI:
All variables are treated as continuous. A matrix consisting of product moment correlations is computed, regardless of the value of MA specified on the DA card. If XM-values are present, pairwise deletion will be used; i.e., each correlation is based on all observations which have non-missing values on both variables.

When MV=2, 3, ..., 9. All versions of LISREL VI:
Each variable is classified as continous or ordinal. A variable is classified as continuous if it has more than MV distinct non-missing values. Otherwise, it is classified as ordinal with category labels 1, 2, ...NC MV. A correlation matrix consisting of product moment, polychoric, and polyserial correlations is computed as described in Section IV.2 of the LISREL VI manual. If XM-values are present, pairwise deletion is used. If the PP-parameter is present on the RA card, the program will output one page of summary statistics for each pair of variables.

Error in the LISREL V and VI Manuals

Kenneth Bollen of Dartmouth College pointed out an error
in Table III.4 of the manual. In the left bottom part of
the table, the direct effect on y by ξ is given as
$\Lambda_y \Gamma$ but should be 0 (zero) and in the expression for
the indirect effect the term $-\Lambda_y \Gamma$ should be deleted.

This error does not affect the program. It is only an
error in the table.